Astrological Calculations:

An Outline of Conventions and Methodology

Bruce Scofield, Ph.D.

THE WESSEX ASTROLOGER

Published in 2021 by
The Wessex Astrologer Ltd
PO Box 9307
Swanage
BH19 9BF

For a full list of our titles go to www.wessexastrologer.com

ISBN 9781910531655

Originally published by One Reed Publications
ISBN: 9780962803185

Cover design by Andy Jay

A catalogue record for this book is available at The British Library

Table of Contents

Preface....5

Chapter I: Coordinate Systems: Astronomical and Temporal
        Frames of Reference....9

Chapter 2: Space and Time Measurement....27

Chapter 3: Using Triangles to Measure the Sky:
        A Short History of Trigonometry....39

Chapter 4: Systems of House Division....75

Chapter 5: Calculating the Astrological Chart....93

Chapter 6: Chart Calculations using Interpolation Tables....113

Chapter 7: Chart Calculations using Algebraic equations
        (Proportions)....129

Chapter 8: Chart Calculations using Logarithms....142

Chapter 9: Chart Calculations using a calculator with
        trigonometric functions....152

Chapter 10: Other Astrological Chart Calculations....162

Chapter 11: Calculations and Certification....199

Tables for Calculations....205

References.... 233

Armillary Sphere

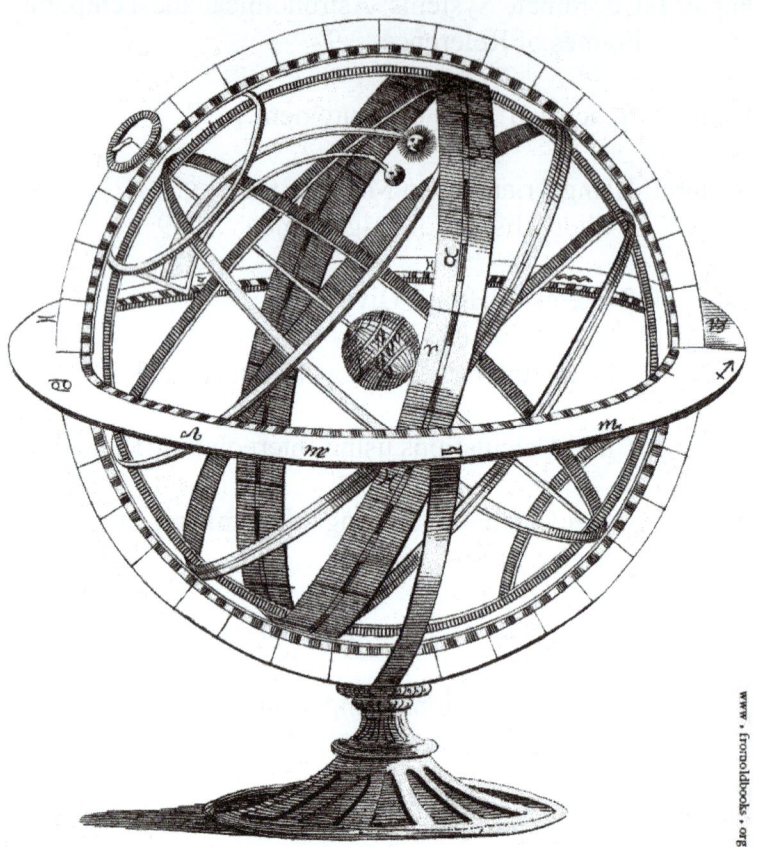

From Ebenezer Sibly, *Astrology* (1791) p. 965

Preface

The material contained in this document has been assembled for two purposes: elucidating the astronomy and mathematics behind the astrological chart and for maintaining the tradition of casting charts by hand (i.e. pencil, paper and tables, calculator, or even slide rule) in a meaningful way. With the advent of the computer, the mathematical skills and astronomical insights involved in chart calculations have become endangered. Today these skills are being kept alive primarily by the requirements of certification exams such as those of the Professional Astrologers Alliance (associated with the National Council for Geocosmic Research), the American Federation of Astrologers, Kepler College, the International Academy of Astrology and a few other schools. While the calculation of astrological charts instantly by computer is certainly labor-saving, it bypasses information that explains what the astrological chart is in reality and how came to be what it is. Today, most practicing astrologers are unable to explain in any detail what the chart, on which they base their insight and analysis on, represents astronomically. Many think that this lack of insight into the mechanics of the horoscope is a serious limiting factor that dilutes interpretation. Some even think that loss of connection to traditional astronomy reduces the subject of astrology to a kind of psycho-therapeutic art form aligned with non-scientific belief systems old and new.

Prior to the 20th century astrological chart calculations were, for the most part, difficult and cumbersome. This was before the age of standardized time, accurate astronomical data, and calculating machines. Astrological textbooks of past centuries routinely included tables of trigonometric functions and logarithms, and many pages were devoted to problems such as determining local time and working with forecasting calculations. During most of the previous two millennia, astrologers who used primary directions as a predictive tool, and that was most of them, had to calculate the positions of the planets and house cusps against two or three coordinate systems. What was called a speculum, a listing of each planet's longitude, latitude, right ascension, declination, oblique ascension, oblique descension, etc., was routinely, and tediously, calculated for each chart using trigonometry and multiple tables. This is the reason that so many ancient, Medieval and Renaissance astrologers were also mathematicians. In fact, astrologers were routinely referred to as mathematicians from Roman times through the Renaissance and they contributed substantially to the development of advanced geometry and trigonometry. With so much space devoted to calculations, many older astrology books left little room for information on the interpretation of planetary patterns.

Astrological chart calculations during the 20th century became more streamlined and far easier than in previous times. Time zones became standards against which birth times could be adjusted, and accurate ephemerides and tables of houses for various systems became widely available. With the rise of easy-to-calculate secondary progressions and solar arc directions, which largely replaced primary directions as preferred predictive techniques, the need for spherical trigonometric calculations to construct a speculum was greatly reduced at first, and then practically eliminated.

Most astrologers in the 20th century learned to calculate astrological charts with proportional tables or logarithms. House cusps were interpolated from tables using simple arithmetic. When the author learned how to cast a chart in the late 1960s, he used both tables of logarithms and a slide rule. By the 1970s pocket calculators became a standard tool for chart calculations, and the first astrological computers appeared later in the decade. It was at this time that the traditional trigonometric formulae for astrological charts were recalled by programmers who were writing software that calculated astrological charts in split seconds. Their software also made it possible to experiment with a wide range of techniques that were previously very difficult to calculate. By the mid 1980s few astrologers were calculating charts by hand and most owned computers or were ordering charts from chart calculation services. Only those who saw value in astrological certification exams kept the relatively simple 20th century methodologies for chart casting alive in the astrological community.

Today many people have become successful practitioners of astrology without ever having to add or subtract logarithms or interpolate a house cusp – or, more rarely, work with trigonometric functions. Some argue that since astrology is now primarily a counseling technique, knowledge of the "nuts and bolts" is irrelevant. Most of us drive cars or use electronic gadgets every day, but only a very few have any idea of how they work. We trust the repair of these things to the experts. I don't think that to be a good analogy for astrology, however.

The astronomical features that lie behind the numbers and symbols in an astrological chart are profound clues to building an interpretation. When the chart is seen as what it really is, a map of the sky at the time and place of an event or a birth, the astrologer truly enters into the spatiotemporal environment within which we exist. It is knowledge of this environment that tells us Aries rises more quickly than Libra, that the Moon's daily motion is constantly changing and that a conjunction shouldn't be measured only in celestial longitude. Without this knowledge, an astrological chart is nothing more than a piece of paper, or a digital image shining back at us in an illuminated rectangle, decorated with circles, numbers and symbols; sadly an appropriate situation for a world in which humans are becoming increasingly disconnected from nature. Further discussion on this issue, the real value of astrological astronomy, is found in the last section of this book.

This document is primarily designed to preserve and teach the methods of the most basic astrological chart calculations along with some history. It attempts to address the disconnect between the actual process of mapping the sky and the simple arithmetic that is required by some astrological exams. Because this is not a rigorous mathematical textbook by any means, but merely a collection of key concepts and practices, and a general reference, some explanations are oversimplified. However, anyone who has passed high school algebra and geometry should be able to follow the explanations and worked calculations in this book. It is hoped that deeper knowledge of this traditional part of astrology, the challenge of mapping the sky and the mathematical ritual of preparing a chart, will allow students to not only glean deeper insights into the subject, but also to allow for a unique contact with astrology's long history.

The first edition of this book was compiled in 2002, itself based on handouts for classes on chart calculations I taught in the 1970s and 80s, some articles I wrote, and also some material from a course on calculations I taught at Kepler College in 2001. This new edition expands the book to include many other topics that I hope will deepen an understanding of what lies behind an astrological chart – in terms of space and time, and also in regard to history. Finally, I wish to thank Karen McCauley who was kind enough to look over the first two chapters, making some edits and suggestions, and Barry Orr who contributed a table of Midheavens and Ascendants.

Chapter 1

Coordinate Systems:
Astronomical Frames of Reference

The Earth in Space

The Sun, located at the center of our solar system, is orbited by planets, moons, asteroids, comets and cosmic debris. Most of these objects revolve around the Sun within the confines of essentially one plane, an outcome of the formation of the solar system from a collapsing nebula or dust cloud. As gravitational forces pulled the debris of the slowly rotating nebula inward (about 4.6 billion years ago), the rotation rate increased as it does when an ice skater in a spin pulls in their arms. The resulting high spin rate flattened out the nebula into the shape of a disk. Most of the nebula's matter became concentrated in the center, forming the Sun, while the remainder formed the rest of the solar system. It is for this reason that the planets orbit the Sun in essentially one plane and can be depicted on a horoscope in one dimension without much of an error. Among the major solar system bodies used by astrologers, only Pluto deviates substantially from this plane, although so do many asteroids and most comets.

From the perspective of the Earth (the geocentric perspective), the Sun and planets appear to move along the plane of the solar system in a relatively narrow band of the sky that we call the zodiac. The zodiac is centered on the *ecliptic,* the Sun's path in the sky on which eclipses take place, and it is divided into sections. The degrees of the zodiac are measured from either the vernal equinox or from a star. The former produces the *tropical zodiac* of astrological signs, the latter the *sidereal zodiac* of constellations. This topic will be considered in more detail on page 31.

There are two primary astronomical perspectives used in astrology. The *geocentric* perspective is one that views the solar system and beyond from the perspective of Earth, the place where human observers live. This Earth-centered perspective is the one used by most astrologers today, although astrologers have long known that the Sun is at the center of the solar system. Among the first Renaissance intellectuals to accept the reality of the Sun-centered solar system proposed by Copernicus in the 16th century were two scientists who also practiced astrology, Rheticus and Johannes Kepler, the former being Copernicus' messenger and the latter being the first scientist to mathematically model the true elliptical orbits of the planets in the solar system.

The standard astrological chart is a geocentric map of the cosmic environment as viewed from our location on Earth. (If one were born on Mars, a Mars-centric chart would need to be calculated.) The *heliocentric,* or Sun-centered perspective views the solar system from the perspective of the Sun. This perspective is used by some astrologers for specific purposes and ephemerides of heliocentric planetary positions are readily available. From an even wider perspective, called *galactocentric*, the Sun revolves around the center of the galaxy, the plane of the solar system being tilted by about 60 degrees relative to the plane of the galaxy.

Poles, Planes, and Orbit

The rotation of Earth on is the basis of the day. Earth's *poles* are the tips or extensions of its axis of rotation which are at right angles to Earth's equator. The axis is tilted at 23.45 degrees relative to the plane of the Earth's orbit around the Sun, shown in *Figure 1* below. This polar tilt, called *obliquity,* is the cause of the seasonal differences during the year. The angle of tilt varies from 21.8 to 24.4 degrees over a 41,000-year cycle and this variation has a powerful influence on climate over long periods of time.

In *Figure 1* Earth is shown in two positions in its annual circuit of the Sun. It is the tilt of the Earth's axis that causes each hemisphere to lean towards the sun (and receive more solar radiation) and then away from it over the course of a year – this being the cause of the seasons.

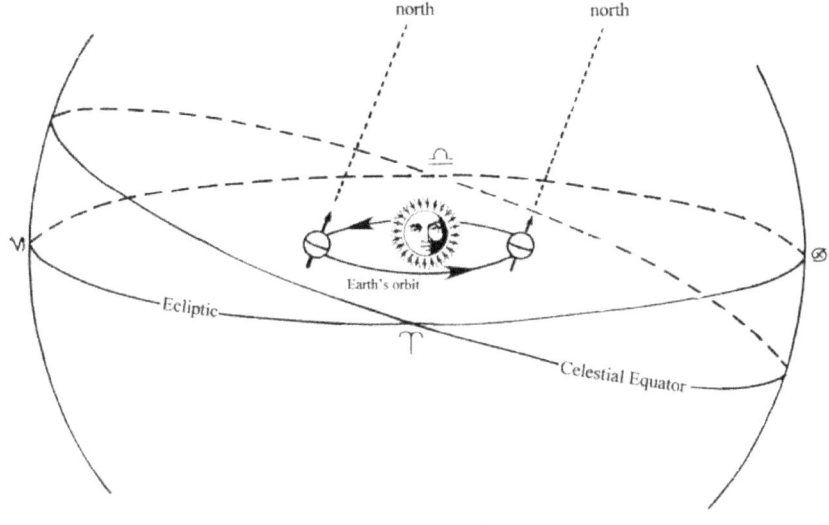

Figure 1

Figure 1. Earth's position at left, where the north pole is tilting toward the Sun, shows northern hemisphere summer and southern hemisphere winter. This is reversed with Earth at the opposite position shown at right. Notice that the plane of the Earth's orbit is the plane of the ecliptic and that the ecliptic's intersection with the plane of the Earth's equator marks the equinoxes as shown by the symbols for Aries and Libra. The Aries/Libra axis is a straight line that is produced by the intersection of two planes.

The shape of Earth's orbit around the Sun is an ellipse, not a perfect circle. *Aphelion* is when Earth is at its greatest distance from the Sun and is moving at its slowest orbital rate. Aphelion occurs around July 4th. *Perihelion* is when Earth is closest to the Sun and at its fastest orbital rate. Perihelion occurs around January 2nd. The seasons during which aphelion and perihelion occur shift over time due to the wobbling of Earth's axis (like the slow oscillation of a rapidly spinning top) which produces two observable effects. First, the direction in space that the poles point towards slowly shifts. The current pole star, Polaris, has not always been the pole star. Second, the equinoxes (intersection of the ecliptic and celestial equator) shift backwards in the zodiac of the constellations at the rate of 50 seconds of arc per year, or one degree every 72 years. The full cycle through the zodiac takes roughly 25,800 years on average (one complete wobble of Earth's axis for every 9,420,000 daily spins). This is called the *precession of the equinoxes*. This motion is more easily understood by watching an animation, many of which can be found online.

There is also a ~21,000 year cycle called truncated or *climatic precession* that has a powerful influence on climate. These two types of precession are related but different. The ~25,800-year precession of the equinoxes, more familiar to astrologers, has a longer length due to the counting of the cycle relative to the stars, not to aphelion and perihelion. The difference between these two kinds of precession is due to the slow rotation (about 112,000 years relative to the distant stars) of Earth's slightly elliptical orbit. This movement is known by several names: precession of the ellipse, perihelion precession, apsidal precession or orbital precession.

Earth is not a perfect sphere. It is a *prolate spheroid*, slightly flattened at the poles and bulging at the equator due to its fast rotation. Earth's polar diameter is 27 miles less than its diameter at the equator. The causes of the wobble that produces precession are the gravitational torques of the Moon, Sun and planets on Earth's equatorial bulge, though other additional factors conspire to make precession variable and not a constant cycle of 25,800 years.

To summarize, Earth rotates on its axis, which wobbles, while it orbits the Sun. The tilt of it's axis accounts for seasonal changes. The wobble of the axis, seen as the shifting of the equinoxes against the background (fixed) stars and changing pole stars, plays a role in gradual climate change cycles. The orbit of Earth around the Sun, which is slightly elliptical, itself rotates around the Sun. The variations of the Earth's orbit and tilt vary the amount of incoming solar radiation and cause climate variations, including ice ages, over long periods of time.

In Western astrology, the precession of the equinoxes, which shifts the position of the signs of the zodiac relative to the stars over time, is currently thought to be transitioning between the signs Pisces and Aquarius marking what is sometimes called a shift of ages. The dating of this change is far from certain because it is denoted by the artificial boundary of those constellations that are near the location of the present day vernal equinox. Many dates for such an age shift have been proposed and there is no consensus on this matter. In Mesoamerican astrology, it is probable that the movement of the winter solstice point was used to designate the cycle of equinox precession. The winter solstice point is currently pointing roughly towards the center of the Milky Way galaxy, and Maya inscriptions unambiguously point to the year 2012 as the transition point between great ages.

The Earth and Space Quantified

All of the data (planets, houses, signs) in an astrological chart, which is a map of the sky from a particular perspective, are located on a grid that is projected onto the sky. This sky grid itself is an extension of the grid used to measure the surface of Earth. In order to locate a particular point on Earth, imaginary lines are drawn that are anchored to some real and fixed features of Earth, such as the equator or the polar axis. This is how geographic maps showing latitude and longitude are made. Celestial coordinate systems on which astrology depends do the same thing, but the grid is projected onto the sky. All terrestrial and celestial map-making is based on the geometry of the sphere.

Geographers of the ancient world divided the surface of Earth into parallels of latitude and meridians of longitude (see *Figure 2*). The scientist Ptolemy (~150 CE) formalized this approach in his writings on geography. The word *latitude* (from Latin, but derived from the Greek word for width) applies to measurements north or south of the equator. All latitude lines are parallel to the equator. *Meridian*, in Latin, means middle (medius) of the day (dies). The word meridian comes from the observation that shadows at noon, the middle of the day, always lie in the north-south direction. All points on that shadow line, from equator to pole, will experience noon at the same time. Meridians of longitude measure distances east or west.

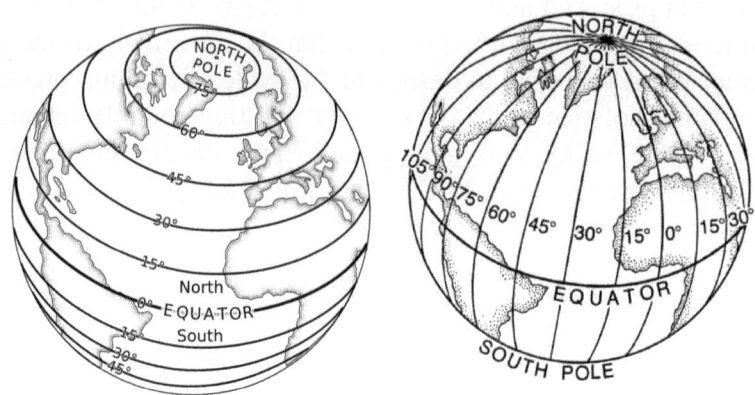

Figure 2.
(image credit: Pearson Scott Foresman, donated to the Wikimedia Foundation)

In *Figure 2* latitude and longitude lines on the globe are shown. On left a grid of horizontal bands or circles (latitude) are projected onto Earth, with the equator being in the center and having the largest diameter. Because the plane of the equator passes through the center of the Earth it is called a *great circle*. All other latitude bands, which are parallel to the equator but do not pass through the center of the Earth, are called *small circles*. On right a series of equidistant bands or circles emanating from the poles of Earth form a grid (longitude) encircling Earth. Each band or circle is the basis for a plane that passes through the poles. Because all longitude circles pass through the center of Earth they are great circles.

Both latitude and longitude are measured in units of degrees, minutes and seconds. The convention of using 360 degrees as a measure for the circumference of a circle was a Sumerian invention established four or more millennia ago. It is likely that 360 was chosen as it closely approximates the number of days in the cycle of the year, though the geometry of an inscribed hexagram (six sides of 60 degrees) may also have been a reason. The Greeks called one 360th of a circumference a *moira*, or part. Later, this unit came to be called in Latin, *de-gradus*, meaning "a step away". Each moira was divided

14

into 60 parts which Ptolemy called the "first small parts" and each of these again divided into 60ths he called the "second small parts." In Latin, Ptolemy's names became *pars minuta prima* and *pars minuta secunda*, or minutes and seconds.

To measure the sky, the planes of measurement on the Earth are *extended* into space. This extension of these planes creates the imaginary *celestial sphere* (see *Figure 3*). The various methods of celestial measurement, grids with different reference points, are called *celestial coordinate systems*. Coordinate systems are mapping techniques that locate things in space. Like a graph with two axes, each coordinate system utilizes a polar-like coordinate and an equator-like coordinate. The exercise of using the celestial sphere to solve problems in astronomy and navigation is called *celestial mechanics*.

In ancient times skywatchers noted the positions of celestial objects both along the horizon (a horizontal measurement) and in terms of altitude or distance above the horizon (a vertical measurement). This was the origin of what is called today the *horizon system*, still used in navigation and also for Local Space astrology (which positions the planets against the horizon as compass directions). Later, two other horizontal planes were used to measure the sky, the projection of Earth's equator into space (called the *celestial equator*), and the *ecliptic* which is the path of the Sun and planets.

Hipparchus (191-120 BCE), the Greek astronomer who made the first extensive star catalog, is thought to have used the *equatorial system* for measuring star positions. The equatorial system is used extensively in astronomy as it tracks the movements of planets and stars as Earth rotates clocklike which facilitates telescope and photographic work. A few centuries later, Ptolemy used the *ecliptic system,* which is far more useful for measuring the Sun, Moon and planets which are always on or close to the ecliptic, and this method also continues to be used today in astrology. (In astrology the equatorial system is used to determine the houses.) It is the translation of the location and position of sky objects or intersection points between these two systems that is at the heart of astrological chart calculations.

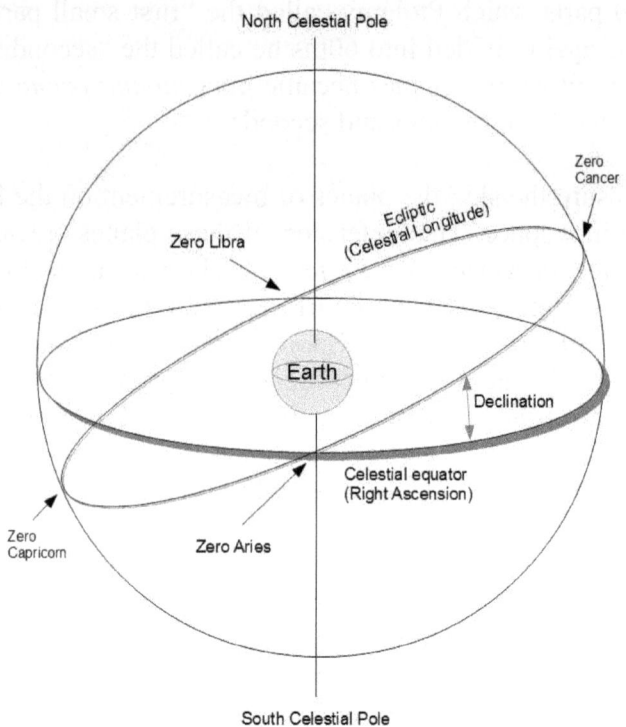

Figure 3. The Celestial Sphere. Earth appears in the center of an imaginary structure that extends into space. Notice that the celestial equator (horizontal in this diagram) is on the same plane as the Earth's equator, and that both are at 90 degrees to the poles. The ecliptic, the path of the Sun and the planets, is tilted by 23.45 degrees to the equator. The intersection of equator and ecliptic marks the first degrees of Aries and Libra (the equinoxes) and the points where they are farthest apart marks the first degrees of Cancer and Capricorn (the solstices).

All coordinate systems, terrestrial or celestial, have the same two features – a horizontal reference plane and a vertical reference plane. We see this methodology in the Cartesian coordinate system credited to Rene Descartes (1596–1650), Pierre de Fermat (1601–1665), and also Isaac Newton, which, long before them, was the framework of terrestrial mapping and celestial mechanics. Used in making graphs, the Cartesian coordinate grid shown below in *Figure 4* has an x-axis (horizontal) and a y-axis (vertical). With just two pieces of information, longitude and latitude, a point can be specified. With such a method applied to the globe, any place on Earth can be specified. Taken further, the Earth-centered grid can be extended into space where these imaginary lines can be used to locate objects such as planets.

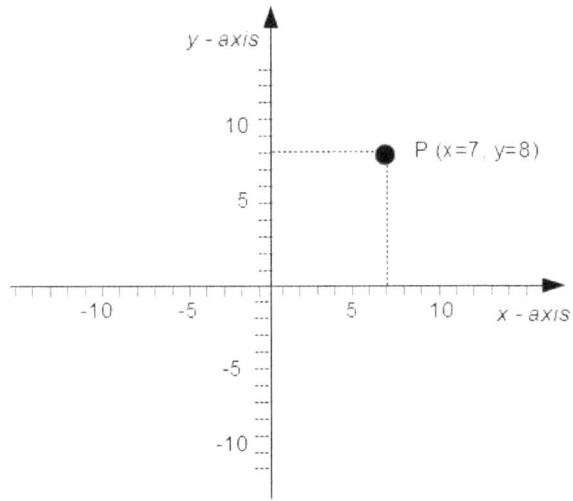

Figure 4. Cartesian Coordinate System. The x-axis, which is equivalent to both the horizon and the equator on Earth and their projections into space, and also the ecliptic, is a horizontal measurement from an origin point which is usually designated as zero. On Earth the origin point is the Greenwich Meridian (0 degrees terrestrial longitude), in space the equinox point (0 degrees Aries) is the origin point for both the equator and the ecliptic. The y-axis, equivalent to latitude on Earth, declination and celestial latitude in space, is a vertical measurement. Notice that there are positive and negative ranges on the grid. Any point can be located with just two coordinates. Here, point P is designated by 7 positive units on the x-axis and 8 positive units on the y-axis. This is basically how planets are located from Earth.

Interested readers are encouraged to download and explore planetarium software such as *Stellarium* to more fully grasp how the coordinate systems described in this chapter appear against the sky. Such software allows the user to not only visualize imaginary frameworks such as the equator and ecliptic against the sky, but also to see how the relationships of these great circles change against the horizon as the Earth rotates. With control over the rotation in terms of speed and time, astronomy software like *Stellarium* will gives a "hands-on" way of visualizing the two dimensional drawings used in this book.

Types of Celestial Coordinate Systems

The *horizon system* is a local system used primarily for navigation and surveying. Its frames of reference (see *Figure 5*) are the *horizon* as seen by the observer and the *zenith* directly overhead. Measurement is noted in terms of *azimuth* along the horizon (the x-axis) usually starting from north, and in *altitude*, or distance above or below the horizon (the y-axis). Astrologers use this system in what is called *local space astrology* where the positions of the planets are applied to a terrestrial map. In the horizon system the extension of the local horizon ignores the spherical Earth making this the most relative (local) of the major coordinate systems.

Figure 5 shows the horizon system which is based on what an observer, located in the center at X, will see – a flat horizon (except in mountainous regions), the four directions, and the dome of the sky above. The line running through points 1 and 2 is a great circle that intersects the object in the sky that is being measured. It passes through the zenith directly above the observer. The distance from the horizon, the distance between points 1 and 2, is the object's *altitude* (y-axis). Point 1, where this great circle crosses the horizon, is the object's *azimuth* (x-axis), which is usually measured along the horizon starting at north (typically designated by 0 degrees azimuth).

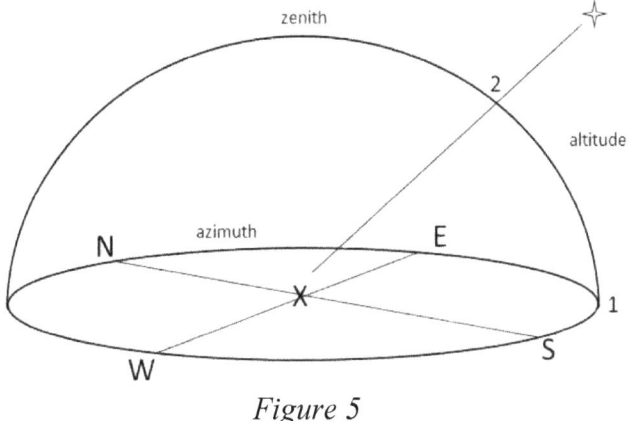

Figure 5

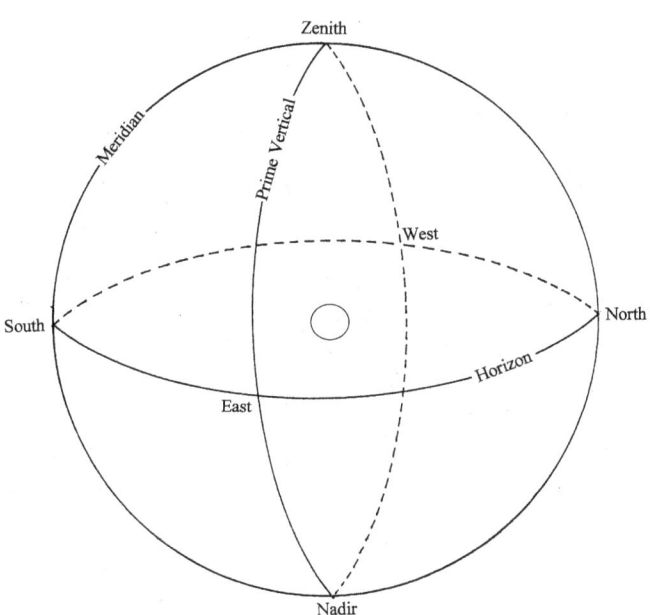

Figure 6

Figure 6 shows the horizon system as it appears from space with Earth at center. Here the horizon is projected into space and it is intercepted by the meridian and the prime vertical, two great circles, that pass through the zenith and mark the four directions where they cross the horizon.

The *equatorial system* (*Figure 7*) uses Earth's equator and its polar axis, extended into space, as reference points. The extension of the equator is called the *celestial equator*. The two key grid measurements are distance along the celestial equator, called *Right Ascension* (x-axis), and distance above or below the celestial equator, called *declination* (y-axis). Because Earth's rotation moves the terrestrial and celestial equator around each day, measurements along the celestial equator in Right Ascension are normally given in hours (but can be converted to degrees). The vernal equinox is used as the zero point in Right Ascension measurements along the celestial equator. Because the spin axis of Earth is very regular the equatorial system functions as a celestial clock.

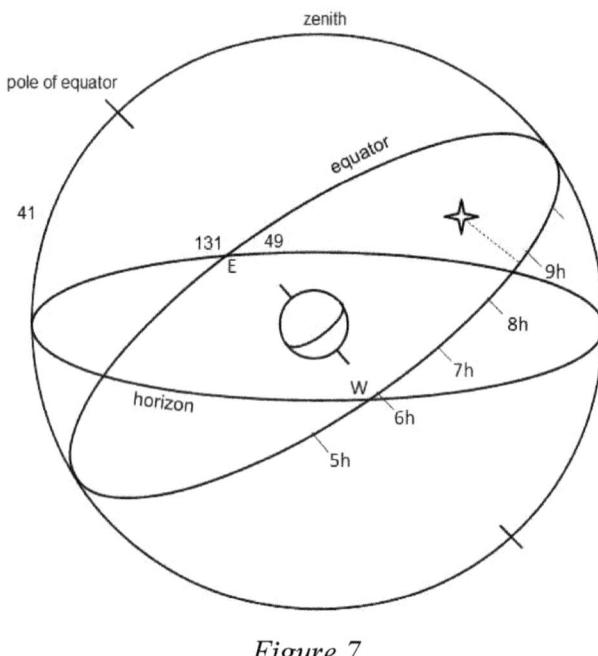

Figure 7

Figure 7: The celestial equator and the poles are shown as extensions of Earth's equator and poles. Where the equator crosses the local horizon, hour markers are shown that designate hours of Right Ascension. The star shown in the diagram is measured in the equatorial system by the hours of Earth's rotation needed (Right Ascension) and distance from the equator (declination).

For an observer anywhere on Earth the celestial equator cuts the horizon at due east to due west, but the angle relative to the horizon varies according to latitude. At low latitudes the angle is steep but moving toward the poles it decreases. A way to think about this is to consider the angle of the celestial poles. The star Polaris is located very close to the north equatorial pole and its elevation above the horizon specifies one's latitude. For example, the North celestial pole would be roughly 41 degrees above the horizon when viewed from New York City which is at 41 degrees of latitude (see *Figure 7*). since the equator is always at right angles to the poles, it would cut the horizon at an angle of 41 + 90 degrees or 131 degrees. since the horizon is a plane of 180 degrees (half a circle) the co-latitude of 131 degrees would be 49 degrees (180 − 131). The colatitude is used in some astrological chart calculations and is found by simply subtracting the event latitude from 90.

The *Ecliptic System (Figure 8)* uses Earth's orbital plane and its axis as reference points. The two key measurements are ecliptic *longitude* (x-axis) and ecliptic *latitude* (y-axis). The orbital plane of Earth around the Sun is more or less in the same plane as the other planets, so it is a practical grid system for plotting planetary positions. Astrologers use this system to mark the planet's places, but also use the equatorial system to establish the houses. As with the equatorial system, it is the equinoxes that are used as a zero point for measurement along the ecliptic. It is the transfer of positions between the equatorial and ecliptic systems that underlies many techniques in astrology including house and predictive systems, and was a major motivation behind the development of trigonometry.

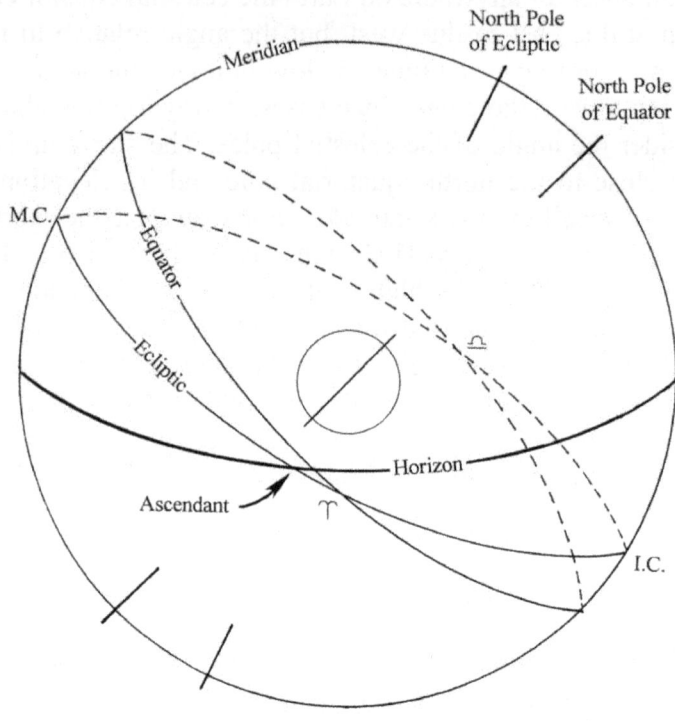

Figure 8

Figure 8: Earth is shown tilted along with the planes and poles of both the equator and the ecliptic. (The poles of any plane are always at right angles to it.) The horizon plane is also shown. Notice that where the ecliptic crosses the horizon marks the Ascendant and where it crosses the meridian marks the Midheaven (M.C.).

The *Galactic System* is a coordinate system used by astronomers to locate the positions of stars and other very distant objects. It uses the plane of the Milky Way galaxy, called the galactic equator, as a fundamental reference (x-axis), and also the polar axis of the galaxy (y-axis). The plane of the solar system is tilted at about 60 degrees relative to the plane of the galaxy. The solar system orbits the galactic center once in every 225 to 250 million years, this being called the galactic year. Galactic system coordinates are not often used in astrology.

Related reference points in four coordinate systems:

Earth	*Horizon*	*Equatorial*	*Ecliptic*
equator	horizon	celestial equator	ecliptic
poles	zenith	celestial poles	ecliptic poles
latitude	altitude	declination	celestial latitude
longitude	azimuth	right ascension	celestial longitude

Uses of coordinate systems:

Earth – maps, surveying, terrestrial navigation, time zones
Horizon – surveying, flight navigation, local space astrology
Equatorial – time-keeping, positional astronomy, astrology
Ecliptic – astrology, astronomy

Greek alphabet designations for the celestial sphere:

Longitude = lambda λ
Latitude = phi ϕ
Right ascension = alpha α
Declination = delta δ
Obliquity = epsilon ε

From Coordinate Systems to the Horoscope

The process of taking planetary positions measured along the ecliptic in longitude, and placing them in a framework of houses determined by Right Ascension, is a use of two coordinate systems. This is not a simple matter and involves triangular calculations handled with trigonometry. The solutions to translations from one system to another require a few known factors. One known is the distance from the meridian to the Aries equinox point, a point which is shared by both the equatorial and ecliptic system. This can be known from the time of an event or birth, or from an astronomical observation. Another known is the 23.45 degree angle between the intersection of the ecliptic and equator, this being the tilt of Earth's axis relative to the plane of its orbit around the Sun. If a line is drawn at right angles from a point on the ecliptic to a place on the equator, a second angle (90 degrees) is then known. Now, with one side and two angles known, the other sides and angle of this triangle can be calculated using trigonometry and the position of the point can be relocated to another set of coordinates. When the resulting data is reconfigured, an astrological chart can drawn up.

The primary tool of the astrologer is astrological chart, basically a map of the sky. It is often called a horoscope, which means "hour observer," a term traditionally applied to just the Ascendant. The astrological chart basically captures the view of the sky in the northern hemisphere looking south, with east and the Ascendant on the left. (The reverse is the case for the southern hemisphere.) The figures on the next pages illustrate how this works.

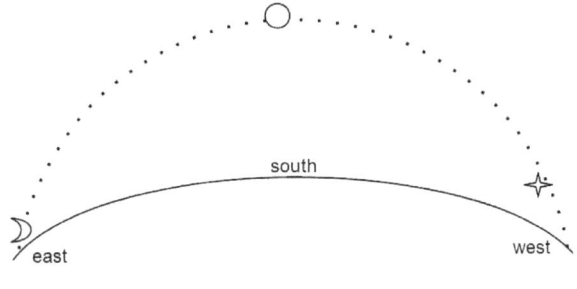

Figure 9

Figure 9 shows the standard northern hemisphere view of the region of the sky in which the planets are found. The observer faces south with east on their left and west on their right. Here, as Earth rotates, the Moon rises in the east as the Sun is near its highest arc in the sky – due south at noon. A star is setting in the west. The path these objects follow, shown as a dotted line, is the ecliptic.

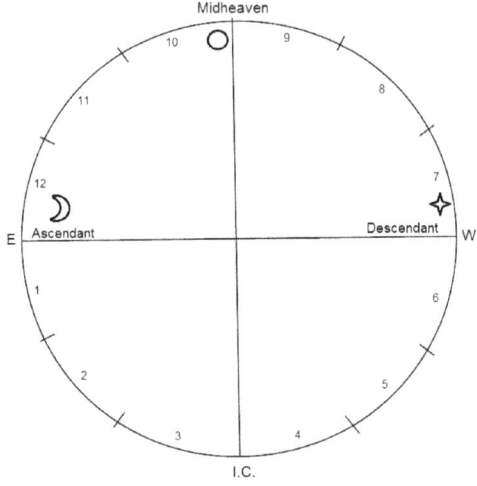

Figure 10

Figure 10 is the standard horoscope form which is used to map what is seen in Figure 9 above. As in Figure 9 the Moon rises in the east, the Sun is near the noon position at the Midheaven (which is south as viewed in the northern hemisphere) and a star is setting in the west. The circle itself here, the boundary of the diagram, is the ecliptic and the Ascendant marks the point where it crosses the horizon. The circle is traditionally divided into 12 sections called domiciles or houses and these are numbered counter-clockwise from the Ascendant.

25

Points on the Celestial Sphere

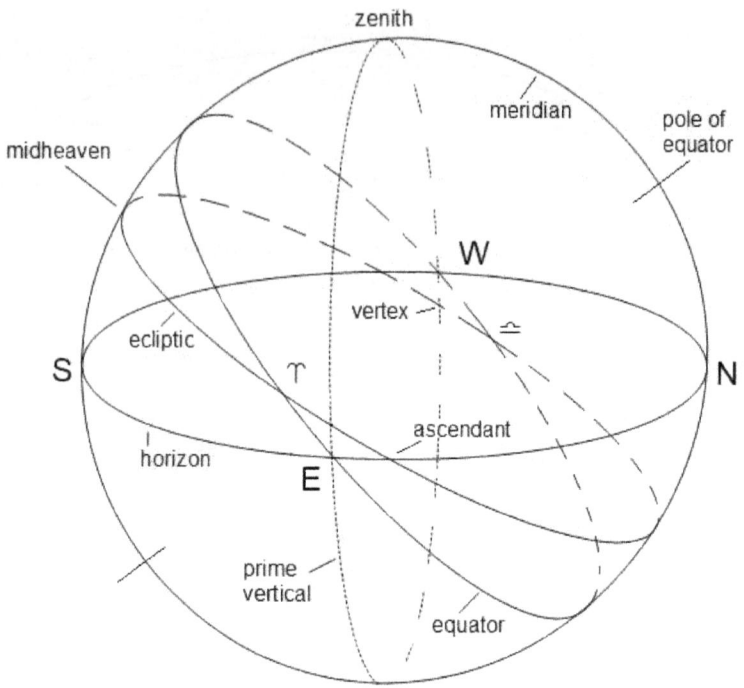

Figure 11

Figure 11 is a composite of three coordinate systems. The horizon system includes the plane of the horizon, marking the four directions, with the zenith at sky center. The nadir, not labeled, is opposite the zenith. The equatorial system includes the celestial equator (the extension of Earth's terrestrial equator) and its pole. The ecliptic system intersects with the equator at the equinoxes, Aries and Libra. Where the ecliptic crosses the horizon marks the Ascendant. Where it crosses the meridian marks the Midheaven (MC).

Chapter 2

Space and Time Measurement

In this section the terminology and most relevant definitions of astrological chart calculations are listed. It is intended as a general reference and a read-through list that students should be familiar with. First are matters related to coordinate systems and the celestial sphere which were introduced in the previous section. Second are definitions concerned with time – its conventions and also conversions.

Consider that the actual structure of the horoscope used by practitioners of astrology today has its origins in naked eye astronomical observations, and the time units used today by humans for social coordination are, or were originally, derived from astronomical facts. Before telescopes, or even astrolabes, humans in many early cultures studied the movements of the stars and planets and devised ways of charting and mapping them. In the mainstream academic world, the study of early astronomical observations is called archaeoastronomy.

Early cultures charted the movement of the Sun throughout the course of the year. In particular they noted its rising and setting positions and its altitude at noon. A wide variety of observatories were built to facilitate this methodical and proto-scientific activity. Some observatories consisted of simply a place to stand and a distant marker on the horizon. Others were buildings that incorporated into themselves the directional features of the annual solar cycle. It must not have escaped these early scientists that the cycle of vegetation moved along with the changes in the Sun's cycle.

The Moon was also an object of study, though one that is not so regular as the Sun's. In the higher latitudes such as the British Isles, the movements of the Moon become quite extreme and its rising and setting positions cover a wide arc. It was discovered that this larger lunar cycle of extreme rising and setting positions was about 19 years in length, this being the nodal cycle and also an eclipse cycle. Again, a number of creatively designed structures were erected in ancient times, including Stonehenge, to chart this cycle.

The study of archaeoastronomy may be seen as a background to the history of both astronomy and astrology. Nearly every convention used in astrology has its origins in the realities of the sky as it was observed in ancient times. In order to grasp the significance of the astrological chart itself, essentially a time-slice map, we need to understand that it is a product of thousands of years of sky-watching and hundreds of years of quantifying these observations.

Coordinate Systems

Great circles pass through the Earth's center cutting it vertically in halves (like orange sections). The equator, terrestrial and celestial, is a great circle. Great circles that pass through the *poles* establish lines of *longitude.* All longitude circles are great circles.

Small circles slice the Earth or celestial sphere, but do not pass through the center. Terrestrial latitude lines, except for the *equator* which is a great circle, are small circles.

Earth Coordinate System – the grid of latitude and longitude lines, and the polar axis, used in cartography, navigation and surveying.

Celestial Coordinate Systems – measure the sky using extensions of the Earth's equator and local horizon, and the plane of the ecliptic.

Horizon – the great circle where the sky meets the Earth that surrounds the observer. While this is technically a local feature of the observer, in astronomy the plane of the horizon is taken as passing through the center of Earth. At great distances this difference is negligible.

Zenith – the point directly above a location, at 90 degrees to the horizon. The zenith is part of the horizon coordinate system.

Nadir – the point on the other side of the Earth opposite the Zenith.

Meridian – for a local observer, the great circle that passes through the zenith and the north and south points on the horizon. The portion that passes above the observer is the upper meridian, the portion that passes under the Earth is the lower meridian.

Prime Vertical – the great circle that passes through the zenith and the east and west points on the horizon.

Prime Meridian – the meridian that passes through Greenwich, England, that serves as the longitudinal reference point (0 degrees) for mapping and navigation as well as astronomy (including astrological chart calculations).

Equator – the great circle that lies midway between the poles of the Earth, dividing it in half.

Celestial Equator – the extension of the plane of the equator into space which measured in Right Ascension or hour angle. Right Ascension is given in hours (time) and converted to degrees (space) by multiplying by 15. The calculation of the Right Ascension of the Midheaven (R.A.M.C.) is generally the first step in calculating an astrological chart.

Ecliptic – the Earth's orbit which, observed from a geocentric position, is seen as the Sun's path. The zodiac is centered on the ecliptic. Zodiacal longitude is *celestial longitude* measured on the ecliptic in degrees and minutes.

Midheaven (Medium Coeli / M.C. - "middle of the sky") – the point on the ecliptic that intersects the upper meridian. The Midheaven is normally the cusp of the 10th house in a horoscope. In astrology it symbolizes the public persona and role.

I.C. (Imum Coeli: "bottom of the sky") – the point on the ecliptic beneath the Earth that intersects the lower meridian. The I.C. is normally the cusp of the 4th house in a horoscope.

Ascendant – the sign and degree of the zodiac at the intersection of the ecliptic and the horizon. In astrology it symbolizes the presentation of self and personal identity. Historically, this point was called the *horoscope* and is also the cusp of the 1st house in most house systems. As Earth rotates, the signs of the zodiac on the ecliptic, measured in celestial longitude, are seen to rise in the east, culminate as they cross the upper meridian, and then set in the west. As Earth rotates on its axis, the celestial equator, which is measured in Right Ascension, always rises exactly east and sets exactly west. Because the plane of the ecliptic is tilted from the plane of the equator by 23.45 degrees, the signs of the zodiac will rise at points either north or south of true east. Only the first degree of Aries and Libra, the equinoctial signs, will always rise due east and set due west because that point is where the ecliptic and equator intersect.

The tilt of the ecliptic relative to the equator and horizon causes the signs near Aries to rise faster than those near Libra in the northern hemisphere, hence the designations "signs of short ascension" and "signs of long ascension." This phenomena can be visualized best in a planetarium, on software, or by spinning a globe that contains its own horizon and markings for the equator and ecliptic.

Equatorial Ascendant – the point in the east where the equator and the horizon intersect. It is always due east and is additionally intersected by the prime vertical. Where a line through this point and the pole of the equator intersects the ecliptic is its zodiacal position.

Vertex – the intersection of the ecliptic and the prime vertical in the west. The anti-vertex is the same intersection in the east. In astrology it is thought to symbolize strong encounters with others.

Diurnal arc – the arc of the daily cycle of the Sun (or other point) as it is carried by the rotation of Earth from rising to setting. Half of the diurnal arc, i.e. from rise to culmination at the upper meridian, or from culmination to set, is called a diurnal *semi-arc*.

Nocturnal arc – the arc of the Sun (or other point) from setting to rising, also divided into two semi-arcs.

House Circles – great circles that radiate from poles that intersect the equator, ecliptic or prime vertical, and are used to determine the location of house cusps in certain house systems.

Obliquity – The inclination of the plane of the ecliptic to the plane of the equator: 23 degrees, 27 minutes (23.45 degrees). Due to an oscillation of the Earth's axis this figure varies by a few degrees over a ~ 40,000-year period and was slightly higher in Hellenistic times.

Equinoxes – the two points where the great circles ecliptic and equator intersect at an angle of 23.45 degrees. The hours of daylight equal the hours of darkness when the Sun is at the vernal (Aries) or autumnal (Libra) equinox. The Sun rises due east and sets due west only when it is at the equinoxes.

Solstices – points where the Sun moving along the ecliptic is at its greatest distance (23.45 degrees of declination) from the equator. These points are 0 degrees Cancer (summer solstice) and 0 degrees Capricorn (winter solstice). Solstice means "sun standstill" because the lengths of day and night remain near constant for a few days around the time the Sun reaches these points, in contrast to the rapidly changing ratio of day and night when the Sun is at the equinoxes.

Node – The points on the ecliptic where the Moon or a planet's orbit intersects it. These intersections are due to the small inclination of the Moon's or a planet's orbital plane relative to the plane of Earth's orbit. The intersection of two planes creates a straight line or axis that shifts over time as the shape of the orbits change. All nodes extend to opposite points of the zodiac and are designated as north or south nodes, the north node being the one that, as the orbit oscillates, crosses the ecliptic from south to north celestial latitude.

Zodiac – the band of sky measured along the ecliptic, extending 8° north and south of it. The *tropical zodiac* is the zodiac of 30 degree sections of the ecliptic (signs) that begins at the vernal equinox. This is the zodiac that most Western astrologers employ in their work. The *sidereal zodiac* is the zodiac of constellations. Its beginning point (fiduciary) varies according to tradition and argument. Hindu

(Vedic) astrology utilizes a sidereal zodiac. This difference in degrees along the ecliptic between the tropical and sidereal zodiac is called the *ayanamsha*. Although there is no exact agreement among astrologers on this matter, it is generally accepted that the tropical and sidereal zodiacs were coincident roughly 2,000 years ago. There is no agreement as to exactly when this occurred. According to Cyril Fagan both coincided in 213 A.D. They coincided in 255 B.C. according to Massey and in 97 B.C. according to Rudhyar. The coinciding of the two zodiacs supposedly marked the beginning of the Age of Pisces.

Conventions of Time

Calendars are civil schedules that approximate astronomical cycles. Calendars which are linked to the lunar cycle (i.e. Islamic calendar) drift over time with respect to the solar cycle and need periodic corrections to keep roughly synchronized with the seasons. Solar-based calendars, which require fewer corrections, fix the equinox to the seasons. In 46 B.C., the Romans adopted the Egyptian solar calendar of 365 days, plus a leap day every four years. This is the 365.25-day year that was the basis of the *Julian Calendar*. But because the tropical year is more accurately 365.2422 days, the equinox retrograded in the Julian Calendar from March 25 in 46 B.C. to March 11 in 1570 A.D. In October of 1582, the improved *Gregorian Calendar* was adopted in much of Europe. Ten days were dropped and other critical time-keeping adjustments were made. The non-Catholic world did not accept this change until much later; Britain in 1752 and Russia in 1918.

Other cultures have developed different calendars and some, like the Islamic calendar, are based on the lunar cycle. Others coordinate both Sun and Moon as in the Hebrew calendar which uses a lunar month but requires adjustments at times over the course of the 19-year Metonic cycle (a common multiple of the solar year and lunar synodic cycle). The Maya civil calendar (Haab') consisted of 18 "weeks" of 20 days followed by 5 extra days. Its start date drifted through the seasons like the Julian calendar did.

Year – the time it takes for one revolution of Earth around the Sun, or viewed from Earth, one complete circuit of the Sun through the signs of the zodiac on the ecliptic. The *sidereal year* marks the return of the Sun to a given point in the background of the fixed stars in the constellations. Its value is 365.2564 days. The *tropical year* marks a return of the Sun to either of the equinoxes. Its value is 365.2422 days (20 minutes shorter than the sidereal year), and it is the basis of our civil year. The reason for the discrepancy is *precession*, the slow wobbling of the Earth's axis.

Day – the most basic time unit is the day, one complete rotation of Earth on its axis that is usually counted from midnight to midnight or noon to noon. The day is marked by the passage of the Sun through the sky and below Earth, its combined diurnal and nocturnal arcs. There are several types of day:

Sidereal day – the true period of Earth's rotation (23h 56m 04s of mean solar time) established by the interval between two successive transits (passages) of a star (not the Sun) over the local meridian. There are 366.2422 sidereal days in one year. The columns below show the consistent vertical alignment between the local meridian and a given star at the same time over the course of 4 days.

Day #	1	2	3	4
Star	✧	✧	✧	✧
Meridian	M	M	M	M

Solar day – also called the astronomical day, marks the interval between two successive transits (passages) of the Sun's center over the same local meridian. The solar day is 24 hours. There are 365.2422 solar days in one year.

Mean solar day – (also called the civil day) is the average of successive solar transits of the meridian, that is the average value of all solar days throughout the year. During summer the Sun moves ahead in the zodiac slightly faster than it does in winter. The small variation in length of day is due to the elliptical orbit of Earth.

The columns below show the alignment between local meridian, a star and the Sun over the course of 4 days. The Sun moves ahead in the zodiac about a degree per day and this means Earth's rotation needs another 3m 56 seconds each day to catch up to it. (In reality, it is the movement of Earth along its orbit that changes perspective and makes the Sun appear as if it is moving.)

Day #	1	2	3	4
Star	✧	✧	✧	✧
Meridian	M	M	M	M
Sun	☉	☉	☉	☉

Notice that the 3 minute and 56 second difference between the sidereal day and the solar day adds up to almost exactly one full day over the course of a year (3m56s x 365.2422 days = 1436.6 minutes ÷ 60 = 24 hours). This is the basis of the roughly 10 seconds-per-hour *solar-sidereal correction* necessary in astrological chart calculations when determining local sidereal time. (The exact figure is 9.8333 seconds per hour.) The solar-sidereal correction is also known as the acceleration correction. Tables for this correction are often found in ephemerides and tables of houses.

Apparent solar time – this is sundial time, completely local. It will vary in length somewhat over the course of a year due to the obliquity or tilt of the axis and the slight eccentricity of Earth's orbit around the Sun.

Mean solar time – this is based on the mean solar day and is also known as civil time or clock time. There may be up to 16 minutes difference between this time and apparent solar time.

The Equation of Time – describes the difference between apparent solar time, which is what is observed, and mean solar time, which is an average and used for civil timekeeping. Apparent and mean solar time can vary by as much as 16 minutes. This variation between apparent and mean solar time can be seen if the Sun were to be sighted at the same time each day over the course of a year. The curve (like a figure 8) produced by daily observations of this variation is called an *analemma* and is often found printed on globes.

Greenwich Mean Time (GMT) – the mean time to which all clocks are synchronized. The Greenwich, England meridian is the standard (prime) meridian for the Earth. Today GMT is considered to be a time zone and UT1 (universal time) or UTC (coordinated universal time) are used by the world.

Zone or Standard Time – local times have been established at intervals of 15 degrees longitude East or West of Greenwich. These were standardized to facilitate train schedules and were adopted in the U.S. in 1883, although it took years for them to become commonly used. 15 degrees longitude = 1 hour of standard time. A standard meridian is adopted for Local Standard Time, such as 75 West longitude (Eastern Time), 90 W (Central Time), 105 W (Mountain Time, 120 W (Pacific Time), etc.

Local Mean Time (sometimes called True Local Time or TLT) – this is a local time that accounts for the difference in time between the location and the longitude of the time zone center. For example, individual cities would have their own local mean time based on their longitude. This kind of time was in common use before time zones were introduced.

Local Standard Time (LT) – refers to clock time that is standardized in a region and based on the local mean time of a standard time zone, these being 15 degrees or one hour apart. The boundaries of a time zone define the use of a single standard time centered on a standard meridian, i.e. Eastern Time is centered on the 75th meridian.

Daylight Saving Time (DST or DT) – a controversial time-keeping convention in which one hour is added in the spring and then subtracted in the autumn. It has been adopted at different times in various states and many countries for varying reasons. It created a nightmare for astrologers due to the complications in record keeping because of regional differences in applying this change. However, historical time change data has now been compiled and published, first in print and then as more easily updated software. *War Time*, similar to DT though in effect all year, was used during World War II in the

United States. In England double summer time was used during World War II.

Daylight Saving Time, which began as a proposal to save lighting (energy) costs and create more time for recreation, was aggressively promoted by the British builder William Willett beginning around 1907. Studies do not show definitively that it saves energy costs though some show it increases motor fuel consumption. Studies do show that it increases revenue for retailers and for golf courses. Daylight Saving Time continues to exist probably because it supports such commercial interests and because it gives more daylight on winter mornings.

Sidereal Time (ST) – this is the angular distance, measured in time on the celestial equator, linking zero degrees of Aries to the local meridian. When zero degrees of Aries is on the local meridian, the sidereal time (S.T.) is 0 hours. 15 degrees of Earth rotation = 1 hour of sidereal time. A sidereal day (23h 56m) is the time between two successive transits of 0 Aries over the local meridian.

S.T. gains 3m 56s per day in the ephemeris in order to catch up with the daily motion of the Sun in the zodiac. The sidereal time listing found in an ephemeris is the local sidereal time given for noon or midnight each day for Greenwich, England. This is the standard time against which local time is adjusted when doing astronomical calculations for astrology charts. It is called sidereal time because it is based on the relation between the rotating Earth and the distant stars that appear to be fixed in space (see sidereal day above, and solar-sidereal correction below).

When converting mean solar time to sidereal time, one must take into account the almost 4 minute (3m 56s) difference between the solar day and the sidereal day. This time difference accumulates at a rate of roughly 10 seconds per hour (1 second per 6 minutes) which must be added to mean solar to get sidereal time. 24 hours of mean solar time = 24h 03m 57s of sidereal time. See below for further explanation.

Solar-sidereal correction (SST) – The solar-sidereal correction is sometimes called the acceleration interval. It is the difference between a single full rotation of Earth relative to the stars, and a single full rotation relative to the Sun. This difference is due to the change in perspective caused by the movement of Earth along its orbit around the Sun. At any location, the meridian, the great circle that runs south to north and through the local zenith, is normally used as a reference point. Using a star or other "fixed" point as a marker, 23h 56m of solar time will elapse between successive passages of that point over the Meridian. Using the Sun as a marker, one daily cycle from noon to noon is 24 hours because Sun appears to have moved ahead in the zodiac during that time by about one degree (actually, the Earth has moved along in its orbit around the Sun). The solar-sidereal correction is 3 minutes and 56 seconds for a full solar day, which is about 10 seconds per hour. Given a time of day that has been converted to Greenwich Mean Time (add 5 hours for times given in Eastern Standard Time, etc.), 10 seconds per hour is then added to that time for the solar-sidereal correction. This rate can be found in tables (p. 217) or calculated by dividing the GMT of an event/birth by 6.1.

Local Sidereal Time (LST) – this is the sidereal time adjusted for a particular meridian. It is used for calculating the local Midheaven, Ascendant, and houses and is listed daily in any ephemeris. When local sidereal time is equal to zero, the first degree of Aries will be at the Midheaven.

Universal Time (UT) – is Greenwich Mean Time expressed in 24-hour format. It is used to regulate civil clocks and is measured by the angle between the mean Sun and the Greenwich Meridian. It is also called zero zone time because it is based on the location of the Greenwich observatory in England which has been agreed internationally to mark 0 degrees Earth longitude. There are several versions of UT that are more or less the same but are derived in different ways. UT1 is based on alignments with very distant quasars. UTC (coordinated universal time) is based on an atomic time scale.

Ephemeris Time (ET) – does not use the Sun for time-keeping. This is a uniform time, introduced in 1940, used to calculate exact planetary positions based on an idealized solar time. It is used in modern astronomical ephemerides. Because the Earth does not rotate at a precisely consistent rate (this being due to earthquakes, tidal forces, and other disturbances) ephemeris time was created. The difference between the ephemeris time system and the solar time system is expressed as a correction, ΔT (Delta T). Ephemeris Time $= UT + \Delta T$. In order to calculate planetary positions exactly, as would be the case with solar or lunar returns, ΔT should be accounted for. (Ephemeris Time is also known as Terrestrial Time or Dynamical Time – see table on page 234.)

Chapter 3

Using Triangles to Measure the Sky: A Short History of Trigonometry

Planetary positions used in astrological chart calculations are given in the ephemeris as daily discreet points along the ecliptic. To locate them in the astrological houses requires computations that involve reconciling the ecliptic (where the planets are found) with the equator which tracks the Earth's rotation. This amounts to the translation of information in the equatorial coordinate system to that of the ecliptic coordinate system and vice versa. Prior to the 19th century, most serious astrologers worked with trigonometry to solve these problems; they were also mathematicians. By the 20th century, practicing astrologers began to rely more on published tables of houses, proportional tables and logarithms to calculate horoscopes. These methods use data derived from trigonometry but reduce it to listings that can be manipulated using arithmetic. When personal computers became readily available and affordable in the late 1970s through the 1980s, chart calculations based on tables were abandoned for instant computer calculations. During this time the use of trigonometry in chart calculations survived only among the few programmers of astrological software.

Trigonometry, which means "triangle measurement," is about conversions of angles to lengths, and vice versa. Plane trigonometry measures triangles on a two dimensional plane, spherical trigonometry measures triangles on a sphere's curved surface. Solving the mathematical problems necessary to calculate an astrological chart inevitably requires the use of spherical trigonometry. The solutions to the spherical trigonometric problems involved in calculating the Midheaven, Ascendant and house cusps, however, does not necessarily require an *understanding* of spherical geometry.

Over the past two millennia some astrologers, discussed in this section, contributed to the development of trigonometry as a technical subject and they certainly understood what they were doing. But for centuries most practicing astrologers who used trigonometrical formulae when casting charts simply followed a standard procedure. During the 20th century before calculators and computers, when all astrologers were calculating charts by hand, it was the same situation, only a very few really knew much about what they were doing. Most just knew how to find the right numbers in various tables. With the rise of the personal computer and the proliferation of astrological software the vast majority of astrologers are now completely ignorant of what lies behind the calculation of a horoscope. This chapter is an attempt to remedy this disconnect by explaining how trigonometry solves the basic problems of horoscope calculation, without going too deeply into the complex proofs behind each operation.

The study, mapping and recording of sky phenomena began in the ancient Middle East during the second millennium B.C.E. This development was the beginning of the exact sciences and it can be argued that, in addition to calendrical concerns, the needs of astrologers were behind these early scientific efforts. The Babylonians recorded risings and settings of astronomical bodies in terms of both position and time, followed the cycle of Venus, cataloged stars and constellations and applied mathematics to their findings. They developed ways to measure celestial phenomena, including sexagesimal notation. Beginning with the Sun's motion through the quarters or seasons of the year, further division of these quarters into thirds likely produced the signs of the zodiac which, was established by the 6th century B.C.E.

During the fourth and third centuries B.C.E., the Greeks, who were concerned with solving problems related to the annual rising and setting of stars, approached sky measurement problems more theoretically. One Greek contribution to mathematical astronomy was the conception of three dimensional geometric models that allowed for accurate measurements of both the globe and sky phenomena. These models were consistent with the Greek notions of the universe being spherical. The solutions to the problems presented by the measurement of angles and arcs on a sphere was the subject matter of what was called *spherics* and several early texts on the subject have survived. It was the merging of spherics and trigonometry that began the mathematical tradition that the fundamental astrological calculations, the translations of positions between coordinate systems, are based on. This tradition is called spherical trigonometry.

The science of spherics was much concerned with the rising times for bodies and degrees on the ecliptic, topics that are crucial to astrology as well as length of day measurement. Recall that the celestial equator is like a clock that rotates in a predictable way spatially and in terms of time. It is always anchored on the horizon at due east and west for any point on the globe at any time of day. (Planetarium software such as *Stellarium* is very useful in visualizing this). If a star or planet is located directly on the equator, or at 0 Aries or Libra (the equinoxes) on the ecliptic, it will rise due east and set due west. But in astrology, or in regard to measuring sunrises and sunsets, the action is on the ecliptic. A body like the Sun, or a degree on the ecliptic some distance from the equinoxes, will not rise due east or set due west, it will follow a trajectory that is located on a small circle that is parallel to the equator. It will also move along with the degree of the equator that was rising at the same time that it was.

So the rising and setting of the Sun, Moon and planets is a problem that involves working with both the equatorial and ecliptic systems. The calculation of when points on the ecliptic will culminate, rise or set, is complicated and, with risings and settings, requires data from all three coordinate systems, equatorial, ecliptic and horizon. The methods the Greeks developed for solving these problems of transferring locations on the ecliptic to the equator, and vice versa, was based on modeling the problem using triangles and making tables of known angles and known sides from which other sides and angles could be calculated.

In a transfer of position from the ecliptic to the equator one such known angle is the one created by the intersection of the celestial equator and the ecliptic, the obliquity angle. Recall the equator and ecliptic are two celestial planes, and also great circles, that intersect at an angle of 23.45 degrees, which is the tilt of the Earth's axis. One known side of a spherical triangle can be determined from the time of an event converted into measurement (Right Ascension) along the equator. The resulting figure is a linear measurement from

0 Aries along the celestial equator of the rotating Earth. With data for distance along the equator, and with one angle known, a right triangle can then be created by connecting the ecliptic and equator with a perpendicular between them – this producing a second known angle of 90 degrees. And with a right triangle, solutions that the astrologer needs become possible. This is the subject matter of this chapter and will be elaborated on ahead. But first let's review some basic geometry.

The geometry of the triangle, usually taught in the second year of high school, states that all triangles must have angles that add up to 180 degrees. Right triangles are composed of a right angle (90 degrees) between two sides, and two other angles that may vary but together must add to 90 degrees. There are five things to know about a right triangle: the lengths of each of the three sides, and the two unknown angles (acute angles). But what if only two sides and the angle between them, or two angles and a side between them are all that is known?

Trigonometry is a branch of geometry. The history of geometry, which intertwines with that of astrology, astronomy, geography, and navigation, begins with the ancient Babylonians and Egyptians. Both cultures used triangles to measure the angular distances of objects on land and in the sky and some evidence suggests their understanding included ratios of the sides and angles, which would be considered trigonometry. The properties of the right triangle were probably known by the second millennium B.C.E. We know that Egyptian surveyors used a rope with knots at 3, 4, and 5 units apart to establish accurate 90 degree corners for buildings. This was practical knowledge and this approach is still used today by carpenters, floor installers and others in the building trades. Many centuries later, the Greek philosopher *Pythagoras* (~580 B.C.E.) expressed this property of right triangles in the form of an equation. He taught that in all right triangles the square of the hypotenuse (side c in *Figure 12* below) is equal to the sum of the square of the other two sides. This is the *Pythagorean Theorem*.

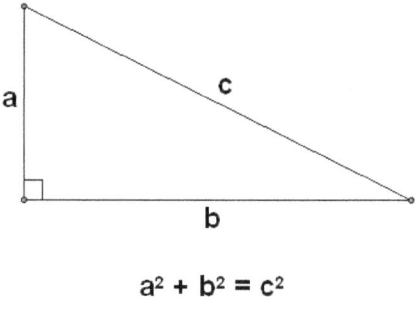

$$a^2 + b^2 = c^2$$

Figure 12

Euclid (active ~300 B.C.E.) published a book on geometry that became a classic work and a cornerstone of Western education right up to modern times. The book, called *Elements*, is a highly organized and accessible work in thirteen parts that was mostly a compilation of the ideas of earlier Greek mathematicians. In Euclid's book are the basic rules of number and geometrical shapes, including the circle and the triangle, both being of critical importance in understanding trigonometry. Euclid's logical proofs, expressed as postulates and theorems in his presentation of the rules of numbers and geometry, is one of the cornerstones of the modern scientific method.

Early Greek scientists used geometry to measure the stars and planets, to make maps and to navigate the oceans. *Aristarchus of Samos* (310-250 B.C.E.) was a Greek scientist who is best known for his advocacy of the heliocentric solar system model. He also argued that the Moon did not produce its own light and that it was illuminated by the Sun. Although his ideas were unable to supplant the geocentric models of Aristotle and Ptolemy that dominated ancient and medieval science, he was probably an influence on Copernicus whose heliocentric model of the solar system played a major role in the scientific revolution some 1800 years later.

Aristarchus also attempted to measure the size and distances of the Sun and Moon using triangles and the Pythagorean Theorem in his surviving work *On the Sizes and Distances of the Sun and Moon.* Based on visual observations of the Moon's first quarter, which should mark a 90 degree angle between the two as view from Earth, he observed that when the Moon was exactly half illuminated, its angle from the Sun was 87 degrees. Therefore, if the angle Sun-Moon-Earth is 90 degrees, and the angle Moon-Earth-Sun is estimated to be 87 degrees (it is really 89.42), then the distant angle Moon-Sun-Earth is 3 degrees.

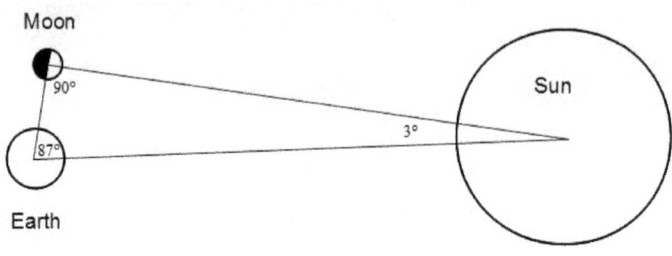

Figure 13

With figures for one side (an estimate of the distance to Moon) and all three angles of a right triangle, Aristarchus constructed a number of other triangles as a proof and concluded that the distance from Earth to the Sun must be 18 to 20 times the distance from the Earth to the Moon (it is really 388 times). Still, this measurement was a feat for its time and it gives a sense of how geometry was crucial to doing astronomy before telescopes.

Eratosthenes (275-194 B.C.E.), educated in several subjects including mathematics, astronomy, and music theory, was the chief librarian at Alexandria. Eratosthenes learned that at noon on the summer solstice in Syene, just south of today's Aswan on the Tropic of Cancer (latitude 23.47), the Sun at noon (directly overhead) was reflected in a deep well. On this same day in Alexandria, 5,000 stadia (11 stadia = ~1 mile) due north on the same longitude line, the shadow of a obelisk or gnomon (part of sundial that casts a shadow) at noon was 7.5 degrees off from vertical. Assuming the Earth is a sphere, a triangular section can be established between Syene, the center of the Earth, and Alexandria as shown (angle exaggerated) below.

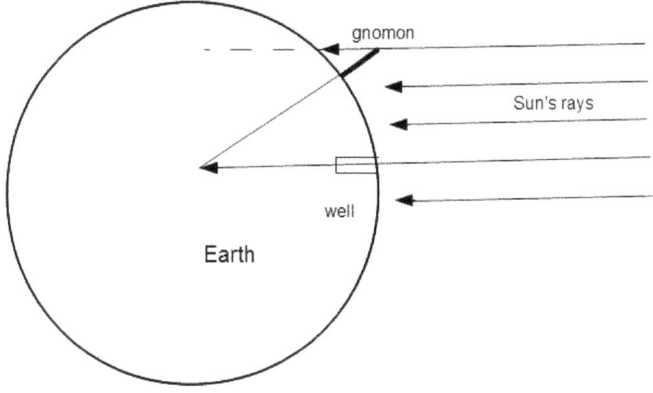

Figure 14

Erathostenes reasoned that if the light rays from the Sun are coming at the Earth in parallel, the arc of the Earth's circumference between Syene and Alexandria must be 7.5 degrees. Further, if 5,000 stadia is 7.5 degrees, and 7.5 degrees is 1/50 of 360, then the circumference of the Earth must be 50 x 5,000, or 250,000 stadia (or 25,000 miles), a figure which turns out to be very close to the actual circumference. In this computation, Eratosthenes was using triangles to solve a problem on a curved surface, which moves us closer to spherics and trigonometry.

Hipparchus (~150 B.C.E.) was one of the greatest astronomers of antiquity. He compiled a catalog of over 800 fixed stars and organized them according to their brightness (his scale is still used today). He is regarded by astronomers as the discoverer of the precession of the equinoxes, he determined the distance to the Moon with accuracy, and measured the length of the year to within 6 minutes. He also introduced to Greek science Babylonian sexagesimal notion for the measurement of angles and is considered by many to be the founder of trigonometry.

Hipparchus made simple trigonometric tables based on extended straight lines from an angle within a circle that touches its edge. Lines drawn from these contact points to the center of the circle establish a triangle ABC as in the diagram of *Figure 15* below. These lines, which as the angle opens up will range from 0 to 180, were called *chords* meaning bowstring, in contrast to the curve of the circle which was called "arcus" or bow. Chords were expressed in numbers relative to the diameter. In the diagram below line BC is the chord of the angle at A. Hipparchus calculated the value of chords for every 7.5 degrees around the circle and used his data to solve astronomical problems such as the Moon' orbit. Unfortunately, his tables and his precise methodology did not survive and are now known only from references made by other ancient authors.

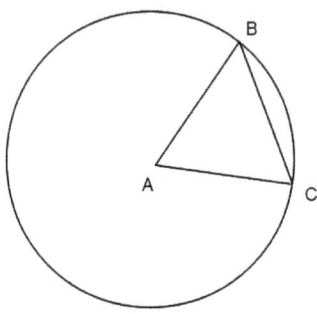

Figure 15

The early forms of spherical trigonometry modeled astronomical motions and aspects of the globe by constructing triangles from the center of a sphere to its surface where contacts with circles were made. For example, consider the equator and the ecliptic as great circles on the surface of a sphere. These great circles have a common center from which lines can connect to points on them forming triangles to be solved using known angles. Solutions to such problems are made easier when there are known relationships between the size of angles from the center and the arc of the great circle. Tables of these relationships, called tables of chords, were calculated and are precursors to modern trigonometry.

Menelaus of Alexandria (70-140 C.E.) is known as the father of spherical trigonometry as he introduced the subject in his three-book work called *Sphaerica*. This book has survived (his six-book treatise on chords is lost) and contains his ideas on spherical triangles, the area enclosed by arcs of great circles on the surface of a sphere, and also his use of chords. He found a way to convert coordinates between the ecliptic system and the equatorial system, known as Menelaus's Theorem, which became the basis for calculations of rising times of planets and the Ascendant. We will come back to spherical trigonometry later as it is the kind of trigonometry that is used to compute Midheavens, Ascendants and house cusps.

Three hundred years after Hipparchus and about two hundred after Menelaus, *Ptolemy* (~150 C.E.) presented a table of chords, and his methodology for constructing it, in his book *Mathematikas Syntaxis*, a massive work of which many copies of which have survived. This piece of writing was so impressive and highly regarded by later astronomers and mathematicians that it was referred to as the greatest, or most majestic, of books. In Arabic it became known as "al-majisti" or in Latin, *Almagest*, and this name stuck.

Ptolemy also authored a number of other books that synthesized the science of his times. One was the *Quadrapartitum*, or *Tetrabiblios*, which means "four books." Its subject matter is entirely astrological and it became the standard reference for astrologers up to the Renaissance and beyond. In it Ptolemy outlined the subject of astrology but it appears that he was not a practitioner or concerned with interpretation – he was an organizer of the astrological knowledge of his times and was more concerned with putting astrology into the context of the Aristotelian and Stoic world view. Ptolemy also wrote books on optics, music theory and geography.

Ptolemy's table of chords in the *Almagest* was calculated for all arcs from 1/2 degree to 180 degrees, in 1/2 degree increments. In his table diameters were measured in 120 units and circumferences in 360 degrees, a 1:3 relationship that approximates π (Pi). In Ptolemy's table, each $^1/_2$ degree of arc is designated by a ratio of the chord to the diameter of a circle – the chord is thus a ratio that varies for all angles up to the 180 degrees of the diameter, the maximum angle. Ptolemy used the term moira (degree), which means "steps away from" to measure the properties of circles. As previously noted, each degree he divided into 60 small parts called "pars minuta prima" and those into "pars minuta secunda," called minutes and seconds today.

Ptolemy's method of tabulating chords began with data obtained from Euclidean geometry. Using the tools and knowledge of his time he inscribed certain geometric solids into circles (regular pentagon, decagon, hexagon, and square) and then, using triangles and the Pythagorean Theorem, calculated the chord ratios for the angles 36°, 72°, 60°, 90° directly. The angles 120°, 144°, and 180° were found as supplements to those already calculated and the remaining angles were determined through bisections and approximations.

Angle in degrees	Chord in diameter units
36°	37° 4' 55"
60°	60°
72°	70° 32' 3"
90°	84° 51' 10"
108°	97° 4' 56"
120°	103° 55' 23"
144°	114° 7' 37"
180°	120°

From this table you can see that as the angle between two radii opens, the chord drawn between their contact points on the circumference of the circle widens. As the angle increases from 0° to 180° (from a single radius to the full diameter of the circle) the chord value is slightly more than the angle and then equals it when the angle is 60°. After this, the chord value decreases relative to the size of the angle until it is 120 (the diameter unit) when the angle is 180°.

For visual clarification *Figure 16* below shows three chord lengths inscribed in three circles. In each circle, AB and AC are radii. Since the diameter has a value of 120, each radius therefore has a value of 60 diameter units. In each circle, BC are chords. In circle 2 where the angle A is 60 degrees, the chord BC completes an equilateral triangle and therefore has the same length as the other two sides. This means that the chord of this figure must have 60 diameter units (see table above). In the first circle, where the angle at A is 36 degrees, the chord BC is smaller and is calculated to be just over 37 degrees. The third triangle, with an angle of 120 degrees has a chord of just under 104 degrees.

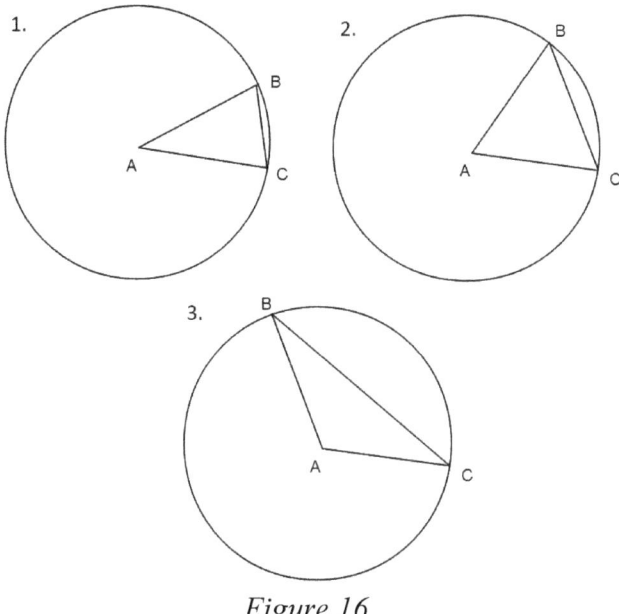

Figure 16

This was the beginning of trigonometry as we know it – a listing of figures corresponding to angles of different sizes that are of use in solving problems involving geography or the celestial sphere. Using the tables, a known angle (or one determined by using a sighting device) could be used to find the arc of the circle being measured and vice versa. With this innovation, mathematicians, geographers, navigators, astronomers and astrologers were able to solve problems requiring very accurate measurement.

Aryabhata (476–550 C.E.) was one of India's greatest mathematicians and a writer on astronomy, which included the math needed for doing astrology. He calculated the value of π to five digits, thought that Earth rotated on its axis, and explained eclipses scientifically. His works had a strong influence on Islamic science of the Middle Ages. More recently, India's first satellite was named for him.

Aryabhata advanced trigonometry by changing the calculations of chords from those set out by Ptolemy to those of 1/2 chord, thus introducing a right triangle into the computations. As seen in *Figure 17* below, he bisected the angle at A that opened into the chord CB creating two right triangles ACm and ABm. The half-chord lengths (Cm and mB) he called "ardha-jya" (Sanskrit for half-bowstring or arc) which later were called simply "jiva." Arabic mathematicians took the word jiva and changed it to the Arabic word jiba (curve, bosom) because it sounded the same. Later translators in Toledo used the meaning of jiba, but expressed it in Latin = sinus (curve), which is how the trigonometric function called the "sine" of an angle came to be.

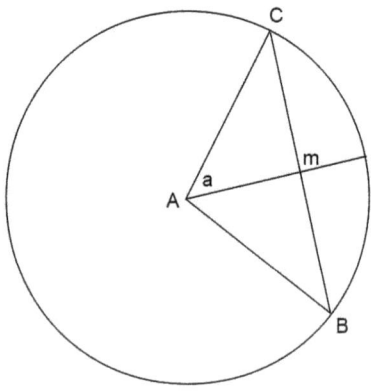

Figure 17

Knowing that the circumference of a circle is equal to twice the radius times pi (C = 2 π r), here's what Aryabhata did. In 360 degrees, the circumference of a circle, there are a total of 21,600 (360 x 60) minutes of arc. Dividing 21,600 minutes of arc by 2 π (2 x 3.1416 = 6.2832) he found that 3,438 is the number of minutes of arc along the circumference of any circle that is equal in length to the radius of that circle. Since Aryabhata was using a half chord to create a right triangle, this figure for the radius (3,438) is the also the value for the hypotenuse (AC in *Figure 17*). The angle (a) from the radius to the base of the right triangle (created by the bisection of the original angle) is then one half the angle of the chord.

Like Hipparchus and Ptolemy he methodically calculated jiva values, but this time by halving chords. For example, take a 60 degree angle, which makes a chord that is the same length as the radius (3,438). Half of that angle, 30 degrees, would therefore have half the length of the value for the full 60 degree chord – which is 1719. So the jiva of 30 degrees = 1719. Likewise the jiva of 15 degrees = 890, of 7.5 = 449, etc.

In the centuries following Aryabhata trigonometry slowly progressed as a number of Muslim scholars tackled, synthesized and improved upon the mathematical and astronomy-related problems of their predecessors the Greeks and near contemporaries from India. Scholars and polymaths such as al-Khwārizmī' (c. 780– c. 850) from Persia, al-Battanī (c. 858–929) from Turkey and Abu Rayhan al-Biruni (973-1048), born in what is now Uzbekistan, wrote influential works on many subjects including trigonometry. Al-Biruni in particular was a prolific author known for his writings on history, geography, mathematics, astronomy and also astrology. Among his many other accomplishments, he summarized Ptolemaic astronomy, described the use of the astrolabe, and devised a method for the trisection of an angle. In regard to trigonometry he formalized the subject and expanded the application of its use in determining directions, notably the direction of Mecca.

This is probably a good point in the chronology of trigonometry to mention the astrolabe (Greek for "star-taker"), an early inclinometer or device to measure angles that is an application of spherical astronomy and trigonometry. It was first described about the time of Hipparchus (2nd century B.C.E. – also the dating of the Antikythera mechanism) who may have invented it or improved upon it. It was used and described by later astronomers including Ptolemy, Theon of Alexandria and his daughter Hypatia. Muslim astronomers improved on the device adding azimuth lines that would help in locating the direction of Mecca. It continued to be used for time-keeping, astronomical measurements, astrological calculations, and navigation from Medieval times well into the 17th century. The astrolabe was an ancestor to other similar time and space measuring devices such as the surveyor's theodolite, the navigator's quadrant and sextant, the planisphere, and mechanical clocks.

A typical astrolabe was essentially a stack of plates or disks, often made of bronze, that could move around a central post. The main outside ring was graduated in 24 hours and the plate over it was specific to the local latitude, but was interchangeable with plates made for other latitudes. This plate also showed the locations of certain stars as they would be seen at that particular latitude. Next was a plate that showed the sun's path and the zodiac. This plate had substantial cutaways that allowed the user to read data off the plate below it. At the top of the stack was a rule which could serve as a pointer for calculation. The back of the astrolabe typically contained an altitude scale and a sighting device like a gunsight (alidade) use to measure the altitude of sky objects when the astrolabe was hung by a string. Often useful tables for data conversions including trigonometry were engraved on the back as well.

With an astrolabe a user could find the time of day by measuring the altitude of the Sun or a star and then using the plates and rule to find the apparent (sundial) time. Other measurements that could be made were the times of sunrise and sunset, sidereal time, Right Ascensions, celestial longitudes, latitudes, and declinations of celestial objects. With this tool and the information it produced, Midheavens, Ascendants, and house cusps, and consequently astrological charts, could be easily calculated.

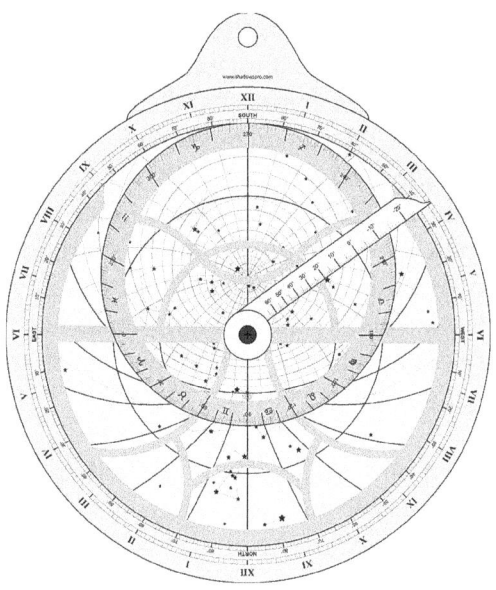

During the 11th and 12th centuries Arab writings began to enter Europe. By the 13th and 14th centuries works on trigonometry were being used by navigators and by the 15th century European astronomers were writing on the subject. *Regiomontanus* (1436–1476) was an outstanding German mathematician, astronomer and astrologer best known in the field of astrology for the house system that bears his name. His real name was Johannes Müller von Königsberg. (Regiomontanus was a name given to him after his death. Both Regiomontanus and Königsberg mean "king's mountain"). Regiomontanus entered college at age 11, was an avid book collector and printer, constructed astrolabes with plates for several latitudes, wrote almanacs with astrological information and made commentaries on classic authors including Ptolemy. He published detailed tables of sines and authored a book on geometry and trigonometry titled *On Triangles* in which he improved upon and formalized the existing methodologies. Modeled after Euclid's *Elements*, it is well-organized and was the first major publication on these mathematical subjects by a European.

By the mid 16th century, the entire way of thinking about trigonometry changed when the sine of an angle became seen as a ratio, not a length, i.e. a chord. This conceptual change from a geometrical view to an algebraic view was made possible by the development of decimals and was completed during the 18th century by the Swiss mathematician Leonhard Euler (1707-1783). Euler changed the sine from a length to a ratio: the sine of any angle is a ratio equal to the length of the side opposite the angle (the half chord) divided by the hypotenuse (the radius). This system of ratios could now be applied to right triangles of any length to solve all kinds of problems in celestial mechanics, navigation and surveying.

Finally, after two millennia we have arrived at the central concept of trigonometry as we know it today: if you multiply a right triangle's sides by the same number, the angles will remain the same. In other words, the angle remains the same as long as the sides remain proportional. It doesn't matter how big or small the triangle is. So if you know something about a right triangle, like an angle and a side, you can use trigonometrical ratios to calculate the other angle and sides of that triangle – and the ratios between the sides will be true for any triangle of any size that has the same angles.

For example, consider the classic right triangle below (*Figure 17*) with an angle at A of 30 degrees. We know the right angle at C is 90 degrees and therefore the third angle at B must be 60 degrees (the angles in a right triangle must add up to 180). Let's say that side AB is 2 units and the side BC is 1 unit. The Pythagorean Theorem tells us that the square of the hypotenuse AB is equal to the sum of the squares of the other two sides. So the square of AB is 4, the square of BC is 1 so side AC must be the square root of 3 which, rounded off to one decimal place, is 1.7. Now multiply all the sides by 4. The angles will all remain the same in this new triangle but side AB will be 8, side BC 4 and side AC roughly 6.9.

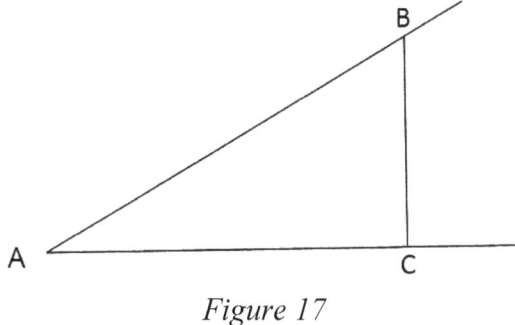

Figure 17

In modern trigonometry, the ratio of the side opposite the angle, here BC (also called the perpendicular) to the hypotenuse AB, is the sine of the angle A. (Recall that AB would be the radius of a circle and BC the half-chord).

To demonstrate this, take Aryabhata's jiva of 30 degrees: 1719. Draw a right triangle with an angle at A of 30 degrees like the one in *Figure 17*. Then from A take a length (any length) and from this point we'll call C, a right angle is drawn to connect with the other side of the angle. This intersection is B. Since AB would be the same as Aryabhata's radius as described above, its value would be 3438. The ratio of BC (which is the jiva 1719) to AB is 1719 ÷ 3438 or 0.5, which is the sine of a 30 degree angle. This ratio remains the same regardless of the size of the triangle. The dimensions of other triangles like this, but with different angles at A, can then be determined by a table of known ratios of these sides – trigonometric tables. While ancient and medieval trigonometry was doing well enough using chords, thinking in terms of ratios opened up more possibilities.

By 1620 all the elements for modern trigonometry were in place. In addition to the sine, which is the ratio of the side opposite the angle to the hypotenuse, other ratios were labeled. The ratio of the side from the angle in question to the right angle (AC in *Figure 18* below – also called the adjacent side or the base) to the hypotenuse (AB) became called the cosine (AC / AB). The other possible combination handles the third angle (B) where the ratio called tangent is the opposite side (BC) to the adjacent side (AB) which is opposite the angle C.

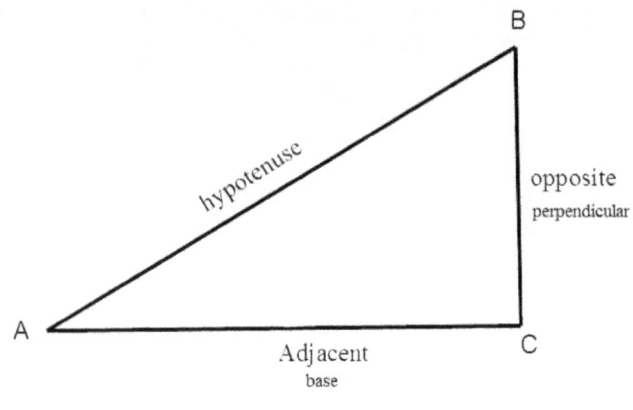

Figure 18

The three main trigonometric functions are:

$$\sin A = \frac{\text{opposite}}{\text{Hypotenuse}} \qquad \cos A = \frac{\text{adjacent}}{\text{hypotenuse}} \qquad \tan A = \frac{\text{opposite}}{\text{adjacent}}$$

These are often remembered using the mnemonic SOH CAH TOA where each first letter stands for the function and the second and third letters the sides of a right triangle. Knowledge of the properties of right triangles can be taken further with the reciprocals of these ratios: the cotangent (cot), secant (sec), and cosecant (csc).

$$\cot = \frac{\text{adjacent}}{\text{opposite}} \qquad \sec = \frac{\text{hypotenuse}}{\text{adjacent}} \qquad \csc = \frac{\text{hypotenuse}}{\text{opposite}}$$

Trigonometry is thus a method of determining the properties of triangles of any size using an established table of ratios. The geometry of the right triangle, which was developed by astronomers, mathematicians and astrologers over the course of two millennia, is the basis of the technique. Only with trigonometry could translations of sky objects or points from one coordinate system to another be managed precisely. The role of astrology as a motivating force in the history of mathematics and science should be appreciated and not ignored as some academic historians of science have.

In astrological calculations the obliquity of the ecliptic (23.45 degrees), which is formed by the intersection of the plane of the celestial equator and the plane of the ecliptic, is a known angle that does not change (except over very long periods of time). This angle, along with the distance from it to a point, can be the basis of a trigonometrical calculation. The distance, a specific distance measured along the celestial equator (using the equatorial coordinate system), is found from the time of an event or a birth. This is because 24 hours of the day corresponds to 360 degrees of Right Ascension measured along the celestial equator, which moves with the rotation of the Earth. In constructing an astrological chart, the time of day of an event or birth is first converted into sidereal time and then into Right Ascension which is distance along the equator measured from 0 degrees Aries. Now with an angle, and a distance, a right triangle can be drawn (to the ecliptic) and trigonometry can be employed to find the Midheaven, Ascendant, house cusps, etc.

In *Figure 19* below, a celestial sphere with Earth at the center, you will see the plane of the equator and ecliptic intersecting and forming an angle of 23.45 degrees at angle A which marks 0 degrees Aries. Notice that the meridian, emanating from the poles, crosses the equator at right angles. A triangle ABC is formed by the intersections of meridian, equator and ecliptic – each of which is a great circle. We know two things about this triangle. We know angle at A (obliquity) and, if we know the time of an event or a birth, we know the distance, given in sidereal time and measured in Right Ascension, along the equator from A (0 Aries) to C.

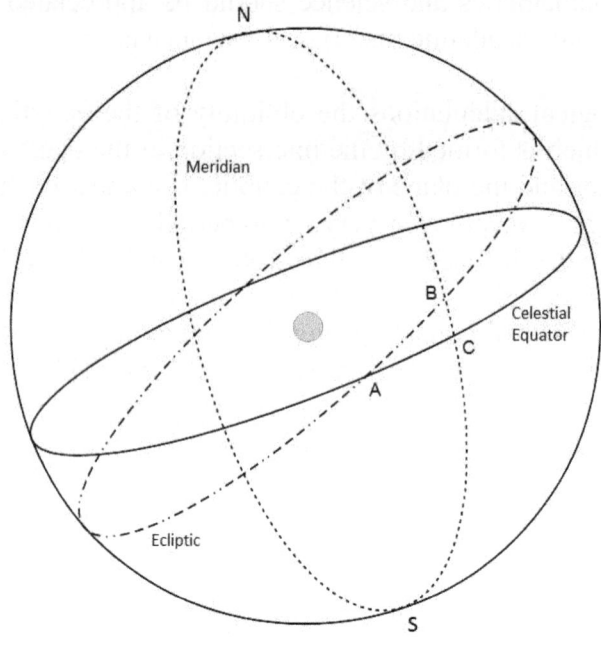

Figure 19

Now let's look at this diagram from the inside (viewed from the surface of Earth – in the northern hemisphere) as shown below in *Figure 20*. Looking toward the south, the celestial equator and the ecliptic intersect at angle A, which we know is 23.45 degrees. The distance AC measured along the celestial equator is known from the time of an event or birth. This is the Right Ascension or RA that is based on the calculated sidereal time for the event or birth. Recall that 24 hours of RA = 360 degrees and 2 hours of RA = 30 degrees. Also recall that when the intersection of the equator and ecliptic, which marks 0 Aries, intersects the meridian, the local sidereal time is 0.

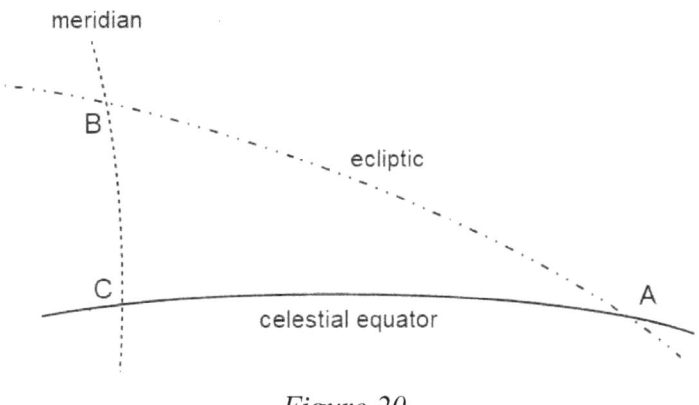

Figure 20

In this example, where 0 Aries (shown here as A) has already passed the meridian due to the rotation of Earth, let's assume we have in this case a sidereal time of 2 hours and 15 minutes. Converted to distance, where 15 degrees of arc on the equator is covered in 1 hour, this would be an RA of 33.75 (2 hours = 30 degrees + 15 minutes [$^1/_4$ of 15 degrees] = 3.75). The equator is always intersected by the meridian at a 90 degree angle, so the angle at C is also known. (Any great circle running through the pole of the equator will intercept the equator at a right angle.) A right triangle is now formed with a known distance, and two known angles. AC is the adjacent side, BC is the opposite side and AB is the hypotenuse.

Now all of this is being mapped out on the surface of a sphere which has its own unique properties due to curvature. But for simplified illustrative purposes, let's just take the triangle ABC out of the sphere and make it a triangle that exists in a plane to demonstrate what we have been looking at so far in terms of plane trigonometry (we'll get back to the sphere ahead). Here's what it looks like extracted from the sphere.

59

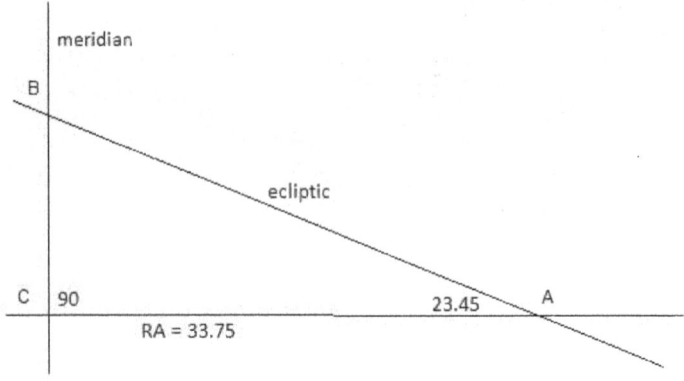

Figure 21

So we know the angle at A (23.45) and we know the distance along the celestial equator from A to C (33.75), which is the adjacent side of the triangle. We also know the angle at C is a right angle and because of this we can apply trigonometry to determine the distance along the ecliptic from A to B, this distance being the hypotenuse of the right triangle. When we know AB we will also know B, which is the Midheaven, the point on the ecliptic that crosses the meridian. This problem can only be solved with trigonometry. The formula is simple; we use one of the three main trigonometric functions.

cos angle A $=$ <u>adjacent (AC)</u>   cos 23.45 $=$ <u>33.75</u>
                         hypotenuse (AB)   AB

Multiply both sides by AB to restate the equation:

cos 23.45 x AB $=$ 33.75

Next find the cosine of 23.45 from a table of cosines or from a scientific calculator. This is 0.917

0.917 x AB $=$ 33.75

Divide both sides of the equation by the cosine of angle A (which cancels out itself on the left side of the equation).

$$AB = \frac{33.75}{0.917} = 36.8$$

Convert to sexagesimal notation = 36d 48m or 6 Taurus 48

In essence, solving right triangles using trigonometry is what happens when a Midheaven, Ascendant and houses are calculated. But it's a lot more complicated (and weird) than this because the problem needs to take into account that the triangle is located on the surface of what is conceptualized as a curved sphere and therefore must be solved by spherical trigonometry.

Spherical triangles have very different properties than plane triangles. One is that the sides of a spherical triangle are measured in degrees, whether this be in right ascension, longitude, latitude, etc. Also, no one side of a spherical triangle can be more than 180 degrees. Another property is that the sum of the angles of a spherical triangle is not limited to 180 degrees. For example, *Figure 22* depicts a sphere with three great circles, the equator and two meridians at right angles to each other. A spherical triangle ABC is formed by the intersection of the two meridians with the equator, and by definition, right angles are formed at each intersection. Therefore, the spherical right triangle ABC has three 90-degree angles for a total of 270 degrees.

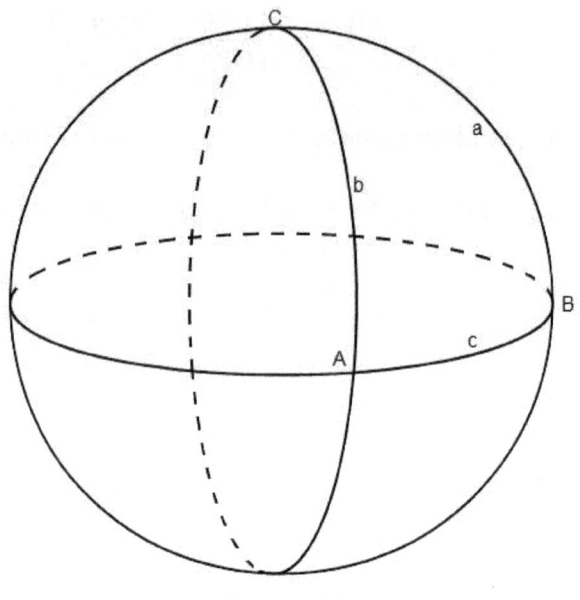

Figure 22

The trigonometric ratios for spherical triangles are different from those of plane trigonometry and these have been worked out by constructing additional plane right triangles that are connected to a spherical triangle. In *Figure 23* a spherical triangle, similar to the one used in the exercise above (*Figure 20*), shows lines connecting the sides to the center of the sphere. Consider that the side AB is measured in degrees and its value will be the same as the angle AOB. Likewise for the other two sides of the spherical triangle ABC. With the center added to the problem, chords can be drawn and arcs along the surface of the sphere worked out over several steps. More modern texts draw tangents to the angles of the spherical triangle forming a geometric solid called a trihedral. From a trihedral other plane right triangles can be constructed by drawing lines tangent to the other angles. In this way, over a series of constructions well beyond the scope of this book, the properties of spherical triangles can be discovered and ratios established.

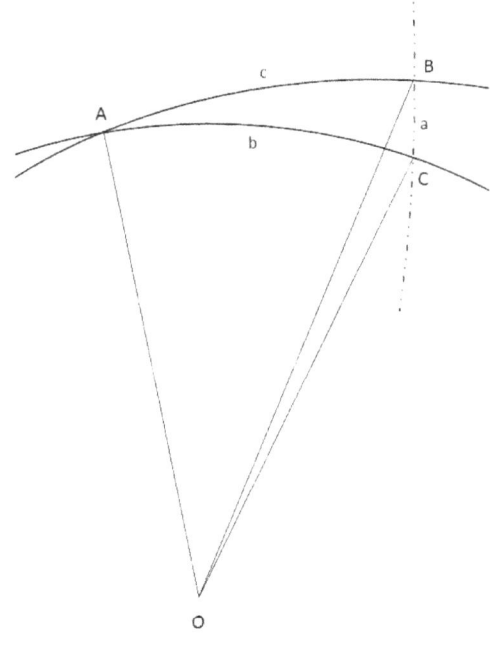

Figure 23

Returning to *Figure 22* above notice that the triangles have sides labeled abc – lower case letters. It is the convention to designate each side of a triangle by the uncapitalized letter of the angle it faces. In a spherical triangle the sines of the angles are proportional to the sines of their opposite sides. This is expressed in the sine law where:

$$\frac{\sin A}{\sin a} = \frac{\sin B}{\sin b} = \frac{\sin C}{\sin c}$$

The sine law, the law of cosines, and other more complex laws concerning the other trigonometric functions, which are ratios of ratios, allow for the solutions of spherical triangles. I will leave this greatly over-simplified explanation of spherical trigonometry here and suggest that adventurous and self-disciplined readers explore the arcane and complex proofs of these relationships on their own.

Returning to *Figure 20* (shown again below) we know ABC is a right spherical triangle and angle C is 90 degrees. We know angle A is 23.45 degrees and we know AC along the celestial equator is 33.75 degrees measured in right ascension. These are given: we want to know the hypotenuse AB, the distance along the ecliptic from A to where it crosses the meridian at B – which will be the Midheaven. One of the traditional formulas for finding parts of spherical triangles, one that is found in many older texts on spherical trigonometry for astrological calculations, is (using the figure below):

cosine A = (tangent AC) (cotangent AB)

A = obliquity angle 23.45
AC = RA of 33.75
AB = the longitude of the Midheaven – which is unknown.

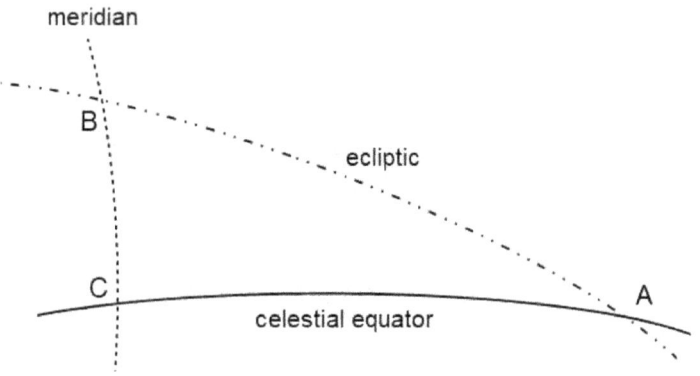

cos A = (tan AC) (cot AB) can be expressed as cot AB = $\frac{\text{cos A}}{\text{tan AC}}$

For this problem A is the obliquity and AC is Right Ascension:

$$\text{cot AB} = \frac{\text{cos obl}}{\text{tan RA}}$$

$$\text{cot AB} = \frac{\text{cos obl } 23.45 = .9174}{\text{tan RA } 33.75 = .6682} = 1.3730$$

Because cot = 1/tan (the reciprocal of tangent)

$$\frac{1}{\tan} AB = 1.3730 \qquad \text{or} \qquad \tan AB = \frac{1}{1.3730} = 0.7283$$

We now have a figure for the tangent, but we want to know the what this is the tangent of. We can look this figure up in trigonometric tables or use the inverse tangent function on a calculator indicated as arctan or tan-1.

tan-1 0.7283 = 36.0658 or 36 degrees 4 minutes, or 6 degrees of Taurus and 4 minutes. Note that this is very close to what was determined using plane trigonometry but more precise.

Today the formula for finding the Midheaven using spherical trigonometry on a scientific calculator is shown below. We will be using this formula in the calculations section of this book.

$$\tan MC = \frac{\tan RA}{\cos obl} \qquad \text{or} \qquad MC = \tan\text{-}1 \; x \frac{\tan RA}{\cos obl}$$

The Ascendant is a far more complicated calculation because in addition to the two coordinate systems utilized in calculating the Midheaven, it requires data from another – the horizon system. The Ascendant is the degree of the ecliptic that crosses the horizon and, if only the Right Ascension and obliquity are known, more than one spherical triangle is needed to solve the problem of transferring information from one coordinate system to another. In fact, the problem of the Ascendant (a.k.a. the horoscope) was one of the central issues in the development of trigonometry and was no doubt driven by the need to make accurate astrological charts. Again, astrology was a powerful motivating force in the development of mathematics and astronomy.

In *Figure 24* below the view is from outside the celestial sphere looking in. Where the equator crosses the horizon at E is due east and where the meridian crosses the horizon at S is due south. At low latitudes the angle of the equator against the horizon is high, moving north the angle decreases. When the latitude of an event is known it follows that the angle of the equator relative to the horizon will be known. Where the ecliptic crosses the horizon is the Ascendant. The Aries symbol in the diagram marks the intersection of the ecliptic and equator, 0 Aries. If this point, or 0 Libra, happens to be rising, then the Ascendant will be due east and coincident with the equator. But at all other times, it is either north or south of the equator. In this example it is north of true east. It's important to consider that as the degree of the Ascendant rises it will follow a path parallel to the point E on the equator.

The phenomena of co-rising points (the Ascendant and E in *Figure 24*) and the translation of these points between coordinate systems is probably the most important concept in understanding the mechanics of the celestial sphere and how it relates to astrology. Any point on the ecliptic (the Ascendant or a planet) rises and sets on a track (a small circle) parallel to the equator. Here is the basis for finding the Ascendant, sunrise and sunset times, for the logic behind time-based house systems like Placidus, and for the technique of primary directions.

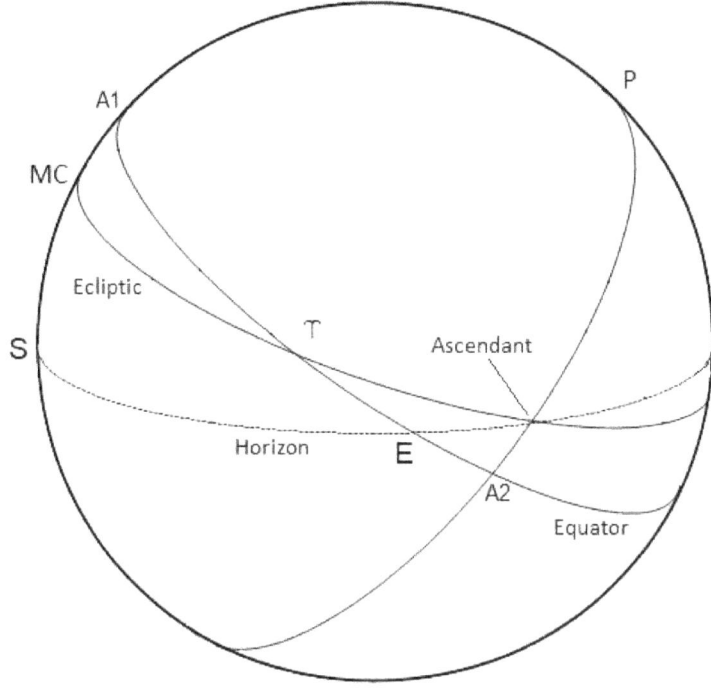

Figure 24

In *Figure 24* a great circle drawn from the pole of the equator P (the north pole) through the Ascendant will necessarily cross the equator at right angles. The angle of the pole to the horizon is the same as the latitude. (A viewer at 40 degrees north latitude will see the North Star at 40 degrees above the northern horizon.) This was referred to in older books as "the elevation of the pole" which is the same as the latitude.

There are several spherical triangles formed by the intersections of these lines that can be solved using spherical trigonometry. The RAMC, the latitude, and the obliquity being knowns, the problem is to find the distance in degrees of longitude along the ecliptic from the MC to the Ascendant. There is another known, however, and this

Oblique Ascension (O.A.), the right ascension of the point on the equator which rises at the same time as the Ascendant. This point is due east (E in *Figure 24*) as it marks the intersection of the equator and the horizon. As the equator is always a 180 degree arc across the sky and cut in half by the meridian (at point A1), the O.A. is found by adding 90 degrees to the R.A.M.C. In the diagram the OA is shown by the arc A1 to E.

(Note that the arc E-A2, which is called the Ascensional Difference or AD, added to the OA would greatly facilitate the solution to the spherical triangle Ascendant-Aries-A2, but it requires knowing the declination of the Ascendant. There are ways of getting at it by using the Sun's position on the day of the event or birth in question, which will include its declination, and then adjusting for the time of the event, something that can be done with tables or an astrolabe. However, since Menelaus the solutions to two spherical triangles were the usual basis of Ascendant calculation. In Figure 24 these are E-A1-S and Ascendant-MC-S.)

The standard trigonometry formula in most books of the 19th century, which solves for these triangles, included the Ascendant as one of the house cusps that were calculated by first adding increments of 30 degrees to the RAMC. The addition of 90 would be used to calculate the Ascendant, or cusp of first house. (Adding 90 to the RAMC gives the Oblique Ascension (O.A.) which is shown as A1 to E in the diagram.) Poles, drawn from the pole of the celestial equator, would then cut the ecliptic at the Ascendant and house cusps. This method of calculating house cusps by trigonometry without house tables, was sometimes referred to as the "ordinary method."

The cumbersome formula for this method, usually worked out using logarithms for the trigonometric functions, requires adjustments for the quadrant location of the equinoxes and was therefore done in two stages. The first stage, using the OA and the latitude gives the altitude of the intersection of the equator and the meridian S-A1.

Log cos OA + log cot latitude (pole of house) = cot Meridian Angle (usually called Angle A or the first angle)

(note: use sin OA if OA is from 90 to 180 and 270 to 360)

The next step takes into account the obliquity angle:

Angle A +/– obliquity (23.45) = Angle B (or second angle)

Note: this adjustment depends on the figure for the OA. If it is less than 90 or more than 270 obliquity would be added to Angle A. If the OA was more than 90 and less than 270, obliquity would be subtracted.

Then log cos B + log cos A + log tan OA = log tan house cusp

In a more modern form this 3-step process would look like:

1. cos OA x cot lat = cot angle A (or sin OA – see above)
2. angle A +/– obliquity (23.45) = angle B
3. [cos A / cos B] x tan OA = tan house cusp

In even older texts (i.e. Benjamin Martin, 1736) the Ascendant is calculated more tediously over many steps that begin by first solving for the Midheaven (MC). Next the meridian angle MC-A1 is found from the triangle MC-A1-Aries, and then the declination of the MC and the altitude of the MC. After that what's referred to as the nonagesima degree, which is the angle the ecliptic makes with the horizon, is found.[1] Then, with two angles (at MC and S, which is 90 degrees) and a side (S-MC), the arc MC-Ascendant can be found, which solves the problem.

One of the biggest problems with calculating the Ascendant is in regard to where, that is in what quadrants, the cardinal points were located at the time of the birth/event. The location of the cardinal points, i.e. the source of the obliquity angle, requires adjustments and these are embedded in traditional descriptions of the trigonometrical methods for calculating the Ascendant and the houses as seen

---

[1] The term nonagesima degree is derived from the nonagesimal point which is on the ecliptic and 90 degrees from the horizon. It is the midpoint between the Ascendant and Descendant and is also the 10th house cusp of the Equal house system.

above. The modern formula for calculating the Ascendant, more direct in certain ways, is shown below but it too requires adjustments based on the quadrant location of 0 Aries as it moves through the diurnal cycle (see Chapter 9).

$$ASC = 1/X \ ARC \ tan \ - \ \frac{(tan \ lat. \ x \ sin \ obl) + (sin \ RAMC \ x \ cos \ obl)}{cos \ RAMC}$$

The calculation of other points on the celestial sphere, for example the Vertex or east point, is similar to that of the Ascendant. Triangles are first established by creating right angles using line drawn from the poles of one plane or another. Then, with the known angles produced by the intersection of planes, i.e. the obliquity angle, plus that of the latitude, enough data is available to solve for the unknown sides and angles. In this way, trigonometry quantifies precisely sky phenomena that would otherwise be very difficult to measure.

Logarithms

In the latter part of the 16th century, solutions to complex navigation problems, astronomical problems, and also compound interest on investment problems, led to the invention and compilation of tables of logarithms. Tables of logarithms allow one to eliminate some of the difficulties in solving trigonometrical problems by changing multiplication and division to addition and subtraction. Credit for the discovery of this method of solving triangulation problems generally goes to *John Napier* (1550-1617), a Scottish mathematician (he introduced the decimal point), physicist, astronomer, and inventor. Napier developed systems to solve problems including Napier's Bones which was very much like a calculating machine, a forerunner of computers. He also drew plans for war vehicles including tanks and submarines, and published a very popular defense of Protestantism in which he attacked the Pope for being the Antichrist and predicted that the Apocalypse would arrive between 1688 and 1700.

Napier's 147-page book on logarithms, the *"Descriptio"* (A Description of an Admirable Table of Logarithms) was published in 1614. His logarithmic tables were a major labor-saving method for doing trigonometry and were adopted by many leading mathematicians, astronomers and astrologers, including Tycho Brahe and Johannes Kepler, who immediately recognized them as a significant innovation. Napier invented the term logarithm; logos = ratio, arithmus = number. These are numbers that move along in such a way to preserve the same ratio to one another.

Numbers progress in different ways. An arithmetical progression is basic counting, i.e. 1, 2, 3, 4, 5, 6, etc. A geometric progression multiplies the terms by the same number: 2, 4, 8, 16, 32, 64, etc., in this case the number 2. This sequence can also be expressed as: 2 to the second power (4), to the third (8), to the fourth (16), to the fifth (32), to the sixth (64), to the seventh (128), etc. At the basis of logarithms is the fact that the exponents can be added. So $2^3 \times 2^4 = 2^7$, or 8 x 16 = 128. Continuing the above example, where the base number is 2, we could say that 3 is logarithm of 8, 6 is the log of 64, and 7 is the log of 128.

Logarithms allow for multiplication by adding, and for dividing by subtracting. Most of today's tables are built on a base of 10 where 10=1, 100=2, 1000=3, etc. Below is a short table of selected logarithms in steps of 0.1, with a few steps that correlate with round numbers (log tables would normally have many more entries). Notice that the table shows that $10^1 = 10$ and $10^2 = 100$. Here the log of 5 is shown as 0.6990 (the table only shows the exponents to four places) which is the same as 10 to the .69897 power. Multiply 3 x 5 and you will get 15. Using the log table below, add the log of 3 (0.4772) to the log of 5 (0.6990) and you will get 1.1761. Look this up in the table and you'll find 15 (this is slightly off because only 4 decimal places are shown in this table). Add the log of 5 to itself and you'll get the log for 25. With logarithms multiplication has been changed to addition and large math problems become much easier to handle.

Exponent	number	log
10	1.000	0.0000
$10^{0.1}$	1.257	0.1000
$10^{0.2}$	1.585	0.2000
$10^{0.3}$	1.995	0.3000
$10^{0.3009}$	2.000	0.3010
$10^{0.4}$	2.519	0.4000
$10^{0.4772}$	3.00	0.4771
$10^{0.5}$	3.162	0.5000
$10^{0.6}$	3.981	0.6000
$10^{0.6990}$	5.000	0.6990
$10^{0.7}$	5.019	0.7000
$10^{0.8}$	6.309	0.8000
$10^{0.9}$	7.943	0.9000

Exponent	number	log
10^1	10.000	1.0000
$10^{1.1}$	12.589	1.1000
$10^{1.1761}$	15.000	1.1761
$10^{1.2}$	15.849	1.2000
$10^{1.3}$	19.953	1.3000
$10^{1.3980}$	25.000	1.3980
$10^{1.4}$	25.119	1.4000
$10^{1.5}$	31.623	1.5000
$10^{1.6}$	39.811	1.6000
$10^{1.7}$	50.119	1.7000
$10^{1.8}$	63.096	1.8000
$10^{1.9}$	79.433	1.9000
10^2	100.00	2.0000

Astrologers have long used log tables for trigonometric chart calculations and also a special type of log table, diurnal proportional logarithms, which were found in many astrology textbooks as well as in most ephemerides.

Diurnal proportional logarithms are logarithms that are specifically made for working with angles and time, as both measurements utilize sexagesimal notation. They can be used for most chart calculations including the Midheaven, Ascendant and houses, and also for planetary motions, which are given in most ephemerides in degrees and minutes in 24-hour intervals. In diurnal proportional logarithms hours, degrees, or minutes are listed at the top of 24 columns of sixty minutes (or seconds), each corresponding to a logarithm of four decimal places. These figures, a total of 1440 logs (24 x 60), are then used for calculations.

The table is produced by starting with the log of 1440, which is $10^{3.1584}$ and subtracting from it the log of each number from 0 to 1440. So the first log, the log of 0 degrees and 1 minute, would be 3.1584. This is 10 to the 3.1584 power which equals 1440.

You can see this in two ways on a scientific calculator. First enter 10, press Y^x or X^y (the symbol for exponent) and then enter 3.1584 and press equals. You should get 1440 (not quite exactly because only 4 decimal points are used). Second enter 1440 and press the log key which should give you 3.1584 (rounded to four decimal places).

Now, given that the log for 0 degrees 1 minute is 3.1584, the log for 0 degrees 2 minutes would be the log for 2, which is 0.3010, subtracted from 3.1584 which is 2.8573 (rounded to four decimal places). Likewise, the log for 0 degrees 45 minutes is obtained by taking the log for 45 and subtracting it from 3.1584. The log for 6 degrees 15 minutes (6 x 60 + 15 = 375) is then 2.5740 subtracted from 3.1584 which equals 0.5844.

Here are some more examples using the table on page 230.
.
Example 1.

What is the log of 12 hours?

$10^{3.1584} = 1440 =$ number of minutes in 24 hours
$10^{2.8574} = 720 =$ number of minutes in 12 hours
Subtracting the second exponent from the first produces the log of 12 hours: $3.1584 - 2.8574 = 0.3010 =$ log of 720 minutes or 12 hrs.

Example 2.

What is the log of 5 hours and 37 minutes?
$5 \times 60 + 37 = 337$ minutes
$10^{2.5277} = 337$
Subtract this exponent from $10^{3.1584}$ (1440)
$3.1584 - 2.5277 = 0.6307$

This figure, 0.6307 is the log of 5h 37m or 5d 37m or 5m 37s

Other examples from the tables on page 230:

The log of 12 degrees and 37 minutes = 0.2793
The log of 60 minutes, or 1 degree = 1.3802
The log of 1 degree and 16 minutes = 1.2775

Chapter 4

Systems of House Division

Planets move against two backgrounds. One movement, motion along the ecliptic which gives their positions in space relative to each other, is mapped using the zodiac. The other motion is their daily (diurnal) cycle relative to the horizon; rising, culminating, setting and lower culmination. House systems are methods of mapping the diurnal cycle, that is the daily rotation of Earth, and they are designed to divide the sky into discrete sectors using the horizon and meridian as anchors or reference points. Attempts at this second kind of space-mapping has ancient roots. Undoubtedly the first division of the sky in early times was simply into day and night, or above and below. Further division of the sky into quarters probably came next, the passage of a planet through the meridian and horizon marking the boundaries of the quadrants. Division of the quadrants into thirds to produce the 12 houses has been a complex and ongoing project in the history of astrology and has involved the use of trigonometry.

Most house systems are based on the astronomy of a rotating sphere and the pure geometry of coordinate systems. One class of house system is static and involves the projection of house circles, which are great circles, from the poles of the horizon, equator, and ecliptic, or from the zenith. Where the projections from these poles intersect the ecliptic, equator, or prime vertical establishes house cusps. Another class is based on the observation that as Earth rotates, planets or any points on the ecliptic will rise, culminate, set, and pass through lower culmination. Both the time it takes for a planet or point to move from the horizon (rise) to the meridian (culmination), and the distance covered during this interval, has been considered important in certain house systems. This motion from rise to culmination, called the diurnal semi-arc, is typically trisected in various ways to produce house cusps for that quadrant; the other quadrants being treated in the same manner.

Most ancient and modern house systems are ideal mathematical constructs applied to the geometry of the sphere or the cycle of the day. They have remained an unsettled issue in astrological theory as there are no easy ways to test for effectiveness. There is more than one way to categorize the many (well over 20 have been described) house systems invented since ancient times, one of which is employed in the listing below. One commonality of the majority of house systems, however, is that the divisions are minimal when near the equator but deviate substantially at higher latitudes.

A variety of clever ways to determine house cusps have been proposed over the past two millennia. In the last century a few more mathematically complex (and possibly elegant to the mathematically inclined) proposals have been added to the list of house systems, two of which, Koch and Topocentric, are listed below. An evidence-based relationship between the complexity of a house system and its actual effectiveness in practice, however, has not been discovered.

Equal House Systems

Ptolemy's Modus Equalis – In this system the ecliptic is divided into twelve equal arcs starting from the Ascendant. Another way of looking at this is by projecting 12 equidistant house circles from the poles of the ecliptic. Where they intersect the ecliptic marks the cusps of the houses. The longitude of the Ascendant is taken as the starting point, and the other house cusps are located in 30 degree increments from this point. In *Figure 25* on the next page the house circles are shown projected from the poles of the ecliptic. Since there are 12 house circles, they are spaced 30 degrees apart, the same distance as one zodiacal sign. Note that the Midheaven, or M.C., is not the cusp of the 10th house. Instead, it falls into the 11th house – in this particular case. In other cases it may fall into the 9th house.

A variant system are *Meridian Equal Houses.* These are the same as the above except that the 30 degree houses radiate from the Midheaven or cusp of the 10th house. This means that the Ascendant would, in most cases, not be the cusp of the first house and would fall into the 12th or 1st houses.

Whole Sign Houses, used in ancient astrology, are another variation on equal houses. In this approach, which has become popular in the 21st century, the first house begins at 0 degrees of the sign of the Ascendant. The other house cusps follow at 30 degree intervals, with 0 degrees of each zodiac sign serving as both a cusp and a sign boundary. In all of the above equal house systems, either the Midheaven or Ascendant, or both, is *not* the cusp of a house. And latitude is not a factor as the house cusps will remain the same at any location.

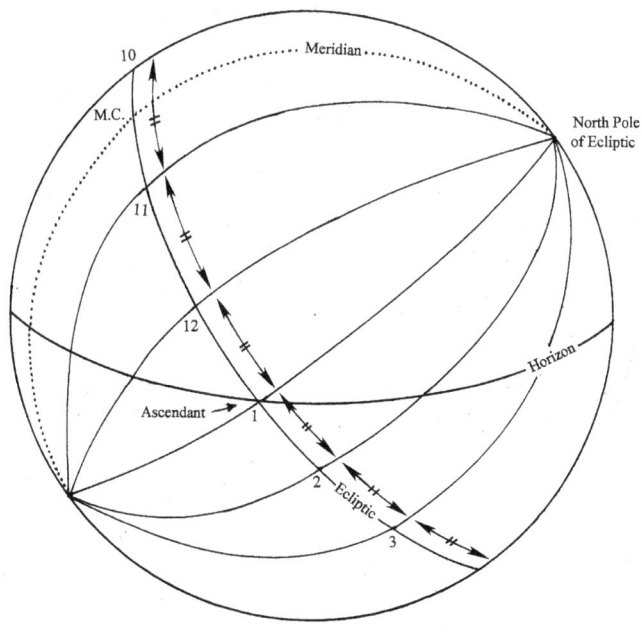

Equal House Method

Figure 25

Quadrant methods of house division

In these systems, the circle of the sky is divided into four sections defined by the horizon and the meridian. Each of these quadrants are then divided into three sections, thus creating a total of 12 houses. A terminology has been established for these four quarters or divisions. The part of the ecliptic above the horizon, on which the planets travel, is called the *diurnal arc*, the part below it the *nocturnal arc*. The eastern quadrant of the diurnal arc, found between the Ascendant and the Midheaven, is called the *diurnal semi-arc*. The eastern quadrant of the nocturnal arc, found between the Ascendant and the I.C., is called the *nocturnal semi-arc*. Normally, house calculations only trisect these semi-arcs establishing cusps that are opposite the cusps of the other semi-arcs.

Porphyry – Possibly the oldest quadrant system, it is attributed to the Neoplatonist Porphyry, the biographer of Plotinus and Pythagoras, though it appears in Valens who lived a century earlier. It is also known in India as the *Sripathi* house system. In this system, the zodiacal longitude of each quadrant is trisected to locate the intermediate house cusps. Another way of looking at it, if you want to see the cusps as projections (which they really don't need to be) is by projecting house circles from the poles of the ecliptic such that the quadrants are divided into thirds. The houses in opposite quadrants are of equal size, but not those of adjacent quadrants. In *Figure 26* below you will notice that the Ascendant is the cusp of the 1st house and the Midheaven, or M.C., is the cusp of the 10th house.

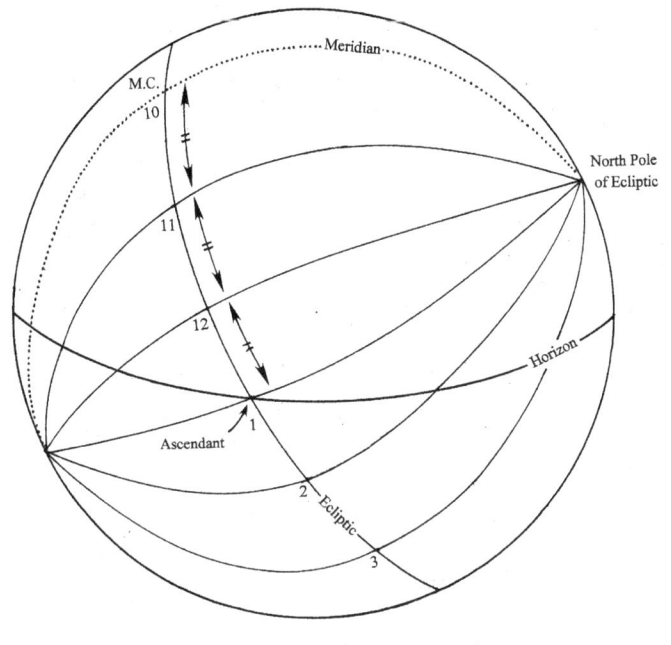

Porphyry Method

Figure 26

Campanus – Campanus of Novara (c. 1220-1296) is associated with this system although it was used centuries earlier. Dane Rudhyar found its rationale supportive of his "person-centered astrology." The meridian, the great circle connecting the north and south points, intersects the prime vertical, the great circle connecting the east and west points, at the zenith – this emphasis on zenith being what Rudhyar thought was most significant about the Campanus house system. The intersection of the prime vertical with the meridian, along with its intersection with the horizon, generates four prime vertical quadrants. Campanus cusps are produced by drawing great circles from the north and south points of the horizon that divide each quadrant of the prime vertical into thirds which are always 30 degree segments. These great circles are then projected to the ecliptic to produce the house cusps. One peculiarity of this system is that the houses near the horizon tend to be larger and it distorts at extreme latitudes.

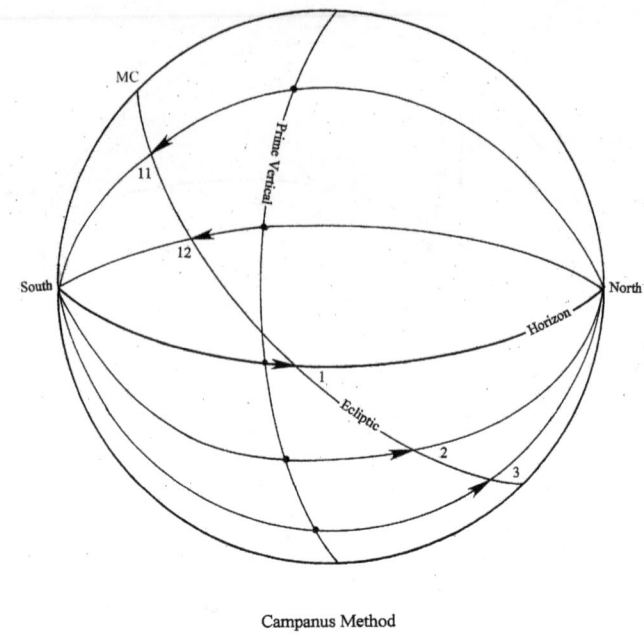

Campanus Method

Figure 27

Regiomontanus – Johannes Müller von Königsberg (1426-1476), who was later named Regiomontanus, is associated with this house system, but it was also used well before his time. It was a commonly-used house system during and after the Renaissance and is much like Campanus except it is the equator that is trisected by means of great circles passing through the north and south points of the horizon. The continuation of the intersection points on the equator, which are again 30 degree intervals, are then projected onto the ecliptic. As with Campanus the horizon itself is one of these house circles and marks the Ascendant and Descendant. The size of the houses in this system change gradually and progressively and are less prone to distortion at high latitudes than Campanus. Both Campanus and Regiomontanus were easily calculated using an astrolabe. There is a similarity between the Regiomontanus system and the "ordinary house system" used by many 19th century astrologers in that the equator is cut in 30 degree intervals and projected to the ecliptic. The difference is that the great circles that evenly divide the equator in the "ordinary" system emanate from the pole of the equator, not the horizon.

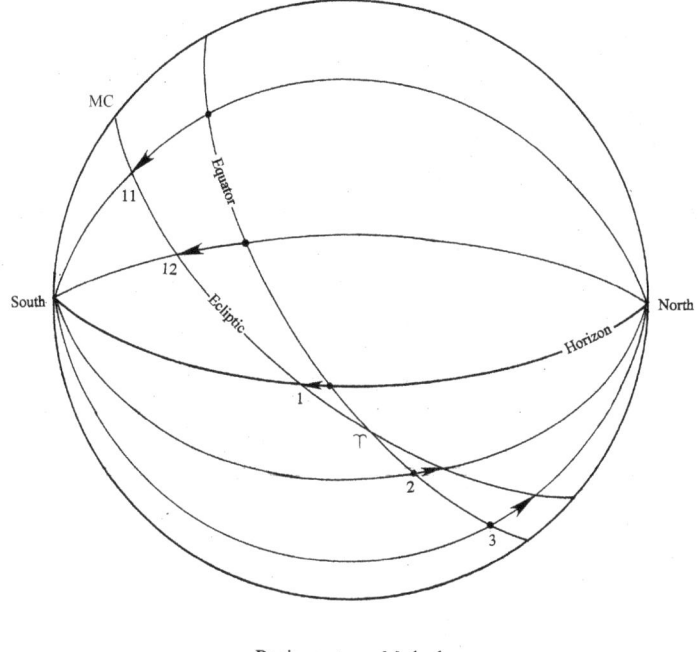

Regiomontanus Method

Figure 28

Time-based house systems

The *planetary hours*, in which the length of both day and night (diurnal and nocturnal arcs) are each divided into twelfths, may be a remnant of early attempts to create additional zones in the celestial environment and may be related in some way to time-based house systems.

Alcabitius – This ancient system of house division is attributed to the Arabic astrologer Al-Qabisi (d. 967), but he did not invent it. It has been dated to Roman times, was very popular in the Middle Ages, and has been called the "standard method." The Alcabitius house system trisects the diurnal and nocturnal semi-arcs of the Ascendant in terms of time. The time trisected is the amount of sidereal time needed for the degree of the Ascendant to be rotated to the Midheaven (the diurnal semi-arc). This amount of sidereal time is divided by three and then the result is added to the sidereal time at birth in two installments; the first new Ascendant becomes the 11th house cusp, the second the 12th house cusp. A similar procedure is used for the nocturnal semi-arc in which the Ascendant is rotated from the I.C. to its birth position and the time taken is trisected to generate the 2nd and 3rd houses. (The house cusps in the other quadrants are the opposite points of those found in these two semi-arcs.) In the diagram below note that, as the Earth rotates, the Ascendant is on its own diurnal circle parallel to the equator.

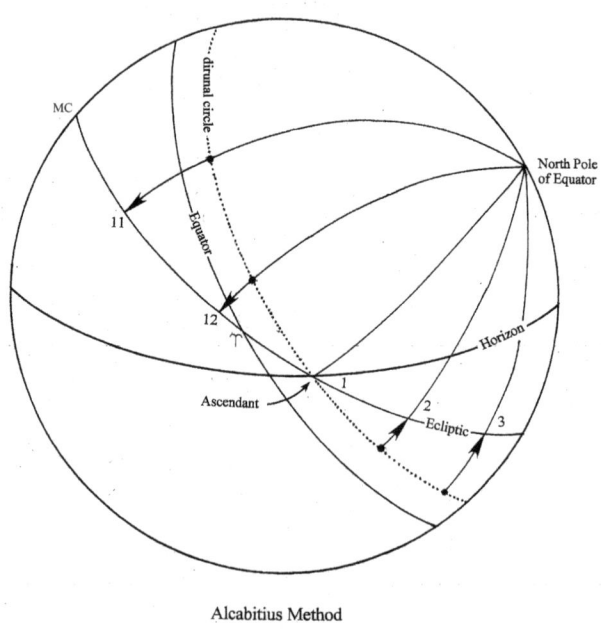

Alcabitius Method

Figure 29

Placidus – Placidus de Titus (1603–1668) was a Spanish monk of the early 17th century whose name is associated with this system. It was previously described and published in 1602 by Giovanni Antonio Magini (1555–1617). Something like the Placidian system may have been used in ancient times as its methodology lends itself to primary directions. Because Placidus has long been widely available in print (not because it has been proven to be the best house system) it has long been the most commonly used system of house division in Western astrology. It does not use projections and is sometimes called the "semi-arc system" because of its time-based nature. The semi-arc of a degree of the zodiac, or a planet, is $\frac{1}{2}$ the time that degree or planet is above the horizon (diurnal arc) or below the horizon (nocturnal arc). This figure can vary considerably depending on the declination of the planet or point. The Placidus system has serious problems in charts set for high latitudes.

Calculations for the Placidus house system are complex and there are several variations in common use. The house cusps are found by tracking the movement of each point (degree) on the ecliptic as it moves along its diurnal circle (parallel to the equator) in each semi-arc. Each point's movement in time during its semi-arc passage is trisected and becomes a house cusp. Conceptualizing the Placidian house system is not easy and diagrams, often confusing, do not reveal its intrinsic time-based nature. Thinking of this way may be helpful. The degree of the Midheaven is a point on the zodiac that has completed one half of its diurnal arc, finishing its diurnal semi-arc. The cusp of the 11th house has completed $\frac{2}{3}$ of its travel through its diurnal semi-arc and $\frac{2}{6}$ of its diurnal arc. The cusp of the 12 house has completed $\frac{1}{3}$ of its diurnal semi-arc and $\frac{1}{6}$ of its diurnal arc.

In *Figure 30* below the numbered points, which are each house cusps on the ecliptic, are seen to belong to small circles parallel to the equator – diurnal circles. Each cusp then has its own track which will move at its own rate and rise and set in a different place than the others.

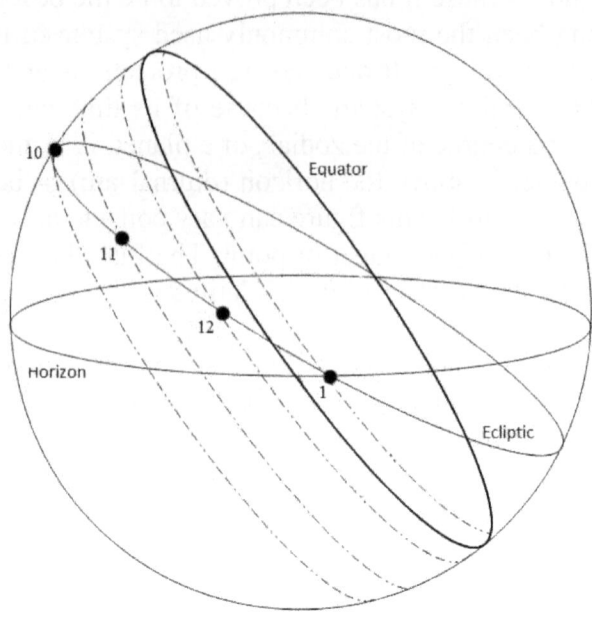

Placidus Method

Figure 30

In many astrology texts of the 19th century a method of making houses cusps was described that takes the Right Ascension of the Midheaven (RAMC) and adds 90 degrees to it. This gives the oblique ascension (OA) of the Ascendant. The degree of the Ascendant is then worked out with trigonometry. Next 30 degrees is added to the RAMC and another Ascendant is calculated, this being the cusp of the 11th. Then 60 degrees is added to the RAMC and the resulting Ascendant becomes the cusp of the 12th. The results give house cusps similar to those of Placidus. Alan Leo calls this the "ordinary method" and others have called it pseudo-Placidus. It appears to be a method based on practicality, not on geometric or rotational idealism, which this author finds refreshing.

Koch - Walter Koch (1895-1970) was a German astrologer who devised a system also known as the "birth-place" method of house division. It attained great popularity in spite of the fact that it was not that well-understood and the alleged birthplace specificity has been criticized as not being astronomically true. It appears to combine some of the qualities of Alcabitius, Regiomontanus and Placidus to arrive at a set of original intermediate house cusps between the Ascendant and Midheaven, which themselves are the cusps of houses 1 and 10. In this system the Midheaven is rotated back to the start of its diurnal semi-arc, when it is on the horizon. The time this takes is trisected, the trisections marking two additional Ascendants which become the cusps of the 11th and 12th houses. The same process is done moving the IC to the Ascendant and trisecting the time elapsed. One way of looking at this is to see each house cusp (except for the 10th and 4th) as like Ascendants with their own horizons or altitude circles, which are small circles parallel to the horizon with their pole being the zenith.

Topocentric – this is another modern system, invented in Argentina by Polich and Page. Even more so than Koch, its rationale is challenging and there are differences of opinion on how it actually works. It appears to be designed roughly as follows: the equator is divided into equal segments and these are projected onto the ecliptic using what are called variable ascension circles, the latter being great circles that are tangent to small circles (parallel to the equator). These small circles relate to the geographic latitude of the birth place in 30 degree intervals. The Ascendant and Midheaven are house cusps. Interested readers may wish to investigate the intricate details of this system on their own.

Other House Systems

Morinus – Jean Baptiste Morinus (1583-1656) is associated with a method of computing houses by dividing the equator into equal arcs, as did Regiomontanus, but then projecting these to the ecliptic via its pole, not the pole of the horizon. These projections are called circles of equal longitude. The Ascendant is not a starting point, and the first house is determined by adding 90 degrees to the longitude of the Midheaven which, where it crosses the horizon, marks the actual east and west directions (called equatorial Ascendant/Descendant or east/west points), directions that the ecliptic Ascendant and Descendant are located in only twice a day when 0 Aries or 0 Libra rises. The Midheaven is not the cusp of the 10th either. This system doesn't distort at high latitudes.

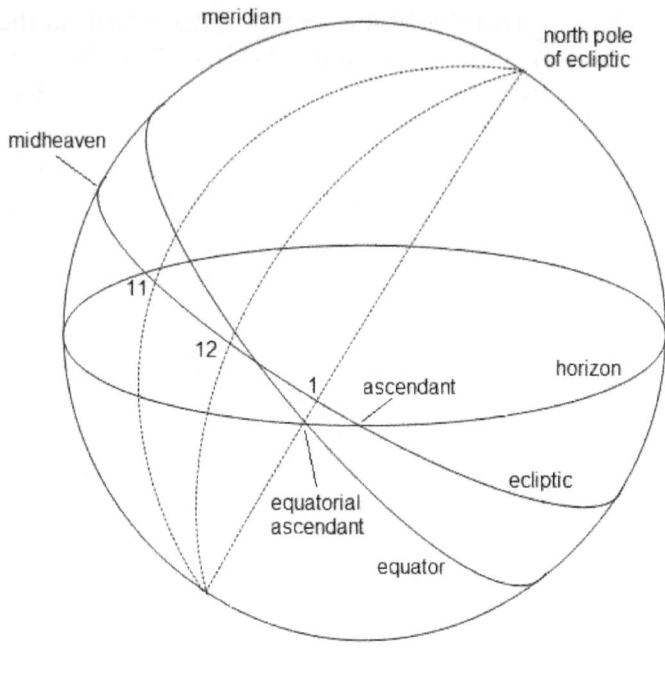

Morinus method

Figure 31

Meridian – also known as the Axial method, Equatorial houses, Equal Division Method or the method of Zariel, an Australian astrologer who promoted it at the start of the 20th century. The celestial equator is divided into 12ths at 30 degree intervals from the meridian (two hours of sidereal time), where the horizon marks one of these intervals. Because there is always 90 degrees of Right Ascension between the horizon and the meridian (upper and lower) each equatorial quadrant has exactly 3 sections. These division points are then projected back to the ecliptic using hour circles from the pole of the equator. This system begins the division of houses at the Midheaven, so the Ascendant is not the cusp of the 1st house in most cases. The first house is the degree on the ecliptic that projected from the equator/horizon intersection. This intersection is called the equatorial Ascendant (and sometimes the east point). This system is a preferred method by many practitioners of the Hamburg School of Astrology founded by Alfred Witte (Uranian Astrology).

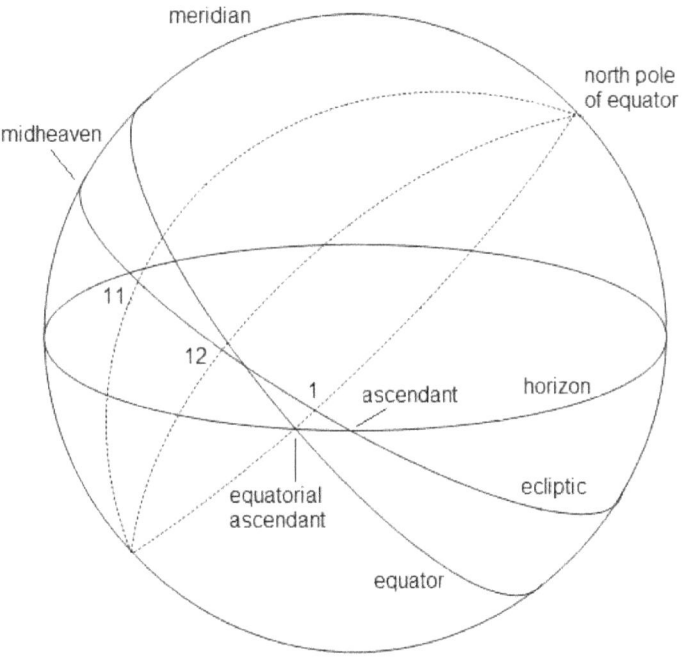

Meridian/Zariel method

Figure 32

Personal Observations on House Systems

"From the interpretation point of view, the only basis for a claim of superiority of one house system over another would be convincing evidence that the house system explained more observable data than any other. No study has been published that supports such claim for any house system." Robert Hand and Joshua Brackett, 1997.

Understanding the logic (and often the geometrical beauty and complexity) of the various house systems is one thing, determining whether or not they work in practice is another. Testing house systems is not a simple problem and has yet to be worked out to a point where an educated consensus on the matter has been reached by the astrological community. Any evaluation of the many house systems in existence must begin with the issue of whether the house cusps are discrete boundaries that cleanly demarcate sections of space as do zodiacal signs, or they are sensitive points that operate with radiating orbs. Consider an example: Mars in a chart is located at 15Ar10 and the cusp of the 6th house is 17Ar21. In the first case Mars would be considered a 5th house planet because it is just over 2 degrees short of the 6th cusp. In the second case, it would be considered conjunct the 6th cusp and therefore constitute a strong influence on the matters of that house. Changing the house system might move Mars well into the 6th or further back into the 5th. Which one corresponds better with reality is highly subjective and difficult to verify. But if the house cusp is regarded as a point, then the problem becomes one of orb of influence.

Most house systems are based on the quadrants formed by the horizon and meridian axes, i.e. the Ascendant/Descendant axis and the Midheaven/IC axis. This means that these points will be the same in most house systems. What differentiates the systems are the intermediate house cusps which may often vary by more than a few degrees and it is logical to focus on these in any kind of test or analysis. It goes without saying that the angles of the chart must be precise, to the minute of arc, in order for the intermediate house cusps to be accurately calculated and adequately tested.

The testing of house systems presents the same problems that any kind of astrological research usually faces – what units are available to test? How does one score Mars in the 6th as opposed to Mars in the 5th? One possible way to do this is to make a list of potential effects of Mars in each house and assign each a score. For example, Mars in the 6th could indicate any of the following each worth one point: self-employment that provides a service, work that is prone to urgencies, enthusiasm and initiative in work, working with tools or sharp objects, work that repairs or heals, acute health concerns, health issues having to do with muscles or blood, difficult or assertive subordinates, etc. Scores attached to each description could then be added and compared.

Several decades ago I did such a test (not to be confused with a thorough scientific study) using my natal chart, which I had rectified the Ascendant and Midheaven to the nearest minute, and also the charts of a few friends where I was also confident of the accuracy of these angles. First I computed all the intermediate house cusps in the following systems: Placidus, Koch, Campanus, Regiomontanus, Meridian, Porphyry, and Alcabitius. I eliminated Equal houses because these cusps are also aspects to the Ascendant. My test was focused on the actual house cusps themselves, not the space between them. The passage over these cusps by slow moving outer planets and progressions were calculated and the kinds of events that occurred at the time were noted. The spread between the cusps generated by these systems was wide enough to catch individual events using an orb of about 7' of arc. (note: my first report was published in Fall/Winter 1992/1993 issue of *The Ascendant*, the journal of the Astrological Society of Connecticut and this article is also posted on the Astrolabe Software website – www.alabe.com.)

Prior to this anecdotal study I had been using Placidus for the same reason nearly all of my fellow astrologers were – tables were readily available and everyone was using them. There was little discussion about this situation and I wondered how many practicing astrologers understood the abstract time/space equations that go into producing these cusps? Not many, it turned out. Worse, the brief explanation for the logic of the Placidian system in Dalton's Table of Houses, for decades the most used table of houses for astrologers, describes something other than Placidus. Astrologers were apparently using a system that they didn't understand, and their source author didn't either, and thus let a faulty explanation continue being reprinted. (Dalton described what was called the "ordinary" method – see above).

After considering transits, progressions and solar arcs to the various cusps over a 20-year period, I concluded that some of cusps generated by the house systems were not effective (or at least not convincing) but Placidus, Porphyry, Koch and Meridian showed consistently appropriate symbolic correlations. Of these four, Meridian and Porphyry appeared, in my estimation, to be the most focused, relevant and significant. These results caused me to adopt the Porphyry system which, in addition to maintaining the Ascendant and Midheaven as house cusps 1 and 10, has the additional bonus of being much easier to calculate than the other far more mathematically complex systems. Porphyry cusps also focus only on the ecliptic, the zone where most of the action in astrology takes place, which I think counts for something. When I made the choice to switch from Placidus to Porphyry, there were no computers, only calculators, so it made good sense to use a house system that could (1) be calculated rapidly and (2) definitely worked, at least as well, if not better, than quite a few others.

Tables of Houses

Tables of houses contain listings of sidereal times; each listing also has the degree of the Midheaven and the zodiacal positions of the Ascendant and half of the intermediate houses. Each degree of the zodiac has a specific sidereal time when it is culminating (at the Midheaven) at any latitude. Sidereal times for Ascendant degrees vary, however, according to latitude. In most house systems the Ascendant is also the cusp of the first house and the Midheaven the cusp of the tenth. The intermediate house cusps listed in a table of houses are typically the cusps of houses 11, 12, 2, and 3, these provide the figures for the opposite cusps 5, 6, 8 and 9.

The table of Midheavens and Ascendants in this book are limited and presented for illustrative and exercise purposes. They list latitudes only at five degree intervals within a range of 30 degrees and do not include intermediate house cusps. But the basic information in regard to sidereal time, Midheavens, and Ascendants is accurate and they are completely usable. Here's a sample of the table that appears in full starting on page 209.

ST	M C	A-25N	A-30N	A-35N	A-40N	A-45N	A-50N	A-55
21h28'	19aq35	4ge18	6ge58	10ge02	13ge40	18ge03	23ge27	0ca15
21h32'	20aq36	5ge21	8ge01	11ge06	14ge43	19ge04	24ge26	1ca10
21h36'	21aq37	6ge23	9ge04	12ge09	15ge46	20ge06	25ge24	2ca04
21h40'	22aq39	7ge25	10ge06	13ge11	16ge47	21ge06	26ge22	2ca57

The sidereal time, in four minute intervals, is listed in the first column, the Midheaven comes next and then Ascendants for latitudes between 25 and 55 north. It is very useful to look over the full table of houses to get a feel for how the Ascendant changes relative to the Midheaven at the varying latitudes. Notice that when the Ascendant is at the equinoxes, at sidereal time 6:00 and 18:00, it is square to the Midheaven which is at the solstices. Also notice how the arc between the Ascendant and Midheaven reaches extremes when the solstice signs are rising, at sidereal time 0:00 and 12:00, this being due to the ecliptic reaching its highest declination north or south at these points.

More typical are tables of houses that list the sidereal time, the right ascension of the Midheaven (RAMC), the Midheaven, the Ascendant and the intermediate house cusps for each degree of a wide range of latitudes. Some even list cusps for the specific latitudes of major cities. There are two general types of house tables. One type lists the sidereal time in four minute increments (as the table in this book does) and the corresponding Midheaven (which is the same for all latitudes) as shown on the next page.

ST = 21h 32m   MC = 20 Aq 36   RAMC = 323

Latitude	11	12	1	2	3
25	21 Pi 50	28 Ar 28	5 Ge 21	0 Ca 43	24 Ca 33
26	21 48	28 39	5 51	1 03	24 42
27	21 46	28 51	6 22	1 23	24 51
28	21 45	29 03	6 54	1 44	25 01
29	21 43	29 16	7 27	2 05	25 10
30	21 41	29 29	8 01	2 26	25 20

A second type of table lists the Midheaven in one degree increments along with the corresponding sidereal time. In the sample below the intermediate house cusps are given in decimals of degrees, but the Ascendant is given in degrees and minutes. Like the example above, the intermediate cusps are Placidus cusps.

ST = 21h 33m 34s   MC = 21 Aq 00   RAMC = 323 23.5

Latitude	11	12	1	2	3
25	22.3 Pi	29 Ar	5 Ge 46	1.1 Ca	24.9 Ca
26	22.3	29.2	6 16	1.4	25.1
27	22.2	29.4	6 47	1.7	25.2
28	22.2	29.6	7 19	2.1	25.4
29	22.2	29.8	7 52	2.4	25.5
30	22.1	0 Ta	8 26	2.8	25.7

What table of houses one should use is really a matter of preference. The first consideration is the house system itself. After that a good table should have listings for all useful degrees of latitude and perhaps contain some other tables as well. If you choose to work with a form of equal houses, or Porphyry, you don't need a table of house, just tables for Midheavens and Ascendants (or a scientific calculator and two trigonometry formulas).

Chapter 5

Calculating the Astrological Chart

The calculation of an astrological chart can be accomplished in several ways. Four methods will be presented in this text:

(1) interpolation tables
(2) proportions (algebra)
(3) logarithms
(4) trigonometry

All methods, however, begin with the same data – the *Local Sidereal Time* and the *Greenwich Mean Time* of a birth or an event.

Required Materials

Ephemeris (singular), *Ephemerides* (plural – Ef-em-MARE-a-dees). This essential component of chart calculation is basically a daily almanac of the planets' positions. These tables are normally calculated for midnight at Greenwich, England. Midnight (zero hour) ephemerides list planetary positions at the beginning of the civil day. In the past ephemerides that list planetary positions at the midpoint of the civil day (noon) were common and are still available. Midnight ephemerides are highly recommended as they are more consistent with modern thinking about the cycle of the day and they simplify calculations. A sample midnight ephemeris is found on page 207 which will be used for examples of the chart calculation methods presented in this book.

Table of Houses. While many systems of house division have been invented only a few are available in printed form, Placidus being the most common. Some tables of houses, and some ephemerides, include *house cusp interpolation tables*. These tables offer an alternative to solving the problem of interpolation by algebra (proportions) or with logarithms. Some tables of houses also contain daylight saving time changes and atlas information (latitudes and longitudes) that add to their usefulness. One alternative to using a table of houses is to use a house system that does not require the calculation of intermediate house cusps such as equal or whole sign houses, or the Porphyry house system which requires only that the arc in longitude between the angles be trisected. Another alternative would be doing the trigonometrical calculations that are required for most complex house systems.

Atlas. For chart calculations an accurate determination of a location's latitude and longitude is necessary. Today, the latitude and longitude of any given location is readily available with an internet search. If the internet is not available, as it may not be if one is taking an exam, a detailed atlas or a book of listings of latitudes and longitudes for cities and towns will be needed. *The American Atlas* and *The International Atlas* are highly recommended, both published by ACS Publications, though now out of print.

Time Changes Tables. A reference for changes in time is required because daylight saving time has not been consistently applied in all locations. This data (one of the great compilation efforts made by a few dedicated astrologers during the 20th century) was published in books listing latitudes and longitudes such as the *The American* and *The International Atlas.* It is also found as a database used by computer software. This information may not be so easily found on the internet.

Scientific calculator. The calculator should have at minimum the ability to convert degrees, minutes and seconds into decimals and vice versa. It should also have at least one memory, and preferably three if the trigonometric method is used. Texas Instruments, Casio and Sharp all produce calculators with these features in the seven to twenty dollar price range. Scientific calculators are also available both online or as software, but make sure these have the features noted above. Microsoft Windows comes with a calculator app that has a scientific mode, but only one memory. See pages 100-101 for more information on this topic.

Tables of Diurnal Proportional Logarithms. Logarithm tables are often found in ephemerides or tables of houses. A complete table of this type of logarithms (used for degrees and minutes, or hours and minutes) appears in this book on page 230.

Chart forms. These are necessary for displaying the information calculated. Historically, astrological charts were written in a square with 12 house divisions. These were easily drawn with only a ruler and show a natural emphasis on the angular houses 1, 4, 7 and 10. The central box was where the event data or any notes could be written. There were other variations of this box-like chart form, some of which are still used in Hindu astrology.

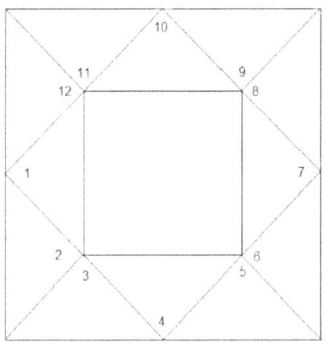

The standard chart form today is basically a circular graph with twelve divisions – like a clock or a pizza. Chart forms, some rather elaborate, can be purchased commercially or drawn by hand using a protractor and ruler.

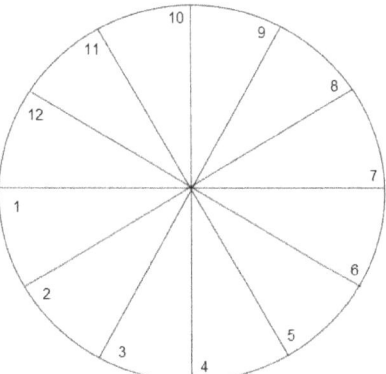

Other Tables. Chart calculations may also be done using a selection of special tables. Tables for determining the solar-sidereal correction, for interpolating house cusps and for interpolating planetary positions are available, one being the *American Book of Tables* that was published by ACS. In addition to tables of houses for Placidus and Koch, it contains a multitude of precision tables (with small increments between listings) for all steps of chart calculation. Interpolation tables for house cusps and planet positions in larger increments are found later in this book and will be used in the examples.

Chart point notations. In addition to the 8 planets of the solar system, modern astrology includes the dwarf planet Pluto. A number of other minor planets like Chiron, and asteroids such as Ceres (which is a dwarf planet), Vesta, Juno, and Pallas are often employed as well. The Sun, Moon and the planets are written into the chart form using standard planet symbols that are the same as those used at times by astronomers (with some minor differences). Planets are also abbreviated in some situations, as they are in many parts of this book. These are listed below:

Planet	Symbol	Abbreviation
Sun	☉	Su
Moon	☽	Mo
Mercury	☿	Me
Venus	♀	Ve
Mars	♂	Ma
Jupiter	♃	Ju
Saturn	♄	Sa
Uranus	♅	Ur
Neptune	♆	Ne
Pluto	♇	Pl

Symbols and abbreviations of the signs of the zodiac:

Aries	♈	Ar
Taurus	♉	Ta
Gemini	♊	Ge
Cancer	♋	Ca
Leo	♌	Le
Virgo	♍	Vi

Libra	♎	Li
Scorpio	♏	Sc
Sagittarius	♐	Sa
Capricorn	♑	Cp
Aquarius	♒	Aq
Pisces	♓	Pi

Time – Space Conversions

The rotation of the Earth is the basis of the day. The movement of the projection of the Earth's equator (celestial equator) under any given meridian during its daily rotation is measured in Right Ascension (R.A.). Twenty four hours of rotation, or one complete rotation, is equal to 360 degrees of distance along the celestial equator. Likewise, distance on the Earth may be converted to time. Note that 360 divided by 24 = 15.

The *Longitude Time Equivalent* (LTE) is used in astrological chart calculations to adjust for the birth location within a given time zone. This is longitude (space) expressed in time and is calculated by dividing the location's longitude by 15.

$$LTE = \frac{longitude}{15}$$

For example, a location on Earth that is 90 degrees west of the Prime Meridian at Greenwich, England has a time value different by 6 hours of rotation on the equator (90 ÷ 15 = 6). Time zones reflect this principle. Eastern time is a 5-hour difference from Greenwich Mean Time, and it is centered on the 75th meridian.

Example: 75 ÷ 15 = 5, or 5 x 15 = 75.

Longitude $\longrightarrow$ time

360° = 24 hours	15° = 1 hour
1° = 4 minutes	1' = 4 seconds.

Time may be also converted to distance:

$$\text{Time} \longrightarrow \text{degrees}$$

24 hours = 360°	1 hour = 15°
4 minutes = 1°.	4 seconds = 1'

Basic Number Manipulations for Chart Calculations

Sexagesimal number system. It has been the convention to measure both time and distance in astrology in units of 60. This counting and measurement, based on 60, was originally used by the Babylonians and later adopted by the Greeks. It is used today as the convention for designating time and also noting location on a sphere. It is also called "base 60" counting.

Time: 1 hour = 60 minutes = 3600 seconds (60 x 60).
Space: 1 degree of arc on a sphere = 60 minutes = 3600 seconds.

Modulus function, or circular counting. This type of counting is done within frameworks, the largest unit being the modulus, the value (a unit of measure) that when reached is then "wrapped around." When doing calculations it is often necessary to subtract the modulus from the figure (sometimes called "reducing to lowest terms"). For example, in time, 24 hours (one day) is the usual modulus, and for degrees and minutes the modulus is 60. In the first case, 30 hours is equal to 24 hours + 6 hours. In the second, 89 minutes is equal to 1 hour + 29 minutes.

Another case of the modulus function are the signs of the zodiac. Although the entire zodiac spans 360 degrees, each sign is 30 degrees in length and any given absolute longitude (see below) needs to be reduced to a figure under 30 degrees. For example 45 degrees of absolute longitude is one full sign of 30 degrees plus 15 degrees of the

98

next sign, this being 15 Taurus. (Example: 225 degrees of longitude is 210 degrees, or zero Scorpio, plus 15 degrees.)

Calculators. Most astrological calculations require the manipulation of figures expressed in either time or degrees. These calculations can be done using arithmetic, but it is far easier to work with these figures when they are converted to decimals. Most scientific calculators have a function key that will make this conversion simple (see below). However, conversion can be handled on a standard calculator in the following way:

Example 1: Convert 29 degrees and 34 minutes to decimal form.

Problem stated as: 29 + $34/60$ = ?
Using calculator: 34 ÷ 60 + 29 = 29.5666

Example 2: Convert 72 degrees and 26 minutes and 10 seconds to decimal form. Note that seconds are divided by 3600 (60 x 60), then minutes are added before the figure is divided by 60. The last step is adding the degrees.

Problem stated as: 72 + $26/60$ + $10/3600$ = ?
Using calculator: 10 ÷ 3600 + 26 ÷ 60 + 72 = 72.4361

Example 3: Convert 72.4361 to degrees, minutes, seconds (dms)

Subtract 72 (degrees), multiply 0.4361 by 60 = 26.166
Subtract 26 (minutes), multiply 0.166 by 3600 = 9.96
Round up 9.96 to 10.
Result is 72 degrees, 26 minutes and 10 seconds.

Converting from sexagesimal notation to decimals on a basic scientific calculator (under $10) is relatively simple, but it should be practiced before doing astrological chart calculations. Buying a more expensive calculator with many features is not necessary and may add confusion. Most keys on scientific calculator keypads serve two functions. One is what's printed on the button, the other is usually printed above the button and it is turned on only after the 2nd function or shift button is pushed.

Note: When using a scientific calculator all conversions from degrees, minutes and seconds to decimals and back must be done with the calculator in degree mode, not radian or other modes.

Texas Instruments*: press yellow 2nd key, then press the DRG key until you see DEG at the top of the display.*

Casio*: press shift key, then mode key, and then the number 4. DEG should appear at the top of the display.*

Sharp*: press 2nd F key, then press the DRG key until you see DEG at the top of the display.*

Texas Instruments (i.e TI-30 series) converts from sexagesimal to decimal as follows:

1. Input degrees (including zero) followed by a decimal point and then minutes and seconds. You will need to precede a single digit in minutes and seconds with a zero.

Example: 17d 21m 45s would look like 17.2145
                      13h 7m 3s   would look like 13.0703
2. Press the yellow 2nd function key at top left of the keyboard and then press the DMS→DD key (which is usually the + key at lower right on the keyboard). You are now in decimals. Using the above examples you should see 17.3625 and 13.1175.

3. To return to sexagesimal notation press the yellow 2nd function key again and then the DD→DMS button (usually the = button).

Casio calculators such as the fx-260 or 300 series are a bit different. They use a special key that has degrees minutes and seconds printed on it. It looks like this: ° ′ ″ The Casio procedure does not require placing a zero before a single digit and calculations can be done entirely in sexagesimal notation without converting to decimals.

1. Enter degrees and press the ° ′ ″ button.
2. Enter minutes and press the ° ′ ″ button.
3. Enter seconds and press the ° ′ ″ button.
4. Press the shift button (upper left) and then the ° ′ ″ button.

Your figure is now displayed as a decimal. To return to degrees, minutes and seconds press the shift key followed by the ° ′ ″ button.

Sharp EL 500 series scientific calculators are similar in operation to Texas Instruments calculators in regard to these conversions. Input degrees followed by a decimal point, then minutes and seconds (with a zero before single digits) and then press the →DEG key. This will convert the figure to decimals. To convert to degrees, minutes and seconds press the second function key (2nd F) at upper left and then the →DEG key.

One consideration in acquiring a scientific calculator is the number of memories it has. Most under $10 scientific calculators will have one memory which is adequate for most purposes, though the Texas Instruments TI-30 series has 3, which is useful in certain kinds of chart calculations.

Absolute or true longitude. Another mathematical convention used in chart calculations is the actual longitude of the planet or point calculated from 0 degrees Aries. The following table shows the number of degrees from zero Aries that each zodiacal sign begins. True longitude is found by adding the degrees and minutes of a planet or point to the appropriate figure below.

Aries: 0	Leo: 120	Sagittarius: 240
Taurus: 30	Virgo: 150	Capricorn: 270
Gemini: 60	Libra: 180	Aquarius: 300
Cancer: 90	Scorpio: 210	Pisces: 330

Examples: 98 degrees = 90 degrees + 8 degrees = 8 Cancer
201 degrees = 180 degrees + 21 degrees = 21 Libra

Steps in Casting an Astrological Chart

The calculation of an astrological chart by any method occurs in three stages. First, the birth data must be converted to two kinds of time, *Local Sidereal Time* and *Greenwich Mean Time*. Second, the Ascendant, Midheaven and houses are calculated from Local Sidereal Time (LST). Third, the planets are calculated from Greenwich Mean Time (GMT). These calculations can be done in several ways which will be described below and will assume the use of a midnight ephemeris. (Using a noon ephemeris may be challenging because it requires conceptualizing noon as the start of the day and also dealing with AM times as part of the previous day.) All methods require the following preliminary steps.

Step 1: Determining the Greenwich Mean Time of birth

1. Take the given time of the event or birth (be clear about AM or PM or express it in terms of 24-hours, i.e. military time).

2. Make corrections for Daylight Saving Time (DST – usually subtract one hour from Daylight Saving Time to obtain standard time).

3. Add the time zone difference (hours west of Greenwich) if location is west longitude – or – subtract time zone difference (hours east of Greenwich) if east longitude.

4. The result is the Greenwich Mean Time (GMT) of the event or birth. If the result is over 24, then subtract 24 – but remember this will move the date you will be working with one day ahead. Use this figure in calculating the Midheaven, Ascendant and house cusps.

Note: When GMT is used to calculate the positions of the planets from the ephemeris, the most precise results will require the ΔT (Delta T) adjustment which is the addition (or subtraction) of a small figure that changes yearly based on astronomical observa-

tions. For most purposes this can be dispensed with, but for solar or lunar return charts it should be factored in.

Step 2: Determining the Local Sidereal Time of birth

1. From a midnight ephemeris take the S.T. (sidereal time) at midnight beginning on the day of birth. (Use the following day if the GMT is greater than 24 hours. With a noon ephemeris use the ST of the previous noon)

2. Add the G.M.T. of birth (without ΔT correction).

3. Add the solar-sidereal correction on the G.M.T. at roughly 10 seconds per hour (more exactly 9.8333 seconds per hour). This figure can be read from a table (see page 217) or by dividing the GMT by 6.1. The resulting figure is then used as minutes with the decimal being seconds. (This correction accounts for the difference between the sidereal day and the solar day, a difference of 3 minutes and 56 seconds.)

Example: for a GMT of 11 hours 45 minutes:

For standard calculator:
11:45 = 11 + $^{45}/_{60}$ = 11.75.
Divide 11.75 by 6.1 = 1.926 (minutes of time).
Subtract 1 minute and multiply remainder 0.926 by 60 = 55.56
Round the figure up = 56 seconds.

For scientific calculator:
Using degree to decimal conversion keys, input time, divide by 6.1 and then press appropriate decimal to degree conversion keys (see section on calculators above).

The solar-sidereal correction is then 1 minute and 56 seconds.

4. This now equals the S.T. at Greenwich for the time of birth.

5. Next *subtract* the west longitude equivalent in time, or *add* the east longitude equivalent in time. This figure can be found in tables of cities, or simply calculated once the longitude is determined from an atlas or from an internet search.

Longitude ÷ 15 = Longitude Time Equivalent.
(15° of longitude = 1 hour, 1° = 4 minutes)

Procedure: convert longitude expressed in degrees, minutes and seconds (DMS) into degrees and decimals. Divide by 15 and then convert back to hours, minutes and seconds. (This is easily done on a scientific calculator with conversion keys but can also be done with many more steps on a standard calculator as shown in the example below.)

Example: for Washington, D.C. = 77 degrees 2 minutes 12 seconds west longitude.

1. Convert to decimals: $12/3600 + 2/60 + 77 = 77.0367$
Divide result by 15: $77.0367 ÷ 15 = 5.1358$ (hours)
2. Convert 5.1358 to hours, minutes and seconds:
Subtract 5 (hours), multiply 0.1358 by 60 = 8.148 (minutes)
Subtract 8 (minutes), multiply 0.148 by 60 = 8.88 (seconds)
Result = 5 hours, 8 minutes and 9 seconds.

6. This adjustment equals the L.S.T. (For births in the Southern Hemisphere, add 12 hours to L.S.T. and then add 180° to the listed house cusps in a table of houses.)

The LST is used to calculate the houses of the horoscope. Normally, a table of houses is employed for this task. For the examples used in this book, the tables of Midheavens and Ascendants found beginning on page 209 will be used.

Step 3: Calculating the Midheaven, Ascendant, and intermediate house cusps

The following steps are necessary to complete the calculation of a horoscope. They are handled in different ways depending on the chart calculation method being used. The logic of these steps is outlined here, but are presented in more detail with examples in the next sections.

1. Using the Local Sidereal Time, calculate the Midheaven from a table of houses using proportions, logarithms, tables – or directly using a calculator with trigonometric functions.

2. Again, using the Local Sidereal Time, calculate the Ascendant from a table of houses using proportions, logarithms, tables or trigonometry. This will normally require first calculating Ascendants for two latitudes, those given by the table of houses. A third calculation must then be done for the exact latitude. Or this can be done directly using trigonometry.

3. Determine the intermediate house cusps. To calculate these exactly from a table of houses, the same calculation done for the Ascendant must be done for the intermediate house cusps in a minimum of two quadrants (the quarters of the horoscope produced by the Midheaven and Ascendant.) Less complicated alternatives are the use of equal or whole sign houses or the Porphyry system which only requires a trisection of the arc between the Midheaven and Ascendant.

4. Place the calculated data on the standard Western chart form.

Step 4: Calculating the Planet's Positions

Planet position calculations require the use of the GMT figure. (For the most precise positions, such as those for needed for solar or lunar returns, make the ΔT adjustment to GMT.)

1. Determine the proportion of the 24-hour day established by the Greenwich Mean Time of the birth or event. For example, the proportion of a GMT of 18 hours to 24 hours is the same as 3/4 or 0.75. This figure is called the *constant fraction*.

2. From an ephemeris, determine the daily motion of each planet. Then multiply the daily motion by the constant fraction. Add the result to the earlier listing of the planet's place in the ephemeris. This is the planet's position at the time of the birth or event. Interpolation tables, examples of which are found in this book, may also be employed to solve the problem of finding the planet's position during the day in question.

3. Place the planets positions into the framework of the chart previously calculated.

Step 5: Miscellaneous Calculations

1. *Mean node:* moves 3'/day (3 minutes per day). Use a rounded-off constant fraction.

2. *Declinations:*
   a. The daily change in the Moon's declination is great. Note whether it is increasing or decreasing in declination. Use the same rules as for calculating the planetary positions.
   b. Use a rough constant fraction for other planets. If declination is listed every 3 days, divide by 3 to get daily motion.

3. *Part of Fortune*. First convert the zodiacal longitudes of the Sun, Moon, and Ascendant to absolute (true) longitude (360 degree notation – see page 102). Use the appropriate formula below and reduce to a figure under 360 by subtracting 360 if necessary.

For diurnal (day) charts: = Ascendant + Moon - Sun
For nocturnal (night) charts: = Ascendant + Sun - Moon

Example from New Horizons launch on next page. Chart is diurnal (Sun above horizon).

Ascendant = 7 Ge 33 = 67 33
Moon = 28 Vi 07 = 178 07
Sun = 29 Cp 33 = 299 33

(Sun) 67 33 + (Moon) 178 07 = 245 40

To subtract the Sun, 360 must be added to the figure:

245 40 + 360 = 605 40   605 40 – (Sun) 299 33 = 306 07

306 07 = 6 Aq 07 = Part of Fortune

4. *Vertex.* This point (the western part of an axis in some ways like the Ascendant/Descendant axis) was promoted by the astrologers Edward Johndro and Charles Jayne and is thought to signify fateful or karmic encounters. Subtract the latitude of the birthplace from 90 degrees; this is the co-latitude of birth place. Use the IC (4th house cusp) as if it were the MC and calculate the Ascendant for the co-latitude (90° – latitude) in Table of Houses. This Ascendant is the vertex. There is a trigonometric formula for this point that is found on page 162.

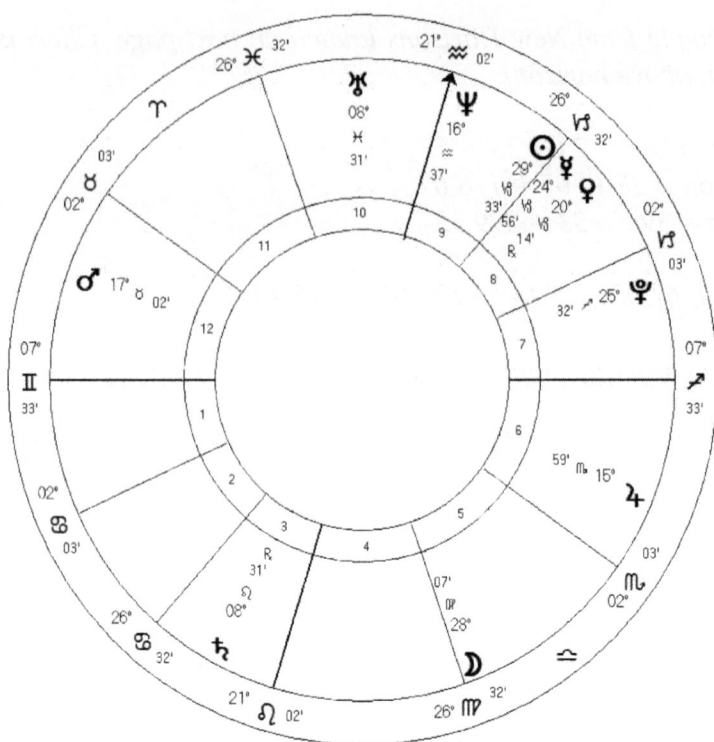

Above: Chart for the launch of NASA's New Horizons spacecraft on January 19, 2006 at 2 PM EST, Cape Canaveral, Florida. This chart will be used as a worked example below and in the next four chapters.

Worksheet for Preliminary Calculations (for all methods)

Basic Chart Data:

Name/Event_____

Year _____ Month _____ Day _____

Time _____AM - PM   Time (24 hour time) _____

Location_____

Time Zone_____

Latitude_____Longitude _____

Calculating Greenwich Mean Time (GMT):

1. Local Standard Time (24 h time)   _____h _____m _____s
2. Daylight/War Time correction: (-) _____h
                   =   _____h _____m _____s

3. Time zone adjustment (+W/-E)   _____h _____m _____s

4. Sum or difference of 3 and 4:
   Result = Greenwich Mean Time: _____h _____m _____s
   (if over 24, subtract 24)   _____h _____m_____s
   (Event/birth will then be on the following day)

Calculating Local Sidereal Time (LST):

1. Sidereal Time from ephemeris: _____h _____m _____s
2. + Greenwich Mean Time: _____h _____m _____s
3. + solar-sidereal correction: _____m _____s
4. Add 1, 2, and 3:   =   _____h _____m _____s
5. Longitude equivalent in time: _____h _____m _____s

6. Subtract 5 from 4 if west long.
   (Add 5 to 4 if east long.)   _____h _____m _____s
7. Result: Local Sidereal Time (LST)_____h _____m _____s
   (Adjust if needed)   _____h _____m _____s

Worked example:

Event: The launch of NASA's New Horizons spacecraft (destination Pluto and beyond) on January 19, 2006 at 2 PM EST, Cape Canaveral, Florida. See the sample ephemeris on page 207 for the source of the sidereal time used below.

Basic Chart Data:

Name/Event__ *New Horizons launch* _____
Year____ *2006* ____Month____ *January* _____Day_ *19* ____
Time_ *2:00* ___AM - **PM**   Time (24 hour time)_ *14:00* __
Location __ *Cape Canaveral, Florida* _____
Time Zone _ *EST* __
Latitude __ *28 N 24* ____ Longitude___ *80 W 36* __

Calculating Greenwich Mean Time (GMT):

1. Local Standard Time (24 h time)   __ *14* _h_ *0* _m_ *0* _s
2. Daylight/War Time correction: __ *0* __h
   Subtract 2 from 1:   __ *14* _h_ *0* _m_ *0* _s

3. Time zone adjustment (+W/-E)   __ *5* _h____m

4. Add 3 & 4:
   Result = Greenwich Mean Time: __ *19* _h_ *0* _m_ *0* _s
   (if over 24, subtract 24.)   _____h ___ m____s

   (Note: if over 24, event/birth will then be on the following day)

5. ΔT adjustment (for planets)   _____h_ *1* _m_ *5* _s
       Result =   _ *19* _h_ *1* _m_ *5* _s

Calculating Local Sidereal Time (LST):

1. Sidereal Time from ephemeris: __ *7* ___h_ *52* __m___ *59* _s

2. + Greenwich Mean Time:	_19_	h	_0_	m	_0_	s
3. + solar-sidereal correction:			_3_	m	_7_	s
4. Add 1, 2, and 3:	_26_	h	_55_	m	_66_	s
5. Longitude equivalent in time: (–)	_5_	h	_22_	m	_24_	s

6. Subtract 5 from 4 if west long.
   (Add 5 to 4 if east long.) _21_ h _33_ m _42_ s
7. Result: Local Sidereal Time (LST)_21_ h _33_ m _42_ s
   (Adjust if needed) ____ h ____ m ____ s

The launch of the New Horizons spacecraft will be used in the next sections on calculations using different methods as the standard example. The computer-generated chart for the event appears below for reference.

Additional example:

Earthquake in Greece: January 8, 2006. Recorded at 1:34 PM (13:34) in Athens, Greece. Epicenter at 36 N 30 latitude, 23 E 43 longitude. Note: The time is given in Eastern European Time (EET) which is 2 hours ahead of Greenwich, England (-2). No daylight time was in effect.

Local Time:	_13_	h	_34_	m	_0_	s
Time zone adjustment:	_-2_	h	_0_	m	_0_	s
GMT:	_11_	h	_34_	m	_0_	s

| (ΔT GMT for planets) | | h | _1_ | m | _5_ | s |
| Result = | _11_ | h | _35_ | m | _5_ | s |

Sidereal Time for 1/8/2006	_7_	h	_9_	m	_37_	s
+ GMT	_11_	h	_34_	m	_0_	s
+ solar-sidereal correction:		h	_1_	m	_54_	s
=	_18_	h	_44_	m	_91_	s

111

Adjust figure:		_18_ h	_45_ m	_31_ s

Longitude equivalent in time:	_+ 1_ h	_34_ m	_52_ s
Local Sidereal Time =	_19_ h	_79_ m	_83_ s
Adjust figure:	_20_ h	_20_ m	_23_ s

Note: For births in the Southern Hemisphere, add 12 hours to L.S.T. and add 180° to the listed house cusps if using a standard table of houses.

When doing chart calculations by hand, Midheaven and Ascendant calculations may vary, depending on the method and the tables used, by a very small amount from figures produced from astrological software. The tables used in this book are for example purposes only and higher accuracy would be obtained using tables that list seconds of arc or more than a few decimal places. However, the accuracy obtainable from the resources in this book, as shown in the above examples and those over the next chapters, is more than adequate for most purposes, including passing an astrological calculations exam.

Chapter 6

Chart Calculations using Interpolation Tables

Interpolation tables may have been the most commonly used method to cast a horoscope during the second half of the 20th century. With a set of detailed tables most of the work in chart construction becomes reduced to a series of additions or subtractions of data found in lists of figures, and the work can be done in sexagesimal notation. It is a convoluted method and certainly doesn't indicate in any way what is actually being done. It is most often recommended for the math-phobic, however.

A table of houses is the first requirement for this method. The Midheaven and Ascendant table in this book that is used for the examples is accurate and should illustrate the procedure clearly, though far more detailed tables can found in other publications like *The Michelsen Book of Tables*. In regard to tables of houses, there are variations and readers should review Chapter 4.

After calculating the GMT and LST as previously explained, you will need to calculate the Midheaven, Ascendant, house cusps and planets, in that order by referring to a second series of tables that sometimes come with a table of houses or may be published separately. Such tables are found in the last section of this book and will be used for the examples.

Calculating the Midheaven:

Here the previously calculated LST for the New Horizons launch will be used as a worked example.

LST for New Horizons launch = *21*h *33*m *42*s
1. Locate the approximate Local Sidereal Time of the event or birth in a table of houses (or the table of Midheavens and Ascendants pro-

vided in this book). In the column listing sidereal times, locate the two listings, one lesser and one greater, that flank the calculated LST. Also locate the two corresponding Midheavens (MC) for these times.

From the Midheaven and Ascendant table on page 209 (portion copied below) the data for sidereal times of 21h 32m and 21h 36m are found, which covers the span within which the calculated LST falls. (Note that this table shows degrees and minutes, but not seconds of arc. This will account for the very small discrepancies that will show up in the results when comparing the different methods.)

ST	MC	A-25N	A-30N	A-35N	A-40N	A-45N	A-50N	A-55
21h28'	19aq35	4ge18	6ge58	10ge02	13ge40	18ge03	23ge27	0ca15
21h32'	20aq36	5ge21	8ge01	11ge06	14ge43	19ge04	24ge26	1ca10
21h36'	21aq37	6ge23	9ge04	12ge09	15ge46	20ge06	25ge24	2ca04
21h40'	22aq39	7ge25	10ge06	13ge11	16ge47	21ge06	26ge22	2ca57

2. Determine the differences between listings.

The difference between the greater sidereal time listing (21h 36m) and the lesser sidereal time listing (21h 32m) is 4 minutes.

$$
\begin{array}{r}
21\text{h } 36\text{m} \\
- \ \underline{21\text{h } 32\text{m}} \\
0\text{h } 04\text{m}
\end{array}
$$

The calculated LST (21h 33m 42s) is 1 minute and 42 seconds greater than the earlier listing:

$$
\begin{array}{rlll}
 & \underline{21 \ \text{h } 33 \ \text{m } 42 \text{ s}} \\
\text{less} & 21 \ \text{h } 32 \ \text{m } 00 \text{ s} \\
= & 0 \ \ \text{h } \ 1 \ \text{m } 42 \text{ s}
\end{array}
$$

The Midheaven given for sidereal time 21h 32m = 20d Aq 36m
The Midheaven given for sidereal time 21h 36m = 21d Aq 37m
The difference between these two Midheavens is 61 minutes, or 1 degree 1 minute.

3. Go to the interpolation tables.

From the Midheaven interpolation tables on page 218 (the relevant section is copied below), find the column closest to 1 minutes 42 seconds and match it with the row closest 61 minutes. In these tables there is a column for 1 minute 40 seconds and a row for 60 minutes.

	1m30s	1m40s	1m50s	2m00s	2m10s	2m20s	2m30s	2m40s
55m	20.6	22.9	25.2	27.5	29.8	32.1	34.4	36.7
60m	22.5	25.0	27.5	30.0	32.5	35.0	37.5	40.0
65m	24.4	27.1	29.8	32.5	35.2	37.9	40.6	43.3
70m	26.3	29.2	32.1	35.0	37.9	40.8	43.8	46.7

The intersection of these two coordinates in the table is 25 minutes. For most purposes this rough interpolation is close enough and serves to demonstrate the procedure.

4. Calculate the Midheaven.

Add the interpolated figure to the Midheaven that correlates with the sidereal time of 21h 32m (the lesser sidereal time).

<pre>
            20 Aq 36m
     +   0   25m
     =   20 Aq 61m
Adjust   21 Aq 01m = Midheaven for LST 21h 33m 42s
</pre>

Note that higher precision is possible with tables that list this same data with seconds, in smaller increments, or by working the problem with proportional calculations. Given that most timed events such as a birth are only given to the minute, the most precise calculation may not always be more accurate in reality. In regard to the accuracy of this example, one option would be to make an estimate of the error. In this example, the difference between the two Midheavens (61m) is one fifth of the distance between 60 and 65. Also note that 1m 42s is also one fifth the distance between the 1m 40s and the 1m 50s listings. In both cases the figures are increasing and so adding a second or two to the result is a reasonable estimated adjustment.

Calculating the Ascendant

Previously Calculated LST: _21_ h _33_ m _42_ s

The calculation of the Ascendant requires *three* operations. Because most tables of houses only give house cusps for round number latitudes, Ascendants for the nearest lesser and nearest greater latitudes must first be calculated. Only then can the Ascendant for the latitude of the birth or event be determined. Note that in most tables of houses the Ascendant (house 1) is listed along with houses 11, 12, 2 and 3.

From the Midheaven and Ascendant tables on page 209 (portion copied below) we have previously calculated the Midheaven located between the listed sidereal times of 21 32 and 21 36. Calculation of the Ascendant requires both the LST and the geographical latitude of the event. In the example this latitude is 28 N 24. After the Midheaven (MC) column, are the Ascendant columns for a range of latitudes at 5 degree increments. The example latitude falls between the listings for latitudes of 25 and 30 degrees. The first step is to calculate the Ascendant for each of these two latitudes in exactly the same way the Midheaven was calculated. Then the Ascendant for the exact latitude of the event is calculated.

ST	MC	A-25N	A-30N	A-35N	A-40N	A-45N	A-50N	A-55
21h28'	19aq35	4ge18	6ge58	10ge02	13ge40	18ge03	23ge27	0ca15
21h32'	20aq36	5ge21	8ge01	11ge06	14ge43	19ge04	24ge26	1ca10
21h36'	21aq37	6ge23	9ge04	12ge09	15ge46	20ge06	25ge24	2ca04
21h40'	22aq39	7ge25	10ge06	13ge11	16ge47	21ge06	26ge22	2ca57

Ascendant at 25 degrees (nearest lesser latitude):

Ascendant for ST 21 32 = 5 Ge 21

Ascendant for ST 21 36 = 6 Ge 23

The difference between these two Ascendants is 62 minutes.

Since we already know that the calculated LST is 1m 42s greater than the earlier ST we go to the Midheaven interpolation tables (copied again below) and find that the closest listings to these figures is again 1m40s and 60m. Again 25 seconds is the approximate figure sought.

	1m30s	1m40s	1m50s	2m00s	2m10s	2m20s	2m30s	2m40s
55m	20.6	22.9	25.2	27.5	29.8	32.1	34.4	36.7
60m	22.5	25.0	27.5	30.0	32.5	35.0	37.5	40.0
65m	24.4	27.1	29.8	32.5	35.2	37.9	40.6	43.3
70m	26.3	29.2	32.1	35.0	37.9	40.8	43.8	46.7

To the earlier Ascendant listing at 25 degrees latitude we then add 25 minutes.

5 Ge 21m + 25m = 5 Ge 46m

Next the same procedure is done for the Ascendant listing at 30 degrees latitude.

Ascendant at 30 degrees (nearest greater latitude):
Ascendant for ST 21 32 = 8 Ge 01
Ascendant for ST 21 36 = 9 Ge 04

The difference between these two Ascendants is 63 minutes, a figure we will need for the interpolation table.

Using the interpolation table again, we locate the nearest figures which in this case is 1m40s and 65m. This combination gives us 27.1 minutes (round off to 27) as the figure sought.

To the earlier Ascendant listing at 30 degrees latitude we then add 27 minutes.

8 Ge 01m + 27m = 8 Ge 28m

We now have two Ascendants each calculated for the example LST at two different latitudes. It is apparent from the tables that the Ascendant increases as latitude increases. The difference between them is calculated by subtracting, which in this case requires rewriting the first figure by taking 60 minutes (1 degree) from the degree column and adding it to the minutes column.

latitude 30:   8 Ge 28m   (7 Ge 88)
latitude 25: - 5 Ge 46m   -   (5 Ge 46)
                              2d   42m

Now it is possible to calculate find the Ascendant for the latitude of 28 degrees and 24 minutes by first calculating the difference between the given latitude and the lesser latitude.

$$
\begin{array}{rl}
 & 28d\ 24m \\
- & 25d\ 00m \\
\hline
= & 3d\ 24m
\end{array}
$$

The Ascendant interpolation table (portion shown below) is used as follows. Find the difference between the two Ascendants (2d 42m) on the far left vertical column and the follow it to the difference between the given latitude and the lesser latitude (3d 24m). The nearest result in the table (using 2d 40 and 3d 20) is 106.6 minutes, or 1 degree and roughly 47 minutes. This figure is then added to the Ascendant calculated for latitude 25.

	2° 50′	3° 00′	3° 10′	3° 20′	3° 30′	3° 40′	3° 50′	4° 00′
2° 30′	84.9	90.0	95.0	99.9	105.0	110.0	114.9	120.0
2° 35′	87.7	93.0	98.1	103.2	108.5	113.6	118.7	124.0
2° 40′	90.6	96.0	101.3	106.6	112.0	117.3	122.6	128.0
2° 45′	93.4	99.0	104.4	109.9	115.5	120.9	126.4	132.0
2° 50′	96.2	102.0	107.6	113.2	119.0	124.6	130.2	136.0

$$
\begin{array}{rll}
  & 5\ \text{Ge} & 42 \\
+ & 1 & 47 \\
\hline
= & 6 & 89 \quad \text{adjusted to 7 Ge 29}
\end{array}
$$

With careful proportioning or a good estimate this figure would increase by about 3 minutes of arc and give an Ascendant of about 7 Ge 32, closer to the computer generated chart above. Again, with more detailed tables that list every degree of latitude and degrees, minutes and seconds, accuracy will be improved. The intention here is merely to show the typical procedure.

Calculating the Houses

After calculating an exact Midheaven and Ascendant, and placing them in the proper positions on a chart form, the intermediate houses cusps typically listed in a table of houses must be added. For most of the 20th century the use of a table of Placidus houses has been the norm and that's what will be demonstrated below. (One alternative is to bypass these calculations and use the Equal House system or Porphyry – see next chapter).

Because of space restrictions and the easy availability of published tables, or one generated by computer software, a full table of houses in not included in this book. To compensate, a portion of a typical table of Placidus houses containing the sidereal time, the Midheaven and the house cusps from 11 to 3 for this example is shown below. The sidereal time and Midheaven degree is on top, degrees of latitude make up the first column. House cusps are listed only for houses 11 to 3 (house 1 is the Ascendant) because the opposite houses will have the same cusp degrees, but in the opposite signs.

ST = 21h 32m   MC = 20 Aq 36

Latitude	11		12		1		2		3	
25	21 Pi 50		28 Ar 28		5 Ge 21		0 Ca 43		24 Ca 33	
26	21	48	28	39	5	51	1	03	24	42
27	21	46	28	51	6	22	1	23	24	51
28	21	45	29	03	6	54	1	44	25	01
29	21	43	29	16	7	27	2	05	25	10
30	21	41	29	29	8	01	2	26	25	20

119

ST = 21h 36m   MC = 21 Aq 37

Latitude	11		12		1		2		3	
25	23 Pi 00		29 Ar 39		6 Ge 23		1 Ca 38		25 Ca 29	
26	22	58	29	51	6	54	1	58	25	37
27	22	57	00 Ta 04		7	25	2	18	25	46
28	22	55	00	16	7	57	2	38	25	56
29	22	54	00	29	8	30	2	59	26	05
30	22	52	00	43	9	04	3	21	26	14

To calculate the intermediate houses cusps exactly, however, the same kind of triple interpolation necessary for the Ascendant just demonstrated must be done.

After calculating the Midheaven which falls between the two given sidereal times, do the following:

1. For each of the two listed sidereal times, calculate each house cusp for the given latitude.

Example: In this table of houses latitudes are given in one degree increments. The given latitude, 28 N 34, is between latitudes 28 and 29. It is 34 minutes into the 60 minute difference between these two latitudes.

For ST = 21h 32m, the 2nd house cusp change between latitude 28 and 29 (2Ca05 – 1Ca44) is 21 minutes.

Using a typical house cusp interpolation table (portion shown below – data is in minutes of arc), find the 34 minute difference between the given latitude and nearest lesser latitude in the first column. Then interpolate between this line and the house cusp interval of 21 minutes (as this table has increments of five, the closest listing is 20) to find the figure 11.3. Then go through the same procedure for ST = 21h 36m.

latitude				house cusp interval				
diff.	5	10	15	20	25	30	35	40
28	2.3	4.7	7.0	9.3	11.7	14.0	16.3	18.7
30	2.5	5.0	7.5	10.0	12.5	15.0	17.5	20.0
32	2.7	5.3	8.0	10.7	13.3	16.0	18.7	21.3
34	2.8	5.7	8.5	11.3	14.2	17.0	19.8	22.7
36	3.0	6.0	9.0	12.0	15.0	18.0	21.0	24.0
38	3.2	6.3	9.5	12.7	15.8	19.0	22.2	25.3
40	3.3	6.7	10.0	13.3	16.7	20.0	23.3	26.7

Results: 2nd house cusp at ST = 21h 32m and latitude 28 degrees:
= 1 Ca 44 + 11m = 1 Ca 56

2nd house cusp at ST = 21h 36m and latitude 28 degrees:
= 2 Ca 38 + 11m = 2 Ca 49

The difference between these two cusps is 53 minutes.

2. Calculate each house cusp for the LST.

Since we already know that the calculated LST (21h 33m 42s) is 1m 42s greater than the earlier ST, we go to the Ascendant interpolation tables (copied below) and find that the closest listings to these figures is 1m40s and 55m for the difference (53m) between the previously calculated 2nd house cusps. The table gives 18.3m as the approximate figure sought. Adding 18m to the earlier 2nd house cusp 1 Ca 56 gives a final 2nd house cusp of 2 Ca 14.

	1° 30′	1° 40′	1° 50′	2° 00′	2° 10′	2° 20′	2° 30′	2° 40′
45′	13.5	15.0	16.5	18.0	19.5	21.0	22.5	24.0
50′	15.0	16.7	18.3	20.0	21.7	23.3	25.0	26.7
55′	16.5	18.3	20.1	22.0	23.8	25.6	27.5	29.3
1°	18.0	20.0	22.0	24.0	26.0	28.0	30.0	32.0

To summarize, finding the house cusps is basically an exercise in working within the limitations of a table of houses – which can't possibly list every single minute of sidereal time, latitude or house cusp. Proportions between the calculated LST and what the tables offer are determined first and then these are used to locate the house cusps. Some tables are more complete than others and often cusps can be easily estimated with no calculation at all. Some tables offer house cusp listings for the latitude of specific cities, which would eliminate step 1 above for events or births that occurred in those cities. There are other options for calculating house cusps that will be described in the next chapter.

Calculation of the planets' longitudes using tables:

Note: Precise calculations of planetary positions require Delta T to be added or subtract to the GMT. (See tables on page 234) This is particularly important for solar and lunar returns, but is optional for most other purposes such as natal and event charts.

1. Determine each planet's daily motion.

Note: the example exercises below assume the use of a midnight ephemeris. The data used to find the positions of the planets are the GMT of a birth or event (in this example GMT = 19h 0m) and the daily motion of each planet, Sun and Moon. From the ephemeris, subtract the planet's position on the day of the event from its position on the day after the event (unless the planet is retrograde which requires doing the reverse). The date of the New Horizons launch was January 19 so the planet listing for that date is subtracted from the listing on January 20. Sections of the sample ephemeris on page 207 are shown below.

Date	S.T.	Moon	Sun	Mercury	Venus	Mars
Jan 18 2006	07:49:02	06°Vi58'	27°Cp44'	22°Cp01'	21°Cp15'	16°Ta22'
Jan 19 2006	07:52:59	18°Vi45'	28°Cp45'	23°Cp39'	20°Cp41'	16°Ta44'
Jan 20 2006	07:56:56	00°Li35'	29°Cp46'	25°Cp16'	20°Cp08'	17°Ta07'
Jan 21 2006	08:00:52	12°Li30'	00°Aq47'	26°Cp55'	19°Cp36'	17°Ta30'

	Jupiter	Saturn	Uranus	Neptune	Pluto
Jan 18 2006	15°Sc46'	08°Le40'	08°Pi26'	16°Aq33'	25°Sg28'
Jan 19 2006	15°Sc53'	08°Le35'	08°Pi28'	16°Aq36'	25°Sg30'
Jan 20 2006	16°Sc01'	08°Le30'	08°Pi31'	16°Aq38'	25°Sg32'
Jan 21 2006	16°Sc08'	08°Le25'	08°Pi34'	16°Aq40'	25°Sg34'

Finding the Moon's position:

To find the daily motion of the Moon subtract 18 Virgo 45 (on Jan 19) from 0 Libra 35 (on Jan 20). since there are 30 degrees per sign, 0 Li 35 can be expressed as 29 Vi 95 to facilitate the subtraction.

$$\begin{array}{rl} \text{Jan 20} = & 29 \;\; 95 \\ - \;\; \underline{\text{Jan 19} = } & \underline{18 \;\; 45} \\ & 11 \;\; 50 = \text{Moon's daily motion} \end{array}$$

Next we turn to the planetary and lunar motion interpolation tables beginning on page 228. In these tables GMT is listed in the first column and the daily motion rates are listed across the top of the other columns. The first table in this book covers the range of all planetary daily motions except that of the Moon which is usually presented as a separate table because of the much larger rate of lunar daily motion. For the purposes of this exercise a small portion of the lunar motion table is shown below.

GMT	11d45m	12d00m	12d15m	12d30m	12d45m	13d00m	13d15m
17	08:19	08:30	08:40	08:51	09:01	09:12	09:23
18	08:48	09:00	09:11	09:22	09:33	09:45	09:56
19	09:18	09:30	09:41	09:53	10:05	10:17	10:29
20	09:47	10:00	10:12	10:25	10:37	10:50	11:02
21	10:16	10:30	10:43	10:56	11:09	11:22	11:35

From the table above we are seeking the distance the Moon traveled in 19 hours (the GMT) at a rate of 11d 50m per day (daily motion). This table only gives lunar daily motion in intervals of 15 minutes, so the closest entry is for 11d 45m which is 9d 18m. Adding this figure to the earlier position of the Moon gives a close approximation of the position of the Moon at the time of the event.

We can refine this figure by noting that 11d 50m is one third from the previous listing at 11d 45m to the next listing at 12d 00m. This means that the exact position of the Moon is one third the distance between the figures given under these two columns for 19 hours GMT. Since this distance is 12, one third of 12 is 4 which added to 9d 18m gives 9d 22m. This calculation would also be done for a GMT figure not on the hour – if using this table. Anyone serious about working with interpolation tables should procure a far more detailed one.

Add the daily motion of Moon to its position in the ephemeris on January 19.

$$+ \quad \begin{array}{r} 18 \text{ Vi } 45 \\ \underline{9 \quad 22} \\ 27 \text{ Vi } 67 = 28 \text{ Vi } 07 \end{array}$$

3. Finding the Sun's position:

Next calculate the position of the Sun. Using the ephemeris shown here again, we find that the Sun's daily motion on January 19 is one degree and one minute, or 61 minutes.

Date	S.T.	Moon	Sun	Mercury	Venus	Mars
Jan 18 2006	07:49:02	06°Vi58'	27°Cp44'	22°Cp01'	21°Cp15'	16°Ta22'
Jan 19 2006	07:52:59	18°Vi45'	28°Cp45'	23°Cp39'	20°Cp41'	16°Ta44'
Jan 20 2006	07:56:56	00°Li35'	29°Cp46'	25°Cp16'	20°Cp08'	17°Ta07'
Jan 21 2006	08:00:52	12°Li30'	00°Aq47'	26°Cp55'	19°Cp36'	17°Ta30'

$$\begin{array}{r} \text{Jan } 20 = 29 \text{ Cp } 46 \\ - \underline{\text{Jan } 19 = 28 \text{ Cp } 45} \\ 1 \qquad 01 \end{array}$$

Using the interpolation table below, 60 minutes (closest to 61) and a GMT of 19h gives 47.5 minutes of motion. That is to say the Sun moved about 47.5 minutes of longitude from the ephemeris listing on January 19 to the GMT of 19 hours.

GMT   Planetary Daily Motion in minutes of a degree

	45	50	55	60	65	70	75	80
15	28.1	31.2	34.4	37.5	40.6	43.8	46.9	50.0
16	30.0	33.3	36.7	40.0	43.3	46.7	50.0	53.3
17	31.9	35.4	39.0	42.5	46.0	49.6	53.1	56.7
18	33.8	37.5	41.3	45.0	48.7	52.5	56.3	60.0
19	35.6	39.6	43.5	47.5	51.5	55.4	59.4	63.3
20	37.5	41.7	45.8	50.0	54.2	58.3	62.5	66.7
21	39.4	43.7	48.1	52.5	56.9	61.3	65.6	70.0

To find the position of the Sun add 47.5 to the position of the Sun in the ephemeris on January 19.

$$\begin{array}{r} 28 \text{ Cp } 45 \\ + \qquad 47.5 \\ \hline 28 \text{ Cp } 92.5 \ = 29 \text{ Cp } 32.5 \text{ (round up to 29 Cp 33)} \end{array}$$

The same procedure is done for the rest of the planets using the table on page 224. Note that retrograde planets require (1) subtracting the later listing from the earlier listing to find the daily motion and (2) subtracting the travel distance (taken from the interpolation table) from the earlier listing. When a planet's daily motion is very slow, it becomes easy to do the calculation in your head (eg. the Saturn calculation below).

4. Finding the position of Mercury:

Using the above ephemeris section again, we see that Mercury was at 23 Cp 16 on the 19th and 25 Cp 39 on the 20th. Subtracting the earlier position from the later one, after changing the figure to facilitate subtraction, we find the daily motion was 1 degrees and 37 minutes, or 97 minutes (60 + 37).

$$\begin{array}{rl} \text{Jan } 20 = & 25 \text{ Cp } 16 = 24 \text{ Cp } 76 \\ - \text{ Jan } 19 = & 23 \text{ Cp } 39 = \underline{23 \text{ Cp } 39} \\ & \qquad\qquad\qquad 1 \quad 37 = 97m \end{array}$$

In the interpolation table below from page 226, we will use 95 as it is closest to 97. Referencing 19 in the first column for the sidereal time, the distance Mercury traveled is then 75.2, or rounded down 75 minutes. This figure is the same as 1 degree (60 minutes) and 15 seconds (75 − 60 = 15).

	85	90	95	100	105	110	115	120
17	60.2	63.8	67.3	70.8	74.4	77.9	81.5	85.0
18	63.8	67.5	71.2	75.0	78.8	82.5	86.3	90.0
19	67.3	71.3	75.2	79.2	83.1	87.1	91.0	95.0
20	70.8	75.0	79.2	83.3	87.5	91.7	95.8	100.0

| 21 | 74.4 | 78.8 | 83.1 | 87.5 | 91.9 | 96.2 | 100.6 | 105.0 |

This figure, 75 minutes or 1 minute and 15 seconds, is then added to Mercury's position on the 19th to obtain its position in the chart. The result is 24 degrees Capricorn and 54 minutes. A more accurate figure would take into account that 97 minutes is 2/5th of the way between the listing under 95 and that of 100. The difference between these listings is 4 minutes, so adding another 2 minutes to our result would make this calculation precise. More detailed tables require fewer adjustments like this one.

$$\begin{array}{lll}
\text{Jan 19:} & 23 \text{ Cp } 39 & \\
+ & \underline{1 \quad\quad 15} & \\
& 24 \quad\quad 54 & + \ 2m = 24 \text{ Cp } 56
\end{array}$$

5. Finding the position of Venus:

In this example Venus is retrograde moving from 20 Cp 41 on the 19th to 20 Cp 08 on the 20th. It's daily motion is then 33 minutes and using the daily motion tables, and the nearest listing of 35, we find the distance traveled to be 27.7. Given that 35 is greater than 33 we could safely use 27 as the figure to be subtracted from the ephemeris listing on January 19.

GMT   Planetary Daily Motion in minutes of a degree

	5	**10**	**15**	**20**	**25**	**30**	**35**	**40**
17	3.5	7.1	10.6	14.2	17.7	21.3	24.8	28.3
18	3.7	7.5	11.3	15.0	18.8	22.5	26.2	30.0
19	4.0	7.9	11.9	15.8	19.8	23.8	27.7	31.7
20	4.2	8.3	12.5	16.7	20.8	25.0	29.2	33.3

$$\begin{array}{ll}
\text{Jan 19} = & 20 \text{ Cp } 41 \\
- & \underline{\quad\quad 27} \\
& 20 \text{ Cp } 14
\end{array}$$

126

6. Finding Saturn's position:

The daily motion of the outer planets (or the inner planets when they are near their stations) is slow and makes the computation of its position relatively easy. From the portion of the ephemeris shown below Saturn's daily motion is indicated to be 5 minutes of arc per day.

	Jupiter	Saturn	Uranus	Neptune	Pluto
Jan 18 2006	15°Sc46'	08°Le40'	08°Pi26'	16°Aq33'	25°Sg28'
Jan 19 2006	15°Sc53'	08°Le35'	08°Pi28'	16°Aq36'	25°Sg30'
Jan 20 2006	16°Sc01'	08°Le30'	08°Pi31'	16°Aq38'	25°Sg32'
Jan 21 2006	16°Sc08'	08°Le25'	08°Pi34'	16°Aq40'	25°Sg34'

The portion of the table of planetary daily motion indicates that for a GMT of 19 hours and a daily motion of 5 minutes the travel distance is 4 minutes of arc. Add this to the position of Saturn on January 19 to obtain the position of Saturn at the time of the event.

8 Le 35 + 4m = 8 Le 39

Once all the planetary positions are determined in this way, they need to be positioned in a horoscope form. Using a 12-sectioned diagram, first write in the Midheaven and its opposite point the I.C. Then add the Ascendant and Descendant which define the horizon. Next add the house cusps and then the planets. Below is a horoscope form with only the points that were calculated in the worked example above. For the computer-calculated chart see page 108.

It is very important to carefully note the position of the Sun in the horoscope you are calculating as a check in your work. In this example, which is for 2 PM, the Sun has to be past the Midheaven because it is afternoon, but still well above the horizon. This would place it in the 8th or 9th houses. If it were not, an error has been made.

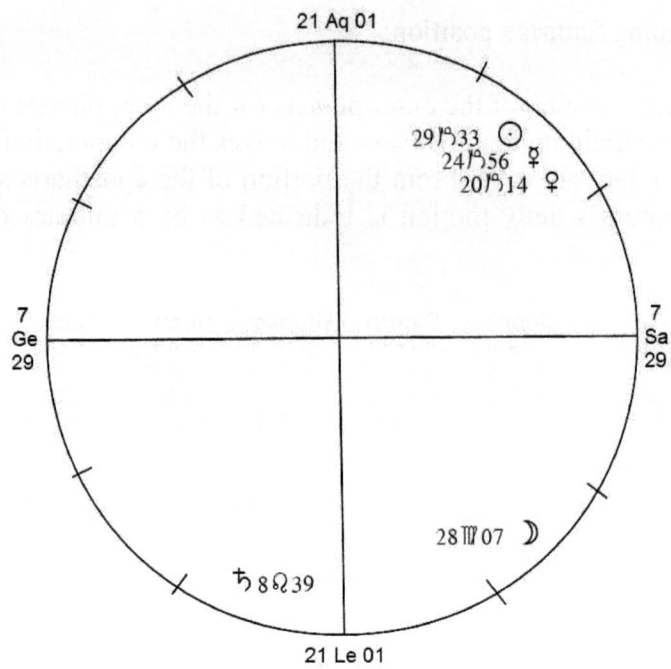

21 Aq 01

29♓33 ☉
24♓56 ☿
20♓14 ♀

7
Ge
29

7
Sa
29

28♍07 ☽

♄8♌39

21 Le 01

Chapter 7

Chart Calculations using Algebraic Equations (Proportions)

An ephemeris and table of houses is required for this method which solves for the Midheaven, Ascendant and planets using proportions expressed as algebraic formulas. It is somewhat more precise than using rough interpolation tables as were used in the previous method (although highly detailed interpolation tables will be just as accurate). After calculating the GMT and LST as previously explained, you will need to calculate the Midheaven, Ascendant, house cusps and planets, preferably in that order. This method can be done using sexagesimal notation in degrees, minutes, and seconds (or hours/minutes/seconds) but is greatly facilitated by converting figures into decimal format at certain points in the process and then reconverting to sexagesimal notation.

Note: Using a scientific calculator with degrees/minutes/seconds to decimal conversion keys is highly recommended. Calculators, both physical and software online, have different ways of moving between sexagesimal and decimal notation (see page 100). Be sure you practice manipulating figures thoroughly before working through chart calculations.

An alternate option workable with an ordinary calculator is to convert all degrees, minutes and seconds into seconds, solve all the equations and then convert the seconds back into degrees, minutes and seconds. There are 3,600 seconds in every hour and 60 seconds in each minute = 86,400 seconds in 24 hours.

Example: the LST for this example is 21h 33m 42s = 75,600 (21 x 3,600) + 1,980 seconds (33 x 60) + 42 seconds = 77,622 seconds. To reconvert, divide 77,622 by 3,600, subtract 21 and multiply the remainder by 60 to get minutes, subtract 33 and multiply the remainder by 60 to get seconds.

129

Procedure for calculating the Midheaven:

Previously Calculated LST: __21_ h __33_ m __42_ s

In a table of houses (portion copied below) first locate the Local Sidereal Time of the event or birth. The sidereal times of 21h32m and 21h36m bracket the calculated LST.

ST	MC	A-25N	A-30N	A-35N	A-40N	A-45N	A-50N	A-55
21h28'	19aq35	4ge18	6ge58	10ge02	13ge40	18ge03	23ge27	0ca15
21h32'	20aq36	5ge21	8ge01	11ge06	14ge43	19ge04	24ge26	1ca10
21h36'	21aq37	6ge23	9ge04	12ge09	15ge46	20ge06	25ge24	2ca04
21h40'	22aq39	7ge25	10ge06	13ge11	16ge47	21ge06	26ge22	2ca57

Use the following formula to calculate the Midheaven or cusp of the tenth house.

Where:

A = the difference in time between the nearest earlier S.T. and the given L.S.T.

$$\begin{array}{r} 21h\ \ 33'\ \ 42'' \\ -\ \ 21h\ \ 32'\ \ 00'' \\ \hline =\ \ 0h\ \ 01'\ \ 42'' \end{array}$$

__1_ m __42_ s, or __1.7__ m (express seconds in decimal form)

B = the difference in time between the nearest earlier S.T. and the nearest later S.T.

$$\begin{array}{r} 21\ \ 36 \\ -\ \ 21\ \ 32 \\ \hline 0\ \ 04 \end{array}$$

__4_ m __0_ s, or __4.0__ m (if needed, express seconds in decimal form)

C = the difference in degrees between the MC at the earlier S.T. and the MC at the later S.T. (Notice that here the figure is in degrees, not minutes as the figures for A and B are.)

$$
\begin{array}{r}
21 \quad 37 \\
- \quad 20 \quad 36 \\
\hline
1 \quad 01
\end{array}
$$

_1_ d _1_ m _0_ s, or in decimals _1.016_ (this figure is usually about 1 degree or 60 minutes)

X = (unknown) the difference in *degrees* between the MC at the earlier S.T. and the MC at the given L.S.T.

$$\frac{A}{B} = \frac{X}{C} \quad \text{or} \quad \frac{A \times C}{B} = X$$

Input the figures for A, B, and C expressed as decimals, then solve the equation for X as follows:

1. (A: _1.7_) x (C: _1.016_) ÷ (B: _4_) = (X: _0.4318_)

2. Convert X into minutes and seconds: _25_ m _54_ s

3. Earlier Midheaven: _20_ d _36_ m _00_ s

4. Add 3 & 2:

$$
\begin{array}{r}
20 \text{ Aq } 36 \quad 00 \\
+ \qquad 25 \quad 54 \\
\hline
20 \qquad 61 \quad 54
\end{array}
$$

Adjust to _21_ d _01_ m _54_ s = exact Midheaven
in _Aquarius_ (sign) = 21 Aq 2 (rounded figure)

Procedure for calculating the Ascendant

Previously Calculated LST: _21_ h _33_ m _42_ s

Latitude of birth or event: _28 N 24' 20"_

The calculation of the Ascendant exactly requires *three* operations. Because most tables of houses only give house cusps for round number latitudes, Ascendants for the nearest *lesser* and nearest *greater* latitudes must first be calculated. Then the Ascendant for the *actual* latitude of the birth or event can be determined.

Note that data from the previous calculation of the Midheaven, specified by letter, is used in these Ascendant calculations.

ST	MC	A-25N	A-30N	A-35N	A-40N	A-45N	A-50N	A-55
21h28'	19aq35	4ge18	6ge58	10ge02	13ge40	18ge03	23ge27	0ca15
21h32'	20aq36	5ge21	8ge01	11ge06	14ge43	19ge04	24ge26	1ca10
21h36'	21aq37	6ge23	9ge04	12ge09	15ge46	20ge06	25ge24	2ca04
21h40'	22aq39	7ge25	10ge06	13ge11	16ge47	21ge06	26ge22	2ca57

*Part 1: Ascendant calculations for the nearest **lesser** geographical latitude =* _25 N 00_

Where:

D1 = the difference in degrees between the Ascendant at earlier S.T. and the ASC at the later S.T.

$$
\begin{array}{r}
6 \ \text{Ge} \ 23 \\
- \ \underline{5 \ \text{Ge} \ 21} \\
1 \quad 02
\end{array}
$$

_1_ d _02_ m _0_ s, or _1.033_ d (express minutes and seconds in decimal form)

Y1 = (unknown) the difference in degrees between the Ascendant at the earlier S.T. and the ASC at the given L.S.T. at the nearest **lesser** latitude.

Using previously calculated figures for the Midheaven:

A = the difference in time between the nearest earlier S.T. and the given L.S.T.

B = the difference in time between the nearest earlier S.T. and the nearest later S.T.

$$\frac{A}{B} = \frac{Y1}{D1} \qquad \text{or} \qquad \frac{A \times D1}{B} = Y1$$

Ascendant at earlier S.T. + Y1 = exact Ascendant for given L.S.T. at the nearest **lesser** latitude.

Worked example:

Input A and B from the Midheaven calculation and D1 as degrees and minutes of arc. Express as a decimal.

1. (A: _1.7_) x (D1: _1.033_) ÷ (B: _4_) = (Y1: _0.4390_)

2. Express Y1 in degrees and minutes: _0_ d _26_ m _20_ s

3. Add earlier Ascendant: _5_ d _21_ m_____ s
4. Result = exact Ascendant   _5_ d _47_ m _20_ s
   (Adjustments if needed)   ____ d ____ m____ s
   Sign = _Gemini_

*Part 2: Ascendant calculations for the nearest **greater** geographical latitude = _30 N 00_*

Where:

D2 = the difference between the ASC at earlier S.T. and the ASC at the later S.T.

$$9 \text{ Ge } 04$$
$$- \underline{8 \text{ Ge } 01}$$
$$1 \qquad 03$$

_1_ d _03_ m _0_ s, or _1.05_ d (express as a decimal)

Y2 = (unknown) the difference between the ASC at the earlier S.T. and the ASC at the given L.S.T.

$$\frac{A}{B} = \frac{Y2}{D2} \qquad \text{or} \qquad \frac{A \times D2}{B} = Y2$$

ASC at earlier S.T. + Y2 = exact ASC for given L.S.T. at the nearest *greater* latitude.

1. (A: _1.7_) x (D2: _1.05_) ÷ (B: _4_) = (Y2: _0.4463_)

2. Express Y2 in degrees and minutes _0_ d _26_ m _47_ s
3. Add earlier Ascendant: _8_ d _01_ m _17_ s
4. Result = exact Ascendant: _8_ d _27_ m _64_ s
   (Adjustments if needed) _8_ d _28_ m _4_ s
        In _Gemini_ (sign)

*Part 3: Ascendant calculations for the **actual** or **given** latitude of birth or the event =* _28 N 24' 20"_

Note: The zodiacal position of the Ascendant may increase or decrease between the lesser and greater latitude positions noted in the table of houses. Make a note of the direction of change in order to determine whether to add or subtract in step 4 below.

Where:

E = the difference in degrees between the nearest *lesser* latitude and the nearest *greater* latitude.

_5_ d ___ m ___ s, or _5.0_ d (express as a decimal)

134

F = the difference in degrees between the given latitude and the nearest *lesser* latitude.

$$\begin{array}{r} 28 \quad 24 \quad 20 \\ - \quad 25 \quad 00 \quad 00 \\ \hline 3 \quad 24 \quad 20 \end{array}$$

___3___d ___24___m___20___s, or ___3.4055___d (express as a decimal)

G = the difference between the Ascendant at the nearest lesser latitude (calculated in Part 1) and the Ascendant at the nearest greater latitude (calculated in Part 2).

$$\begin{array}{r} 8 \ \text{Ge} \ 28 \ \ 4 \ = \ 7 \ \text{Ge} \ 87 \ 64 \ (\text{adjusted}) \\ - \ 5 \ \text{Ge} \ \ 47 \ 21 \ = \ 5 \ \text{Ge} \ 47 \ 21 \\ \hline 2 \qquad 40 \ \ 43 \end{array}$$

$$\begin{array}{lr} & 8 \ \text{Ge} \ 28 \ \ \ 4 \ = \ 8.4678 \\ \text{or} \quad - & 5 \ \text{Ge} \ \ 47 \ 21 \ = \ 5.7892 \\ \hline & \qquad\qquad 2.6786 \end{array}$$

___2___d___40___m___43___s, or ___2.6786___d (express seconds as a decimal)

Z = (unknown) the difference between the Ascendant at the nearest lesser latitude and the Ascendant at the actual or given latitude.

$$\frac{F}{E} \ = \ \frac{Z}{G} \qquad\qquad \text{or} \qquad\qquad \frac{F \ x \ G}{E} \ = \ Z$$

1. (F: ___3.4055___) x (G: ___2.6786___) ÷ (E: ___5___) = (Z: ___1.8244___)

2. Convert Z to DMS: ___1___ d ___49___ m ___28___ s
3. Nearest lesser lat. Asc   ___5___ d ___47___ m ___21___ s
4. Add 2 and 3 (in this case)   ___6___ d ___96___ m ___49___ s
    Adjustments: ___7___ d ___36___ m ___49___ s

In ___*Gemini*___ (sign) = 7 Ge 37 (rounded figure)

The results obtained, using the example tables which only contain degrees and minutes, not seconds, are within a few minutes of arc of the computer-generated positions. This is close enough to pass an astrology exam, however. A more detailed table of houses listing latitudes at one degree intervals with degrees, minutes and seconds will give far more accurate results.

Note: this calculation can also be done in a different order. First calculate the Ascendant at the lesser sidereal time for the given latitude, then do the same for the greater sidereal time. Last, calculate the Ascendant for the LST.

Calculating the Houses

After calculating an exact Midheaven and Ascendant, and placing them in the proper positions on a chart form, the intermediate houses cusps must be accounted for. This has traditionally been done using a table of houses. To calculate the intermediate houses cusps exactly, however, the same kind of triple interpolation necessary for the Ascendant must be done, which is a time-consuming prospect.

1. Calculate each house cusp for the nearest lesser latitude.
2. Calculate each house cusp for the nearest greater latitude.
3. Calculate each house cusp for the actual latitude.

An alternative to these time-consuming calculations is to use an *Equal House* system from the Ascendant (or Midheaven), or to use the *Porphyry* system which is explained below and can be calculated using simple math. Porphyry does not require a table of houses.

Equal Houses

This method requires no calculations. The degree of the Ascendant is simply carried around the zodiac at intervals of 30 degrees each being the cusp of a house. The Midheaven is not the 10th house cusp in this system. Equal houses may also be radiated from the Midheaven, in this case the Ascendant is not the cusp of a house. A variant that was commonly used in ancient astrology is called *Whole Sign Houses* where 0 degrees of the rising sign becomes the cusp of the first house and all other houses are marked at intervals of 30 degrees. The Ascendant will then fall in the first house but not mark the first house cusp. These methods of house division are generally not accepted in astrological certification exams but they have a long history and have many advocates in the astrological community.

Porphyry Houses

In the Porphyry system of house division, the difference in zodiacal longitude between the Ascendant and the Midheaven, that is the diurnal semi-arc in longitude, and the nocturnal semi-arc between the IC (4th house cusp) and the Ascendant, is trisected. The figure for the trisection is then used to determine the intermediate house cusps. This is a division of quadrants based on space along the ecliptic. To calculate the intermediate houses according to the Porphyry system:

1. Convert the degrees of the Midheaven and Ascendant to true longitude (see page 102) and convert to decimals. This can be done by hand or with a calculator. Subtract the Midheaven from the Ascendant. (It may be necessary to add 360 to the Ascendant in order to subtract.) Divide this figure by 3 and write down the result or store it in the calculator. (We will use the figures calculated above knowing that these are not as precise as they could be.)

Ascendant = 7 Ge 37 = 60 + 7d 37m = 67d 37m = 67.62
Midheaven = 21 Aq 02 = 300 + 21d 2m = 321d 2m = 321.03

Ascendant adjustment: 67.62 + 360 = 427.62

Ascendant _427.62_ – Midheaven _321.03_ = _106.59_

divide by 3 = _35.53_ (trisection)

2. Add the trisection to the Midheaven. The result is the cusp of the 11th house. Next add the trisection to the figure for the 11th house. This is the cusp of the 12th house.

Midheaven _321.35_ + trisection _35.53_ = _356.56_ (11th)

_356.56_ (11th) = _356_ d _45_ m = 26 Pi 33

+ trisection _35.393_ = _392.09_ (-360) = _32.09_ (12th)

_32.09_ (12th) = _32_ d _5_ m = 2 Ta 5

3. Locate the 2nd and 3rd house cusps. The same procedure outlined above is done to the quadrant formed by the IC and the Ascendant. Trisect the quadrant and add the figure to the Ascendant to find the 2nd house, then add it again to find the 3rd house. Houses 5, 6, 8, and 9 are exact opposites of houses 11, 12, 2 and 3.

Note: After you do the second trisection for the 2nd and 3rd houses, look closely and you will notice that the degrees on the cusps match the degrees on the 12th and 11th houses, though, of course, the signs will differ. The 2nd house is exactly the same degree and minutes as the 12th but usually two signs ahead in the zodiac. (For this example = 2 Ca 5.) The 3rd house is the same degree and minute as the 11th but usually four signs ahead. (For this example = 26 Ca 33). Notice the number symmetry of this system and realize that no calculation other than that for the 11th and 12th houses is required! However, attention must be paid to sign placement as quadrant size is not always 90 degrees, which occurs only when the equinoxes are rising. Quadrant size is affected by the latitude of the event/birth, most obvious when the signs near the solstice are rising.

Calculation of the planets' longitudes:

Note: Precise calculations of planetary positions require Delta T to be added or subtract to the GMT (see tables on page 234). This is particularly important for solar and lunar returns, but is optional for most other purposes. Also note that in most ephemerides the daily position of the Sun and Moon is often given in degrees, minutes, and seconds to facilitate more precise calculations which are needed for solar and lunar returns.

The calculated GMT for the example is 19h 0m. Delta T for 2006 (from table) is 65 seconds.

1. Determining the Constant Fraction: GMT/24 = CF

GMT: __19__ h __1__ m __5__ s *(with Delta T adjustment)*
Express minutes and seconds in decimal form: __19.0181__

Divide GMT by 24 = __0.7924__

This is the constant fraction (CF). Store it in the calculator's memory. Remember that in some cases the GMT of birth or the event will fall into the *next day.* (This adjustment is also important if using a noon ephemeris).

2. Determine daily planetary motions by subtracting the earlier position from the later position (or the reverse for retrograde planets).

Note: When the later ephemeris position is a lower number than the previous position, add 30 degrees to the previous position. Similarly, if the planet's longitude after calculation is over 30, subtract 30. It is highly recommended to convert degrees and minutes into degrees and a decimal as was done in the calculations for the Midheaven and Ascendant.

3. Planet's daily motion x constant fraction = distance traveled.

4. Add this figure to the planet's previous ephemeris listing. This equals the planet's position at the GMT. (If the planet is retrograde,

subtract from the previous ephemeris listing.)

Worked examples for January 19, 2006 with a ΔT adjusted GMT of 19h1m5s and constant fraction of 0.7924.

Date	S.T.	Moon	Sun	Mercury	Venus	Mars
Jan 18 2006	07:49:02	06°Vi58'	27°Cp44'	22°Cp01'	21°Cp15'	16°Ta22'
Jan 19 2006	07:52:59	18°Vi45'	28°Cp45'	23°Cp39'	20°Cp41'	16°Ta44'
Jan 20 2006	07:56:56	00°Li35'	29°Cp46'	25°Cp16'	20°Cp08'	17°Ta07'
Jan 21 2006	08:00:52	12°Li30'	00°Aq47'	26°Cp55'	19°Cp36'	17°Ta30'

Sun

1. Later ephemeris position: 29 Cp 46 = 29.766

2. Earlier ephemeris position = 28 Cp 45 = 28.75

3. Subtract earlier from later position: 29.766 – 28.75 = 1.016

4. Daily motion = 1.016 (1d 1m)

5. Multiply by the constant fraction: 1.016 x 0.792 = 0.805

6. Add to earlier ephemeris listing: 28.75 + 0.805 = 29.555

7. Convert to degrees and minutes = 29 Cp 33 = Sun's position

Moon

1. Later ephemeris position: 00 Li 35 = 30 d 35 m = 30.583

2. Earlier ephemeris position = 18 Vi 45 = 18.75

3. Subtract earlier from later position: 30.583 – 18.75 = 11.83

140

4. Daily motion = 11.83 (11d 50m)

5. Multiply by the constant fraction: 11.83 x 0.792 = 9.374
6. Add to earlier ephemeris listing: 18.75 + 9.369 = 28.124

7. Convert to degrees and minutes = 28 Pi 07 = Moon's position

Note: Unlike the Sun and Moon, Mercury and the other planets may have retrograde motion. In such a case, the daily motion of the planet is determined by subtracting the later ephemeris position from the previous position. When this figure is multiplied by the constant fraction, it is then subtracted from the previous position. The example below illustrates this as Venus was retrograde at the time of the event.

Venus

1. Later ephemeris position: 20 Cp 08 = 20.133

2. Earlier ephemeris position = 20 Cp 41 = 20.683

3. Subtract *later* from *earlier* position: 20.683 – 20.133 = 0.55

4. Daily motion = 0.55 (0d 33m)

5. Multiply by the constant fraction: 0.55 x 0.792 = 0.436

6. *Subtract* from *earlier* position: 20.683 – 0.436 = 20.247

7. Convert to degrees and minutes = 20 Cp 15 = Venus' position

Chapter 8

Chart Calculations using Diurnal Proportional Logarithms

This method is basically the same as the previous method except that multiplication and division are replaced with addition and subtraction with no conversion to decimals. The use of logarithms for chart calculation began about 400 years ago and was popular until very recently. *Diurnal Proportional Logarithms* are a specialized log table that allows for computations of both time (hours and minutes) and degrees and minutes. See the table of diurnal proportional logarithms on page 230.

Below is a section of the table of houses from which the data needed to calculate the Midheaven and Ascendant is derived. Example LST = 21h 33m 42s

ST	MC	A-25N	A-30N	A-35N	A-40N	A-45N	A-50N	A-55
21h28'	19aq35	4ge18	6ge58	10ge02	13ge40	18ge03	23ge27	0ca15
21h32'	20aq36	5ge21	8ge01	11ge06	14ge43	19ge04	24ge26	1ca10
21h36'	21aq37	6ge23	9ge04	12ge09	15ge46	20ge06	25ge24	2ca04
21h40'	22aq39	7ge25	10ge06	13ge11	16ge47	21ge06	26ge22	2ca57

Calculating the Midheaven to the nearest minute:

Where:
A = the difference between the nearest earlier S.T. and the given L.S.T.

$$LST = 21h\ 33m\ 42s$$
$$- \underline{21h\ 32m\ 00s}$$
$$1m\ \ 42s = A$$

Table of Diurnal Proportional Logarithms (excerpt from page 230).

	0	1	2	3	4	5	6	7
41	1.5456	1.1540	.9515	.8140	.7097	.6256	.5552	.4947
42	1.5351	1.1498	.9488	.8120	.7081	.6243	.5541	.4937
43	1.5249	1.1455	.9462	.8101	.7066	.6231	.5531	.4928

The log of A, 1m 42s, is found in the log table, a portion of which is shown above. The figures across the top are used as minutes and the figures vertically on the left as seconds. The log of 1m 42s is 1.1498.

B = the difference between the nearest earlier S.T. and the nearest later S.T.

$$
\begin{array}{r}
21\text{h } 36\text{m} \\
-\quad 21\text{h } 32\text{m} \\
\hline
4\text{m} = \text{B}
\end{array}
$$

	0	1	2	3	4	5	6	7
	3.1584	1.3802	1.0792	.9031	.7782	.6812	.6021	.5351
1	3.1584	1.3730	1.0756	.9007	.7763	.6798	.6009	.5341
2	2.8573	1.3660	1.0720	.8983	.7745	.6784	.5997	.5331

The log of B, 4m, is .7782

C = the difference between the two Midheavens corresponding to the earlier and later S.T.s

$$
\begin{array}{r}
21 \text{ Aq } 37 \\
- 20 \text{ Aq } 36 \\
\hline
1 \quad\quad 1 \;=\; 1\text{d } 1\text{m} = \text{C}
\end{array}
$$

Using the section of the log table above, the log of C, 1d 1m, is 1.3730

Find X = (unknown) the difference between the MC at the earlier S.T. and the MC at the given L.S.T. The equation is the same as used in the proportional or algebraic method of the last chapter.

$$\frac{A}{B} = \frac{X}{C} \quad \text{or} \quad \frac{A \times C}{B} = X$$

But using logarithms, the multiplication and division are handled by addition and subtraction.

$$\log A + \log C - \log B = \log X$$

1. log A		*1.1498*
2. plus log C	+	*1.3730*
Result =		*2.5228*
3. minus log B	–	*.7782*
Result =		*1.7446* = log X

Log X is then found in the log tables and the data in sexagesimal form is read by interpolation. The closest figure to 1.7446 in the table is 1.7434 which corresponds to 0 d 26m.

	0	1	2	3	4	5	6	7
25	1.7604	1.2289	.9970	.8466	.7351	.6465	.5729	.5100
26	1.7434	1.2239	.9940	.8445	.7335	.6451	.5718	.5090
27	1.7270	1.2188	.9910	.8424	.7319	.6438	.5707	.5081

4. interpolate X:	*0* d *26* m
5. plus earlier Midheaven +	*20* d *36* m
6. exact Midheaven =	*20* d *62* m
Adjust	*21* d *2* m
In _Aquarius_ (sign)	

Calculating the Ascendant:

Given:
LST = 21h 33m 42s
Latitude = 28 N 24

ST	MC	A-25N	A-30N	A-35N	A-40N	A-45N	A-50N	A-55
21h28'	19aq35	4ge18	6ge58	10ge02	13ge40	18ge03	23ge27	0ca15
21h32'	20aq36	5ge21	8ge01	11ge06	14ge43	19ge04	24ge26	1ca10
21h36'	21aq37	6ge23	9ge04	12ge09	15ge46	20ge06	25ge24	2ca04
21h40'	22aq39	7ge25	10ge06	13ge11	16ge47	21ge06	26ge22	2ca57

*Part 1: Ascendant calculations for the nearest **lesser** geographical latitude =*   __25 N__

Using previously calculated figures for the Midheaven and the log tables on page 230.

A = the difference between the nearest earlier S.T. and the given L.S.T. 1m 42s = log A = 1.1498

B = the difference between the nearest earlier S.T. and the nearest later S.T.   4m = log B = .7781

D1 = the difference between the Ascendant at earlier S.T. and the ASC at the later S.T.

$$
\begin{array}{r}
6 \text{ Ge } 23 \\
- 5 \text{ Ge } 21 \\
\hline
1 \qquad 2
\end{array}
$$

1d 2m = log D = 1.3660

Find Y1 = (unknown) the difference between the Ascendant at the earlier S.T. and the Ascendant at the given L.S.T.

$$\frac{A}{B} = \frac{Y}{D1} \qquad \text{or} \qquad \frac{A \times D1}{B} = Y$$

Using logarithms: log A + log D1 – log B = log Y

1. log A	_1.1498_
2. plus log D1	+ _1.3660_
Result =	_2.5158_
3. minus log B	− _.7782_
Result =	_1.7376_ = log Y1
4. interpolate Y1	_0_ d _26_ m
5. plus earlier ASC	+ _5_ d _21_ m
6. exact ASC =	_5_ d _47_ m
Adjust	_____ d _____ m

in _Gemini_ (sign)

*Ascendant calculations for the nearest **greater** geographical latitude*
= __30 N__

Using log A and log B from above calculations:

D2 = the difference between the Ascendant at earlier S.T. and the Ascendant at the later S.T.

$$9 \text{ Ge } 04$$
$$- \ 8 \text{ Ge } 01$$
$$1 \quad 03 \ = \ \log D \ = \ 1.3590$$

Y2 = (unknown) the difference between the Ascendant at the earlier S.T. and the Ascendant at the given L.S.T.

$$\frac{A}{B} = \frac{Y2}{D2} \qquad \text{or} \qquad \frac{A \times D2}{B} = Y2$$

Using logarithms: log A + log D2 - log B = log Y2

1. log A	_1.1498_
2. plus log D2	+ _1.3590_

Result =   _2.5088_
3. minus log B   – _.7782_
Result =   _1.7306_   = log Y2
4. Interpolate Y2   _0_ d _27_ m
5. plus earlier ASC   +   _8_ d _01_ m
6. exact ASC =   _8_ d _28_ m
     Adjust   d   m
       in _Gemini_ (sign)

*Ascendant calculations for the **actual** latitude of birth or the event =*
28 N 24

Note: The zodiacal position of the Ascendant may increase or decrease between the lesser and greater latitude positions noted in the table of houses. Make a note of the direction of change in order to determine whether to add or subtract in step 5 below.

E = the difference between the nearest lesser latitude and the nearest greater latitude.
    _5_ d _0_ m

F = the difference between the given latitude and the nearest lesser latitude.
    _3_ d _24_ m

G = the difference between the previously calculated Ascendant at the nearest lesser latitude and the previously calculated Ascendant at the nearest greater latitude. If necessary, adjustment figures to facilitate subtraction.

   8 Ge 28 – 5 Ge 47 = G   7 Ge 88
                          – 5 Ge 47
                       2   41 = G

Z = (unknown) the difference between the ASC at the nearest lesser latitude and the ASC at the given latitude.

$$\frac{F}{E} = \frac{Z}{G} \qquad \text{or} \qquad \frac{F \times G}{E} = Z$$

Using logarithms: log F + log G − log E = log Z

1. log F		.8487			
2. plus log G	+	.9515			
Result =		1.8002			
3. minus log E	−	.6812			
Result =		1.1190	= log Z		
4. Interpolate Z		1	d	50	m
5. Plus earlier ASC*	+	5	d	47	m
7. exact ASC =		6	d	97	m
Adjust		7	d	37	m
in __Gemini__ (sign)					

Note: These results are the same as those obtained using algebraic proportions and they are within a few minutes of arc of the computer calculated example chart. The small discrepancy is due to the fact that the example tables used in this book do not contain seconds of arc and latitudes are spaced by 5 degrees. Small differences in seconds of arc accumulate and affect the final results. Given the fact that times of births and events are rarely record to the second, these small errors are negligible and would not be critical if taking an astrology exam.

Calculating the Houses

Exact house cusps are found in the same manner as the Ascendant – you must first calculate the cusps for the nearest lesser and greater latitude, and then find the cusp for the given latitude. There are other options such as using equal houses or the Porphyry method of houses (recommended) as described in the previous section.

Calculating the Planet's Places using Logarithms

In the era before calculators, logarithm tables were commonly used to determine where planets were located in astrological charts. The planet's places can be calculated by adding the logarithm of the daily motion (DM) to the logarithm of the GMT. The sum is then found in the tables and interpolated to determine the distance traveled.

Note: Precise calculations of planetary positions require Delta T to be added or subtract to the GMT. This is particularly important for solar and lunar returns, but is optional for most other purposes such as natal and event charts.

The basic formula for calculating the planet's places is quite simple: log GMT + log DM = log distance traveled and added to the earlier ephemeris listing. Note that in planet calculations the log table is used for degrees and minutes.

Table of Diurnal Proportional Logarithms

	16	17	18	19	20	21	22	23
	.1761	.1498	.1249	.1015	.0792	.0580	.0378	.0185
1	.1756	.1493	.1245	.1011	.0788	.0576	.0375	.0182
2	.1752	.1489	.1241	.1007	.0785	.0573	.0371	.0179

GMT is 19h 0m. Log GMT = .1015

1. Calculating the Sun's longitude using logarithms:

Example event: January 19, 2006, GMT = 19h

Date	S.T.	Moon	Sun	Mercury	Venus	Mars
Jan 18 2006	07:49:02	06°Vi58'	27°Cp44'	22°Cp01'	21°Cp15'	16°Ta22'
Jan 19 2006	07:52:59	18°Vi45'	28°Cp45'	23°Cp39'	20°Cp41'	16°Ta44'
Jan 20 2006	07:56:56	00°Li35'	29°Cp46'	25°Cp16'	20°Cp08'	17°Ta07'
Jan 21 2006	08:00:52	12°Li30'	00°Aq47'	26°Cp55'	19°Cp36'	17°Ta30'

Sun's daily motion (DM) from ephemeris shown above:
29 Cp 46 – 28 Cp 45 = 29d 46m
                    – 28d 45m
                    1d   1m = DM

	0	1	2	3	4	5	6	7
	3.1584	1.3802	1.0792	.9031	.7782	.6812	.6021	.5351
1	3.1584	1.3730	1.0756	.9007	.7763	.6798	.6009	.5341
2	2.8573	1.3660	1.0720	.8983	.7745	.6784	.5997	.5331

Log of DM = 1.3730

1. log of GMT	*.1015*
2. + log of Sun's daily motion	+ *1.3730*
3. = log of distance traveled	*1.4745*

	0	1	2	3	4	5	6	7
47	1.4863	1.1290	.9356	.8023	.7005	.6180	.5488	.4890
48	1.4771	1.1249	.9331	.8004	.6990	.6168	.5477	.4881
49	1.4682	1.1209	.9305	.7985	.6975	.6155	.5466	.4872

4. Interpolate *1.4745* =   _0_ d _48_ m

5. Sun's previous ephemeris listing + _28_ d _45_ m
6. Equals Sun's longitude   _28_ d _93_ m
       Adjust   _29_ d _33_ m
       in _Capricorn_ (sign)

2. Calculating the Moon's longitude using logarithms:

00 Li 35 – 18 Vi 45 = 30d 35m = 29d 95m
                                – 18d 45m
                          11d 50m = DM

	8	9	10	11	12	13	14	15
49	.4349	.3882	.3461	.3077	.2724	.2398	.2095	.1811
50	.4341	.3875	.3454	.3071	.2719	.2393	.2090	.1806
51	.4333	.3868	.3448	.3065	.2713	.2388	.2085	.1802

Log of Moon's DM = .3071

1. log of GMT	*.1015*
2. + log of Moon's daily motion	+ *.3071*
3. = log of distance traveled	*.4086*

4. Interpolate from tables		9	d	22	m
5. Moon's previous listing	+	18	d	45	m
6. Equals Moon's longitude		27	d	67	m
Adjust		28	d	7	m

      in __Virgo__ (sign)

3. Calculating Venus' longitude using logarithms:

In this example Venus has a retrograde daily motion.

20 Cp 41 to 20 Cp 08 = 20d 41m

$$- \quad \underline{20d\ 08m} \quad = 33m$$

	0	1	2	3	4	5	6	7
32	1.6532	1.1946	.9765	.8320	.7238	.6372	.5651	.5032
33	1.6398	1.1899	.9737	.8300	.7222	.6359	.5640	.5023
34	1.6269	1.1852	.9708	.8279	.7206	.6346	.5629	.5013

Log of Venus' DM = 1.6398

1. log of GMT		.1015			
2. + log of Venus's daily motion	+	1.6398			
3. = log of distance traveled		.7413			
4. Interpolate from tables		0	d	26	m
5. Venus's previous ephemeris listing		20	d	41	m
6. Subtract distance traveled	−		d	26	m
Adjust		20	d	15	m

      in __Virgo__ (sign)

Chapter 9

Chart Calculations using a
Scientific Calculator

Materials needed: A midnight ephemeris, an astrological atlas (with latitudes, longitudes and Daylight Saving Time information), a scientific calculator, a pencil and a piece of paper. A table of houses is optional but useful for checking results. The scientific calculator is the key tool. At minimum it should have the trigonometric functions and an easy way of changing degrees and minutes into decimals, as well as the reverse. *Note: the calculator must be in degree mode (see page 100) in order to properly convert from degrees, minutes, and seconds to decimals.* It does not need to have any other higher math or statistics functions, so a more complicated and expensive calculator is not better for astrological calculation purposes. It should have at least one memory and preferably a few more.

Texas Instruments, Casio and *Sharp* offer quality products of this description for roughly $10. Online calculators are also available. All of the important calculations in this method are done in decimals, not degrees. Practice changing degrees (and minutes and seconds) to decimals and back again. Also, make sure you know how to input data using the parentheses keys. By trying out different brands you may find one is easier for you to use than another.

You will also need to understand that the answers you get from the calculator for the Midheaven, Ascendant, and houses will be expressed in true longitude. This means degrees, minutes, and seconds ranging from 0 to 360 starting at 0 Aries. Below is the list of signs, and the degrees they begin with, which you should become familiar with. To convert a figure in true longitude to zodiacal sign and degree, simply subtract the closest lesser value below. Example: 118 degrees. Cancer (90) is the closest lesser value, so 118 minus 90 equals 28, or 28 degrees of Cancer.

Aries: 0   Taurus: 30   Gemini: 60
Cancer: 90   Leo: 120   Virgo: 150
Libra: 180   Scorpio: 210   Sagittarius: 240
Capricorn: 270   Aquarius: 300   Pisces: 330

When using a calculator it is most efficient to convert all figures normally expressed in degrees, minutes and seconds, or in hours, minutes and seconds, to decimals. This includes the figures for GMT and LST.

Example: New Horizons Launch: Jan 19, 2006. 2:00 PM EST. 28N24, 80W36. Previously calculated GMT = 19.00 h, LST = 21.5616 h

Calculating the Midheaven

We will now use trigonometry to locate the Midheaven on the ecliptic, or Sun's path, along which the zodiac extends. The triangle used to perform this operation is the one designated by the following known figures: 1. The line along the celestial equator (expressed in Right Ascension) from the vernal point (the intersection of the equator and the ecliptic, or 0 Aries) to the meridian. 2. The angle created by the intersection of the equator and the ecliptic, which is the obliquity of the ecliptic, or 23.45 degrees. With one side and one angle known, we can then determine, by making a right spherical triangle and using trigonometry, the other side that runs along the ecliptic – which will give us the longitude of the MC.

1. Take the calculated LST and multiply by 15. This figure is the Right Ascension of the Midheaven (RAMC) which locates the intersection of the meridian and the celestial equator. Put this figure, the RAMC, in the calculator's memory. If it has another memory, you may also store the obliquity (OBL) of the ecliptic (Earth's tilt on its axis) which is 23.45.

The formula for calculating the Midheaven is:

$$MC = ARC \tan \quad x \quad \frac{\tan RAMC}{\cos OBL}$$

2. With the RAMC displayed, press tan (tangent) on the calculator, then divide by the cosine of 23.45 (OBL). The sequence on most calculators should be (starting with the RAMC in the display) tan (divide) 23.45 cos (equals).

3. Now press either ARC tan or tan-1, whichever one your calculator has. These are the same function but with different names. (ARC tan is the tangent multiplied by -1). On many calculators, this will require first pressing a Shift, F, or INV key (for second function or inverse function) and then ARC tan or tan-1 (which may be printed above the tan key).

You now have a figure that may need to be adjusted. Check your original LST and if it is between 0 and 6, add nothing; between 6 and 18, add 180; and between 18 and 24, add 360. (This adjustment is for the quadrant the calculation requires. It accounts for the distance of 0 Aries from the Midheaven which affects the spherical triangle at the basis of the calculation.)

4. Convert the result back into degrees and minutes. Check this Midheaven against a table of houses or computer.

Example:

1. LST (21.5616) multiply (x) 15 equals (=) RAMC (323.424).

2. Next, 323.424 tan (-0.7420) divided by (÷) 23.45 cos (0.9174) equals (=) (-0.8088)

3. ARC tan (-38.9665). Because the LST was between 18 and 24, you will need to add (+) 360 which then equals (=) (321.0334). This figure is the Midheaven. Converting to degrees, minutes and seconds, the Midheaven is 321 degrees, 2 minutes and 0 seconds. Since

the sign Aquarius starts with 300 degrees (see table of absolute longitudes above) this corresponds to 21Aq02 at the Midheaven. Compare with the computer calculated chart on page 108.

Calculating the Ascendant

This is the toughest calculation because it requires so many buttons to be pushed impeccably. Before you begin, make sure you have the RAMC stored in the memory of the calculator, and also the obliquity of the ecliptic (23.45) and the geographical latitude of the birth (also expressed in decimals) handy. If your calculator has only one memory, you should probably use it for the RAMC. You should also make sure that you know where the parentheses are on your calculator. In the formula we are using, the proper use of the parentheses is critical.

The formula for calculating the Ascendant is:

$$1/X \text{ ARC tan} \quad - \frac{(\tan \text{ lat. x sin OBL}) + (\sin \text{ RAMC x cos OBL})}{\cos \text{ RAMC}}$$

Notice the negative sign that precedes the main part of the equation. When you get to this part of the problem, multiplying it by -1 will work, but with calculators its much easier to just push the change sign key which looks like this (+/-) or this (+⇆ -). The equation can also be expressed as below which facilitates calculations.

$$\frac{(\tan \text{ lat. x sin OBL}) + (\sin \text{ RAMC x cos OBL})}{\cos \text{ RAMC}} \text{ x (-1) } 1/X \text{ ARC tan}$$

1. Begin with the data that will be divided by the cos of the RAMC. Press the left-handed parenthesis key, input the latitude and press tan. Press multiply (x), input the obliquity (OBL) and press sin. Then press the right-handed parenthesis key.

2. Press the plus (+) sign. Next, press the left-handed parenthesis key again, recall the RAMC and press sin. Press multiply (x), input

the obliquity (OBL) again and press cos. Next, press the right-handed parenthesis key and then press equals (=).

3. Now press the divide (÷) sign and recall the RAMC and press cos. Press the equals (=) sign.

4. Next, press the change signs (+/-) key (or multiply by -1) and then the 1/X key (You may need to press a second function key here. The 1/X key means the reciprocal of the number, that is the multiplier that produces a product of 1.). Then press ARC tan or tan-1, which-ever your calculator uses (this usually requires pressing a second function key to activate) and take a good look at what you've got.

5. Now check your original LST. If it is greater than 0 and some-where between 12.0 to 14.0, add 180. The exact change point will depend on the latitude. The change is around 13.25 for 40 degrees north. If the figure is over this value (12.0 to 14.0) and under 18.0, add 360. If it is over 18.00 and less than 24, add nothing.

6. After making the above correction, change your figure into de-grees and minutes and locate the sign it falls in. You've got the As-cendant! Check it against a table of houses or computer printout, and use common sense to confirm that you've got your data in the right quadrant.

Example: GMT = 19.00   LST = 21.5616
LST (21.5616) multiply (x) 15 equals (=) RAMC (323.424)
Latitude = 28N24 = 28.4

The RAMC for the example above is 323.424. The obliquity (OBL) is 23.45 and the geographical latitude is 28.4 degrees north latitude. Store the RAMC in the memory of your calculator and, if you have additional memories, the obliquity and latitude as well.

$$\frac{(\text{tan lat.} \times \sin \text{OBL}) + (\sin \text{RAMC} \times \cos \text{OBL})}{\cos \text{RAMC}} \times (-1) \; 1/X \; \text{ARC tan}$$

1. First use the latitude and the OBL. Don't forget the parentheses! Input (28.4 tan x 23.45 sin). Press = and you should have 0.2152 in your display.

2. Press plus (+) and then, using the parentheses again, input (323.424 sin x 23.45 cos). Hit the equals (=) key. You should have -0.3315 in the display.

3. Press divide (÷), then recall or input the RAMC, hit cos and then equals (=). You should now have – 0.4128 in the display.

4. Now hit the change signs key (+/-) (or multiply by -1) and then the 1/X key. Next hit ARC tan or tan-1. Your display should now read 67.5694.

5. Since the LST is over 18 and less than 24, add 0. Our result is 67.5694, or converted to degrees, minutes and seconds, 67 degrees 34 minutes and 9 seconds. This corresponds to 7Ge34 and it is the Ascendant for our example chart. Check it against a computer or table of houses. Use common sense – the Ascendant must be located further ahead in the zodiac than the Midheaven!

Hint: Once you've got this procedure down, list the sequence of buttons to push on your calculator for the Midheaven and Ascendant calculations on a file card. It will be your crib sheet. You could also program the sequence on a programmable calculator, though you may not be able to use that if taking an exam.

Calculating the Houses

There are many house systems in that have been invented for astrologers to use (see Chapter 4) and not one of them has been proven decisively to be better than the others. Most people don't even make a choice about what house system they use – they just follow whatever their teacher used or use the default setting on their astrological software, which is usually Placidus. This is because for many years, tables of houses according to the method of Placidus were the only ones readily available, so nearly everyone used them. Abundance does not necessarily make something right. In the late 20th century Koch, a modern system, became popular especially in Europe, mostly because some influential astrologers favored it, though very few understood how the system worked. If something is fashionable, that doesn't necessarily mean it is proven. However, both of these house systems do have tables readily available. They can also be handled with trigonometrical calculations if done with a calculator. (For those who wish to experiment with calculating the house cusps in other systems, see *An Astrological House Formulary* by Michael Munkasey.)

The first house system was probably the system called Equal houses. In this one, the Ascendant is calculated and the rest of the houses are located at exactly 30 degree intervals. Or, the cusp of the Ascendant's sign becomes the boundary of the first house, this being called whole sign houses. These are easy solutions to getting house boundaries in a chart but may not be allowed on exams. Classically-oriented astrologers using computers generally prefer the Regiomontanus house or Campanus systems. Tables for these systems exist and they can be calculated with trigonometry. But there is a good alternative to the tedious calculations required for such systems. As previously stated in several places, Porphyry houses are very easy to calculate, are based entirely on the ecliptic where nearly all the action in astrology takes place, and you can pass an exam with them. Until there is strong, verifiable and compelling evidence that one system of houses is better than another, there is no reason to not use Porphyry.

Calculating Porphyry house cusps

In the Porphyry system, the houses are created by a simple tri-section of the ecliptic arc between the Midheaven and the Ascendant, or any other quadrant. The beauty of the system is that once you've found the cusps of the 11th and 12th, you've got the rest. Here's how you do it.

1. Store the Midheaven (in decimals) in your calculator's memory.

2. Input the Ascendant (in decimals). If the Ascendant is a lower figure than the Midheaven, add 360.

3. Subtract the Midheaven from the Ascendant.

4. Divide this figure by 3. This is the trisection of the quadrant between the Ascendant and Midheaven. Write down the result or store it in an extra memory if you have one.

5. Next, add the Midheaven (recall it) to this dividend. The result is the cusp of the 11th house.

6. Add to the above (11th cusp) the figure from step #4. This is the 12th house cusp.

7. The 2nd and 3rd house cusps are found by trisection of the quadrant between the Ascendant and the IC (4th house cusp which is opposite the Midheaven) as above. Houses 5, 6, 8, and 9 are exact opposites of houses 11, 12, 2 and 3.

But it turns out no further calculations other than those for houses 11 and 12 are necessary in the Porphyry system. The degrees and minutes of the calculated 11 and 12 cusps are replicated in the cusps of 2 and 3, just the signs differ. When the quadrants are of roughly equal size, house 2 will be one sign ahead of the Ascendant and will have the same degrees and minutes as house 12. House 3 will be two signs ahead of the Ascendant and its cusp will have the same degrees and minutes as the house 11. But with more unequal quadrants the choice of sign will need to be thought out. This has also been described on page 138.

Calculating the Planets' Places

For this step you will need the GMT and an ephemeris. Basically, you will be calculating how far each planet traveled in one day (its daily motion) and then determining how far it moved in the zodiac up to the moment of the event. For the Sun, Moon, and inner planets, use the rules below.

Note: Precise calculations of planetary positions require Delta T to be added or subtracted to the GMT. This is particularly important for solar and lunar returns, but is optional for most other purposes.

1. Divide the GMT (in decimals) by 24. Store this figure, called the *Constant Fraction*, in your calculator's memory.

2. Figure the daily motion of the planet in question according to the following formula: Daily Motion = the planet's longitude on the day after the event (or later longitude if retrograde) minus its longitude on the day of the event (or earlier longitude).

3. Multiply the daily motion of the planet by the constant fraction in your calculator's memory.

4. Take the result of step #3 and add it to the planet's longitude on the day of the event (earlier longitude) or subtract if retrograde. This equals the planets zodiacal position exactly. (If the GMT is over 24 be sure to used the next day as your planetary calculation date.)

You may come across a few quirks now and then. One is in regard to the two longitude positions being in different signs. For example, suppose the Moon on the day of birth is at 25 degrees of Aries, and on the next day at 10 degrees of Taurus. Add 30 degrees to the latter and subtract the former so it becomes 40 minus 25, or 15 degrees. Another quirk is in regard to retrogradation. Just do the subtracting in reverse here. If Mercury was at 20 degrees on the day of birth and 18 the next, then figure the difference (2), multiply by the constant fraction and subtract from the day of birth (earlier) longitude. This is the same method used in Chapter 7. See page 139 for the worked example.

Equations for other points:

Vertex = arc tan $\dfrac{\cos \text{RAMC}}{(\cot \text{lat} \times \sin \text{obl}) - (\sin \text{RAMC} \times \cos \text{obl})}$

Note: Input cot lat as tan lat 1/X. The cotanget function is the inverse of tangent. The Antivertex = Vertex ± 180 degrees

Equatorial Ascendant = arc tan $\dfrac{\tan (\text{RAMC} + 90)}{\cos \text{obl}}$

This point, also called the east point, is the degree of the zodiac that would rise if the birth or event took place right on the terrestrial equator. At other latitudes, it is the ecliptic position of the degree of the celestial equator on the horizon, which is always due east.

Chapter 10

Other Astrological Chart Calculations

Western astrology has produced a range of techniques designed to assess the qualities of past, present and future time. Through the use of astrological symbolism, conditions well into the future can be evaluated and timed, but precise predictions cannot be made. In some cases long-range predictions may be broad-based, in others limited to single categories. Since astrology concerns itself primarily with time and general qualities, very accurate predictions must also utilize information from other sources.

The material in this chapter considers Western astrological predictive techniques of the past 2000 years in the order of most common usage followed by other historical techniques including primary directions and Hellenistic time periods. Following this summary a few other miscellaneous calculations will be presented.

Transits

Transits relate the moving positions of the Sun, Moon and planets in real time relative to a static horoscope, itself a time-slice diagram with diurnal cycle positional data on these bodies for a specific date, time and place. In modern times, transits are probably the most-used predictive technique, in part because no real calculations are needed. In Hellenistic times two millennia ago, transits were used as potential triggers or temporary rulers within the context of larger periods of time and were considered more significant when occurring near the birthday.

The most important factor in judging the effects of transits may be the daily motion or rate of speed of the transiting planet. Mercury, for example, normally moves much faster than the other planets (except the Moon) and its transits last for not much more than a day – unless it is reversing direction when its retrograde period begins or ends. For a few days at these stations Mercury is moving at the rate comparable to one of the outer planets and its astrological effects can be substantial. This observation suggests that the strength of a transit can be described in a general sense by the following equation:

$$AE = \frac{1}{DM}$$

Here the astrological effect (AE) is a function of the daily motion (DM) of a planet shown as a fraction: 1/DM. The larger the daily motion, the smaller the fraction and therefore the shorter, and weaker, the astrological effect. Since the Moon's daily motion varies from about 11 to 15 degrees per day, it would follow that the strength of its several hour-length transits (and also natal imprint) may vary accordingly.

Lunations and Eclipses

While the transits of the Sun may last a few days, and those of the Moon a few hours, the combined influence of these two bodies, when in conjunction or opposition as measured on the ecliptic, can be substantial. Such events, new and full Moons, are called *lunations*. Lunations so precise that the bodies overlap in space as seen on Earth are *eclipses*. These will occur when the Sun is near one of the lunar nodes, which mark the points where the Moon's orbit crosses the ecliptic. Only then can the Moon cover the Sun (solar eclipse) or fall into the Earth's shadow (lunar eclipse).

A precise new Moon is a solar eclipse and a precise full Moon is a lunar eclipse. Both are quite powerful in terms of astrological effect and, when precisely contacting sensitive points in a horoscope, can often sustain an observable effect for months. Most ephemerides will list the date and time of lunations and eclipses. It has been observed that the effects of eclipses often precede the actual alignment of Sun and Moon by days or even weeks, something that challenges conventional notions about time.

Transit Calculations

Outer planet transits involve no calculations as their effects are broad and encompass periods of days, months or even years. But inner planet transits often correlate with effects within hours of their exactness. In these cases it may be useful to determine the precise time a transit becomes exact. This is especially appropriate for the Moon and Mercury. Such a calculation is done as follows:

1. Begin with the degree and minute of the point (usually from a natal or event chart) that will be transited, i.e. receiving a transit. This could be a conjunction or any aspect. Then determine the day that the transiting planet will pass over this degree and minute.

2. Next determine the transiting planet's earlier position (EP) in the ephemeris (midnight ephemeris much preferred), and its later position (LP). Subtracting the former from the latter (or the reverse if retrograde) will equal its daily motion (DM). This procedure has been explained in the previous sections on chart calculations. These ephemeris positions will be in GMT which will be converted after the calculation.

3. Determine the distance the planet must travel from the EP to reach the point sought. This is called the travel distance or TD. Then set up the following equation:

$$\frac{TD}{DM} = \frac{GMT}{24} \quad \text{or} \quad GMT = \frac{TD \times 24}{DM}$$

4. The result in GMT will require adjusting for the local time zone (subtract if west longitude, add if east) and accounting for daylight time if in effect. If over 12 hours, subtract 12 for civil clock time.

This equation is the same used for solar and lunar returns, and also *ingresses* – the entry points of planets into signs. One common ingress considered important for millennia is the entry of the Sun into Aries, that is the moment when the Sun crosses the intersection of the ecliptic and equator. Ingresses will be discussed below.

Solar and Lunar returns

Solar and lunar returns are basically a form of transits. Other names for the technique, which has a long history, include solar or lunar revolutions and birthday maps. In Hellenistic astrology no actual return chart was calculated but transits to natal planets were noted at the time of the birthday. The first major work on solar returns, circa 800, was Albumasar's *Revolutions of the Years of Nativities*.

Although solar returns were known in ancient times, they have long been a staple of the modern astrologer's predictive arsenal. The exact time that the Sun returns to its natal position is first determined and then a chart is calculated for that time. For lunar returns the same procedure is applied to the return of the Moon to its natal position. Once the time of day that the Sun or Moon returns to its birth position has been determined, a horoscope can be calculated for this time in the usual way. As solar and Lunar returns are charts that require much precision, locating the exact positions will require the use of the Delta T correction. Theoretically, returns for all of the planets are possible with extreme astronomical precision, and astrological software can do this, but to calculate by hand will require an ephemeris with planetary positions given to fractions of seconds of arc.

A solar or lunar return is the return of either of these bodies in zodiacal longitude to its event or birth position. This does not take into consideration the fact that this point has shifted over time relative to the background stars of the galaxy due to the precession of the equinoxes. Many astrological practitioners have argued that the natal position of the Sun, Moon, or other body for which a return is to be calculated, should be corrected for precession by adding the precession correction value, which increases over time. See below for more discussion on this problem.

There are two other variants on solar and lunar returns. One is the practice of calculating charts not only for the return of Sun or Moon, but also for their return to the opposite position (demi-return) or the quarters (quarterly-return). Some historical texts say that if the solar return has cardinal signs on the Ascendant it will be effective for just a few months and therefore quarterly returns will be needed over the course of the year for more detail. If mutable signs are angular, the return is said to be effective for six months. If fixed are angular, the return is good for a year. To my knowledge, this idea has not been tested except anecdotally.

Many astrologers believe that the solar return chart should be calculated for the current location rather than the natal location. This can change the angles considerably if someone lives far from their birthplace. Given this notion, the assumption that a person's experience during the year ahead can be modified by temporary relocation for the birthday has taken a hold in certain sectors of the astrological community and has become a service offered by consulting astrologers. Personal experience suggests a relocation on the birthday will correlate with experiences at that location, but upon return to the home base, the power of the chart for that location will assert itself. This is a practice that has not been studied in any serious way, largely because of the difficulties in assigning units to personal experiences. It appears, however, to be of financial benefit to astrologers who confidently offer the service.

Calculating Returns

The procedure for calculating a solar or lunar return is similar to the calculation for the time of a transit, but with more precision. In this situation it is advisable to add the ΔT (delta T) correction to the calculated GMT.

1. In an ephemeris with daily listings of planetary positions, find the day during which the return will occur. This day will be bracketed by the first ephemeris listing called the earlier position (EP) and second called the later position (LP). The difference between these two listings is the daily motion (DM). (When a planet is retrograde, this difference is determined in reverse.)

To determine the exact degree, minute, and second of the Sun or Moon's natal (or event) position use ΔT corrected GMT and the constant fraction (CF) which is GMT divided by 24. The constant fraction is used for calculating all planetary positions from an ephemeris as described in the horoscope calculations of the previous chapters of this book.

DM x CF + EP = exact position of Sun, Moon or planet. (In the case of a retrograde planet, the result of DM x CF would be subtracted from EP).

2. Find the date on which the return will occur in the ephemeris. Then, from the ephemeris, determine the distance the Sun or Moon travels on this day in degrees, minutes and seconds. This is the daily motion or DM – *for the return.*

3. For the date of the return determine the distance traveled in degrees, minutes and seconds between the first and earlier ephemeris listing (EP) and the event or natal position of the Sun or Moon previously calculated – call this TD for travel distance.

Event/natal Sun or Moon position – EP = TD

5. Calculate the time of day for the return using the formula:

$$\frac{TD}{DM} = \frac{GMT}{24} \quad or \quad \frac{TD \times 24}{DM} = GMT$$

5. Using this GMT and the location required, convert to local time if desired, calculate the Local Sidereal Time (with ΔT compensation) and then cast a chart as described in the previous chapters.

Example: Solar Return

New Horizons launch January 19, 2006, 2 PM Cape Canaveral FL, 28N24 (28.4)

Calculate a Solar Return for 2015, the year the probe reached Pluto. The launch location will be used in the exercise.

Note: the sample ephemeris used in this book for previous examples gives the Sun, Moon and planet positions in only degrees and minutes. For solar and lunar returns more precision is required. The tables below include seconds in addition to degrees and minutes for the Sun and Moon. These will give results closer to the far more precise values from the best computer software. The first is for the launch date (the "natal" chart), the second is for the year of the return.

Calculations in the example below are done in both sexagesimal notation and using decimals. The calculations can be done using logarithms, but they need to be five place Ternary Proportional logarithms to achieve the precision required for returns.

Date	S.T.	Moon	Sun
Jan 18 2006	07:49:02	06°Vi58'43"	27°Cp44'30"
Jan 19 2006	07:52:59	18°Vi45'59"	28°Cp45'34"
Jan 20 2006	07:56:56	00°Li35'09"	29°Cp46'37"
Jan 21 2006	08:00:52	12°Li30'43"	00°Aq47'41"

Date	S.T.	Moon	Sun
Jan 18 2015	07:48:20	22°Sg50'41"	27°Cp33'02"
Jan 19 2015	07:52:17	07°Cp11'04"	28°Cp34'08"
Jan 20 2015	07:56:13	21°Cp54'42"	29°Cp35'15"
Jan 21 2015	08:00:10	06°Aq53'49"	00°Aq36'21"

1. Calculate Sun's exact event/natal position (January 19, 2006). Make the ΔT correction to the GMT.

a. GMT = 19h + ΔT 65s = 19h 1m 5s or 19.0181 = GMT

b. Sun's daily motion: 29d 46m 37s – 28d 45m 34s = 1d 1m 3s

or...   29.7769 – 28.7594 = 1.0175 = DM

c. Constant fraction = GMT/24 = 0.7924 = CF

d. DM (1.0175) x CF (0.7924) = 0.8062 (48m 23s) = TD

e. Sun on Jan 19 (28.7594) + TD (0.8062) = event Sun (29.5656 or 29Cp 33m 56s)

2. The solar return occurred on January 19, 2015.

Jan 19 Sun = 28d 34m 8s
Jan 20 Sun = 29d 35m 15s

29d 35m 15s – 28d 34m 8s = 1d 1m 7s = 1.0186 = DM

3. The Sun's travel distance TD on January 19, 2015:

a. natal/event Sun (29Cp33m56s) – Sun on Jan 19 (28d 34m 8s) = 0d 59m 48s = TD

    or...   29.5656 – 28.5689 = 0.9967 = TD

4. Find the GMT of the solar return:

SR GMT = $\dfrac{\text{TD x 24}}{\text{DM}}$

$\dfrac{\text{TD (0.9967) x 24}}{\text{DM (1.0186)}}$ = 23.4839 (23h 29m 2s) = SR GMT

5. Subtract ΔT (page 234) and adjust for local time.
GMT = 23h 29m 2s – 68s = 23h 27m 54m (23.4839 – 0.0189 = 23.4650).

For Eastern Time (the launch site), subtract 5 hours. 23h 27m 54s – 5h = 18h 27m 54s local time (6:27:54 PM). This result should be close to a value calculated by quality computer software.

6.Calculate LST for chart angles and houses:

ST on January 19 2015 = 7h 52m 17s = *7.8714*

+ GMT	23.4650
+ SST (GMT/6.1/60)	0.0642
	31.4006
– LTE (80.6/15)	– 5.3733
	26.0273
Adjust	– 24
LST =	2.0273 = 2h 1m 38s

Or in the form of sexagesimal notation:

ST on January 19 2015 = 7 h 52m 17s
+ GMT   23 h 27m 54s
+ SST   h   3m 51s
                    =   30 h 82m 122s
– LTE (80W36/15)   –   5 h 22m 24s
                    =   25 h 60m 98s = 26h 1m 38s
Adjust = (-24)   2 h   1m 38s = LST

See previous chapters for horoscope calculation procedures. Remember that the houses are calculated with the LST but the planetary positions are calculated with GMT + ΔT.

Lunar and planetary returns

Lunar returns are calculated in the same way as solar returns, the major difference being the much larger daily motion of the Moon. The important thing in doing solar and lunar returns is to account for the seconds in the equation, which should be found in the ephemeris listings, and also the ΔT correction as these can make a difference in the angles and house cusps of the final charts. High precision in calculating a return is the goal but it may not always be clear that it has been achieved. Given minor differences in individual ephemerides and different computer algorithms built into astrological software, results may vary slightly. Comparison of hand-calculated charts vs.

computer generated charts is an important check on one's work, but only be concerned if there are differences of over 15 minutes of arc on the angles. Most professional astrological exams are tolerant of these small variations.

Other planetary returns are possible but accurate results are even more dependent on the precision calculations of planetary orbits, these being subject to perturbations from other planets and consequently vary by small amounts over time. Due to their faster motions, the returns of the inner planets will be more accurate than those of the outer planets where motions are only a few minutes of arc per day.

Ingresses

Ingress charts are horoscopes calculated for the time an astronomical body enters a sign. The most commonly calculated ingresses are those of the Sun into the cardinal signs, especially the Sun's ingress into Aries, a chart that has been used as reference for prediction by astrologers for millennia. Ingresses are mostly used to interpret and forecast collective and environmental events and trends including politics and weather. They are always calculated for a specific location; i.e. the capital of a country.

Like returns, ingresses require precision in calculations. The timing of a transit to a natal or event chart can tolerate some margin of error, but a return or ingress does not because it requires the calculation of a chart with accurate angles (Midheaven and Ascendant). Precision is obtained through the use of seconds in calculations provided in most ephemerides for the Sun and Moon, the most commonly used points in returns and ingresses.

Calculations for ingresses are basically the same as those for returns. Consider the entry of the Sun into Aries, that is 0 degrees Aries, as the degree sought in the calculation. This degree is then treated like the Sun or Moon in a return.

1. After locating in the ephemeris the listings that bracket the Sun's transit of 0 Aries, first the daily motion (DM) of the Sun on that day

is calculated by subtracting the earlier position (EP) from the later position (LP). (Because 0 Aries begins a new sign you will have to add 30 degree to the LP in order to subtract.)

LP – EP = DM

2. Next the travel distance (TD) from the earlier position of the Sun to 0 Aries is calculated. (Do this by using 30d 0m 0s for 0 Ar)

0 Ar – EP = TD

3. Using the equation, find the GMT of the ingress.

$$\frac{TD}{DM} = \frac{GMT}{24} \quad \text{or} \quad \frac{TD \times 24}{DM} = GMT$$

4. Calculate planet positions using this GMT and follow standard procedures for calculating an event or natal chart.

Sidereal time (ST) from ephemeris for the day of the ingress
+ GMT
+ solar sidereal correction (SST) for GMT
– longitude time equivalent in time LTE
= Local Sidereal Time (LST)

Note that the GMT calculated will need to be adjusted for ΔT before calculating the Ascendant and Midheaven for the location desired (usually subtracted).

The Sidereal Correction Issue

Due to the roughly 26,000-year wobble of the Earth's axis the difference between the tropical zodiac, the basis of the seasons, and the sidereal zodiac, as measured against the distant background stars (referred to in astrology as the fixed stars), increases. The vernal point, the first degree of Aries marked by the intersection of the ecliptic and equator, retrogrades in the zodiac at a rate of roughly 1 degree every 72 years. This means that the positions of the points in an event or natal chart relative to the background stars, but located in the tropical zodiac, will slowly increase in zodiacal longitude as the equinox retrogrades against them. For example, the position of a planet located at 0 degrees of tropical zodiac Aries in 1940 will in 2012 actually be at 1 degree of tropical Aries. But this point viewed against the distant background stars will not appear to have moved at all. So the issue is whether or not this difference, the sidereal correction, should be accounted for in solar and lunar returns. The general consensus is that both charts probably have merit, although there are vocal proponents for each method. Like most techniques in astrology, it has never been adequately tested because of the immense difficulty of establishing units to measure.

The annual rate of precession is about 50.26 seconds of arc. In the example above, a solar return calculated for 10 years after launch, this difference would amount to over 8 minutes of arc. It would take the Sun about 3 hours later to reach this point than it would take to reach its Tropical zodiac position. This means that the Midheavens of these two returns would differ by roughly 45 degrees. Such differences between returns calculated in the tropical zodiac and those with a correction for precession are therefore substantial and this issue remains an unresolved, or at least unclarified in terms of testable information, problem for the field of astrology.

Diurnal Charts

A diurnal chart is cast daily for one's birth time using the current (transiting) planets. It is the daily repeat of the event or birth time that forms the basis of this system. One needs only to examine the time of birth for each successive day to see when natal or transiting planets become angular, that is conjunct the Ascendant, Midheaven and their opposite points in the zodiac. Such contacts are considered significant and are then interpreted.

A diurnal chart could be considered a type of progressed chart. This method uses the ratio of 1 day = 1 day, the same ratio used by standard transits. There is a way of graphing planets in the diurnal chart. For many years Valliere's *Natural Cycle's Almanac* was produced by James Valliere and published by Astrolabe. It offered a set of monthly graphic calendars showing the hourly angularities of the planets during each day. A line drawn through at the birth time on the x-axis of each month's graph would show when daily planetary angularities were personally relevant.

Secondary Progressions

Secondary progressions are based on a one to one relationship between the rotation of Earth and its revolution around the Sun (a ratio of 1 day to 1 year). In this system one rotation is regarded as equivalent to one year of life and the planetary activity during that single rotation is seen as a fractal of the trends, developments and events of a full year. The changing planetary positions of the rotation period, called the progressed planets, are evaluated in two ways: (1) progressed planetary aspects to natal positions, and (2) progressed planetary aspects to progressed positions.

Secondary progressions, which have also been called Arabian Directions, are thought to be of more recent origin than primary directions or time-periods (see below). The are often attributed to Placidus who used them, but apparently so did Kepler before him which puts their use in Europe at least as early as the 17th century. It wasn't until the later part of the 19th century that they became widely used when they were reintroduced by Sepharial and then popularized by Alan Leo. The technique soon became the most used astrological predictive technique, along with transits, of the 20th century.

Calculating Secondary Progressions

Progressed charts are charts cast for a specific time and date after an event or birth corresponding to the following formula: 1 day = 1 year. This technique is based on a fractal-like analogy between two fundamental motions of the Earth, rotation and revolution. If one 24-hour day is equal to all the days in one year, then the following correlations are also established:

12 hours = 6 months

2 hours = 1 month
30 minutes = 1 week
4 minutes = 1 day

The date of the progressed chart can be based on age or by the year in question. For progressed charts a few days after the event/birth (for events/births of only a few years in age) count ahead beginning with the event/birth date as zero. For longer periods take the day of the event/birth and subtract it from the number of days in that month. Then add the total number of days in each succeeding month until reaching the required age. This is the progressed date for that age.

Example: Given a birth on February 15, 1970 at 9 AM in NYC, calculate a progressed chart for age 46. (February 1970 was not a leap year and thus had 28 days).

February: 28 – 15 = 13 days
March: + 31 days
                 = 44 days + 2 days = April 2

A progressed chart is then calculated for April 2, 1970 9 AM, NYC.

Another way of calculating a progressed chart is to seek a specific year. First subtract the year of birth from the year sought and then cast a chart for that day using the event/birth time.

Example: Using the above example find the progressed chart for 2016: 2016 – 1970 = 46. From February 15 add 46 days to reach the date of the progressed chart. Begin with 13 days from February + 31 days from March = 44 days. Two more days comes to April 2. A chart is then calculated for April 2, 1970 9 AM, NYC.

Calculating a progressed chart in the manner just explained is essentially the same as calculating a diurnal chart. Diurnal charts, which are calculated for the same time each day, illustrate how the Midheaven moves about one degree ahead per day while the Ascendant will move ahead at a similar but variable rate according to the sign it is in. A series of progressed charts will, like diurnal charts, show the same movement of the angles. Consider that during a day the Midheaven will actually have moved through the entire zodiac plus one degree during the course of the progressed day – it will be a degree ahead of where it was the day before. This fact raises the issue of how the Midheaven and Ascendant should be progressed, which will discussed in some detail below.

Probably the most popular, and also efficient, method of calculating a progressed chart is to find the date that corresponds with the planetary listings in the ephemeris, what is called the *adjusted calculation date* or ACD. This is the date in the year when the planet's places in the ephemeris correspond to the actual progressed positions. Finding this date eliminates the need to calculate the planets zodiacal positions.

Example: New Horizons launch on January 19, 2006 at 2 PM Eastern Time. The GMT = 19 (14h + time zone 5). Calculate a progressed chart to a date in the 10th year from the launch that corresponds to the positions of the planets in the ephemeris.

The simplest way to find the ACD is to multiply 365.24 by the constant fraction used when calculating the planets in a chart. The constant fraction (CF) is GMT divided by 24. The result will be the number of days before the day of the event or birth.

$$\frac{GMT\ (19.0)}{24} = 0.7917 \qquad CF\ (0.7917) \times 365.24 = 289.16\ days$$

Using a 30.43 day average month (365.24 ÷ 12), 289 days is roughly 9.5 months before January 19. Nine months before January 19 is roughly April 19. The additional 0.5 of a month corresponds to 15 days. This yields an ACD of April 4 which is close but may be off by a day or two because an average month figure was used in the calculation. Counted backwards month by month the ACD is found to be April 5. Yet another way is to find the ACD is to count forward. By subtracting 289 from 365, we can count forward 76 days from January 19 to reach April 4.

The following formula can also used to determine the ACD from an ephemeris.

Sidereal time (ST) on day of event/birth + (24 – GMT) + solar-sidereal correction (SSC) on GMT = ACD.

Example:

Date	S.T.	Moon	Sun	Mercury	Venus	Mars
Jan 18 2006	07:49:02	06°Vi58'	27°Cp44'	22°Cp01'	21°Cp15'	16°Ta22'
Jan 19 2006	07:52:59	18°Vi45'	28°Cp45'	23°Cp39'	20°Cp41'	16°Ta44'
Jan 20 2006	07:56:56	00°Li35'	29°Cp46'	25°Cp16'	20°Cp08'	17°Ta07'
Jan 21 2006	08:00:52	12°Li30'	00°Aq47'	26°Cp55'	19°Cp36'	17°Ta30'
Jan 22 2006	08:04:49	24°Li37'	01°Aq48'	28°Cp34'	19°Cp06'	17°Ta53'
Jan 23 2006	08:08:45	07°Sc01'	02°Aq49'	00°Aq13'	18°Cp38'	18°Ta17'
Jan 24 2006	08:12:42	19°Sc47'	03°Aq50'	01°Aq53'	18°Cp12'	18°Ta41'
Jan 25 2006	08:16:38	02°Sg59'	04°Aq51'	03°Aq34'	17°Cp49'	19°Ta05'
Jan 26 2006	08:20:35	16°Sg41'	05°Aq52'	05°Aq16'	17°Cp27'	19°Ta29'
Jan 27 2006	08:24:31	00°Cp53'	06°Aq53'	06°Aq58'	17°Cp08'	19°Ta54'
Jan 28 2006	08:28:28	15°Cp32'	07°Aq54'	08°Aq40'	16°Cp51'	20°Ta19'
Jan 29 2006	08:32:25	00°Aq31'	08°Aq55'	10°Aq23'	16°Cp36'	20°Ta45'
Jan 30 2006	08:36:21	15°Aq43'	09°Aq56'	12°Aq07'	16°Cp24'	21°Ta10'

1. The sidereal time ST (at midnight) on January 19, 2006 was 7h 52m 59s. Convert to decimals = 7.8830.

2. Convert GMT to decimals: = 19.00

3. Subtract GMT from 24 hours: 24 – 19 = 5

4. Find the solar-sidereal correction (SSC) on the GMT. Use the tables (page 217) or calculate as follows: First divide GMT by 6.1: 19 ÷ 6.1 = 3.1147 minutes. Then divide this figure by 60 so that it is expressed in a 24-hour context: 3.1147 ÷ 60 = 0.0519.

5. Add 7.8830 (ST) + 5 (24-GMT) + 0.0519 (SSC) = 12.934990.

6. Convert to degrees, minutes and seconds: 12h 56m 5s

7. Find the day of the year (it could be any year) in an ephemeris that is closest to this sidereal time. The answer is April 5, give or take a day, depending on the year. This is the day that corresponds

to the planetary positions in the ephemeris. No planetary calculations are then necessary.

This means that the planetary positions as listed in the ephemeris for January 20 will be the progressed planetary positions on April 5 (after the launch) in 2006. The positions on January 21 will then correspond to April 5 2007 and January 29 will correspond to April 5 2015, ten years after launch. The ephemeris shows that the progressed Moon just entered Aquarius on the ACD for the year 2015.

Another way of looking at all this is to see the planetary positions listed in the ephemeris for the day of the event/birth as denoting a point before the event/birth, which in this case occurs in the previous year – April 5, 2005.
8. Calculate the progressed Midheaven and Ascendant: A very simple and effective way to do this is to subtract the natal Sun's longitude from the progressed Sun's longitude.

In this case the Sun's position on January 29 being 8Aq55 and on January 19 it is 28Cp45. (Add 30 degrees to the January 29 list in order to subtract.)

January 29   38d 55m
January 19   –   28d 45m
                    =   10d 10m

Add this figure, 10d 10m, to the natal Midheaven to locate the progressed Midheaven. This progressed Midheaven will then advance at the same rate as the progressed Sun, about a day a year. A corresponding progressed Ascendant will need to be calculated for this progressed Midheaven from a table of houses for the latitude of birth, or current location (relocated Ascendant). This will require first calculating the Ascendant for the greater and lesser latitudes in the table of houses, and then for the given latitude.

Progressions may also be calculated backwards in time, these being called converse progressions. Opinion varies as to their effectiveness but they are easy enough to calculate. The method is the same as that for standard progressions but it is applied to a date in the ephemeris that occurs the same number of days before the event or birth date.

Methods of progressing angles

In secondary progressions the day is equated to the year. During each day the planets will change position relative to each other (progressed to progressed) and relative to the event/natal chart the progressions stem from (progressed to natal). Over the years planets will be seen to move to other places in the progressed chart and they can also form entirely new aspects with each other. The movement of the Midheaven, Ascendant and house cusps is another matter. In one 24-hour day, the Midheaven moves 361 degrees so it would be logical to follow that moving Midheaven (and the accompanying Ascendant and house cusps) around the natal chart throughout the year. Quotidian is the Latin word for daily and in *quotidian progressions* the Midheaven and house cusps cycle completely around the chart in the course of a year. Quotidian progressions produce nearly the same cusps as diurnals.

The following are alternatives for handling the movement of the angles in secondary progressions. The siderealist astrologer Cyril Fagan was concerned with these distinctions and interested reader should search for technical information on these techniques in his writings and those of other siderealists.

1. *Mean Quotidian* (based on mean solar day) – moves the chart angles ahead at the rate of one solar day per year.

2. *Apparent Quotidian* (based on apparent solar day) – moves the chart angles ahead as in mean quotidian, but makes adjustments for the changing *equation of time* which is a result of the slight eccentricity of Earth's orbit.

3. *Neo-Quotidian Rate* (based on a portion of the day) – Cyril Fagan's method. Normally, 6 hours of a progressed day = 1 year/4. In this case its 6 hours of a progressed day = 90 degrees of solar motion in RA. The formula is RAMC progressed – RA progressed Sun + RA transiting Sun + RAMC natal Sun.

4. *Progressed Daily Meridian in Longitude* is a Uranian astrology technique. The formula is longitude of progressed Sun − longitude of natal Sun + longitude of transiting Sun + longitude of natal Midheaven. The principle here is that the Midheaven moves so that it is always the same distance from the transiting Sun as the natal Midheaven is from the natal Sun + the progressed solar arc in longitude.

Another far simpler, and more popular, alternative is to move the Midheaven approximately 1 degree per year such that it moves about 5 minutes of arc per month. Here is a list of methods used to progress the angles in this way.

1. *True Solar Arc in Longitude* − directs the Midheaven by the true rate of solar motion for any time of year. It is one of most common methods and very easy to calculate. Progress the Sun, subtract its longitude from the longitude of the natal Sun, and add this to the longitude of the natal Midheaven. This is the method used in the Hamburg School (Uranian astrology).

2. *Naibod in Longitude* − a solar arc method that directs the Midheaven by 59'08", the mean daily motion of Sun. This figure is added annually to the Midheaven in longitude, not RA.

3. *True Solar Arc in R.A.* − advances the RAMC by the mean rate of the Sun. To calculate, progress the Sun, find its RA, subtract the RA of the natal Sun from the progressed Sun and add this figure to the RAMC of the birth chart.

4. *Naibod in R.A.* − moves the sidereal time ahead 3m56s per year of life. This rate is based on the mean solar day for the date of birth.

Other kinds of progressions

Secondary progressions were initially viewed as a complement to primary directions. Other forms of secondary progressions, or more accurately modifications of the system in general, include lunar minor and tertiary progressions. *Minor progressions* were popularized by C.C. Zain and the Church of Light and equate one lunar return after birth to one year of life. *Tertiary progressions* were apparently invented by E.H. Troinski in the 20th century and equate one day after birth with one month of life. Lunar progressions are then based on a relationship between the lunar cycle and the solar year, or between the day (rotation on axis) to the lunar month.

All progressed rates are a ratio of real time to progressed time. This is a case of what might be called astrological fractology where there is an exchange of one time unit for another while respecting proportions. Calculations are done proportionally as with secondaries.

Secondary progressed rate (1 day = 1 year)$$\frac{1 \text{ day}}{365.2422 \text{ days}}$$

Lunar tertiary rate (1 day = 1 month)$$\frac{1 \text{ day}}{27.3216 \text{ days}}$$

Lunar minor progressed rate (1 month = 1 year)$$\frac{27.3216 \text{ days}}{365.2422 \text{ days}}$$

Symbolic Directions

Symbolic directions are a simplified form of "directing" points in a chart that is less rigorous than either primary directions or secondary progressions. Most of the several variations of symbolic directions move the planets and angles at a rate of a degree for a year, much like primary directions, though in these methods the complex astronomical coordinate system realities are dispensed with and nearly all action takes place on the ecliptic. Several English astrologers of the 19th and early 20th centuries proposed "radix systems" which combine the natures of primaries and secondaries. They are called radix systems because the entire radix (natal chart) is essentially rotated against itself. In one version all the planets are moved forward in RA by the Naibod rate (Simonite). This is procedure is far easier to calculate than standard primaries. Another version applied this idea to zodiacal positions in longitude. The Naibod rate, the mean annual daily motion of the Sun which is 59'08", is only one of a number of time measures that have been forwarded by other astrologers.

Today, the most popular time measure is the true movement of the Sun, known as the *Solar Arc*. From the mid 20th century Solar Arc directions have spread in general astrological practice largely as the result of the influence of the Hamburg School of Astrology (known as Uranian Astrology in the USA), though its origins appear to go back at least as far as Kepler. The solar arc is simply the difference between the progressed Sun and the natal Sun. This makes solar arc directions both a radix system and a subspecies of secondary progressions. Many would argue, based on anecdotal evidence, that this technique actually works better in practice than the others.

Solar Arc Directions

Solar arc directions are calculated by adding the distance between the progressed Sun and the natal Sun, which is called the solar arc, to each of the planetary positions and the Midheaven and Ascendant. This is easily done by expressing the position of the progressed and natal Sun in absolute longitude.

Progressed Sun – Natal Sun = Solar Arc

Natal planetary positions + solar arc = solar arc directed positions

The solar arc can be doubled, creating a moving reflection point of the progressed Sun, or halved, creating a moving midpoint of the natal and progressed Suns. The half and double solar are employed in Uranian Astrology and may be that movement's original contribution to the technique. The half solar arc is the distance in degrees midway between the natal and progressed Sun. This figure is then added to the other points in the natal chart. The double solar arc is the reflection point of the natal Sun using the standard solar arc as the midpoint axis. This arc, double the solar arc, is then added to the other points in the natal chart.

Double Solar Arc = solar arc x 2

Half Solar Arc = $\dfrac{\text{solar arc}}{2}$

Primary Directions

Primary directions are based on the axial rotation of Earth. A rate of 1 degree of RA over the MC is said to be equal to one year of life. This means that one's life events are symbolized during the first six hours of life (or a bit longer for very old people).

Primary directions are very ancient. Ptolemy vaguely described "modes of prorogation" or what are more properly called equatorial arcs. This system was based on the ancient idea of the power of planets as they bodily rise and set – that is appear on the horizon. Placidus, who called them "arcs of direction," expanded upon these ideas. Here the semi-arcs of the planets are used to determine the amount of time needed to make contact with an angle or another planet. A semi-arc (diurnal or nocturnal) is one half the time a planet remains above or below the horizon. It is this is the kind of thinking that lies behind the Placidian house system.

In directing by equatorial arcs or primary directions one directs the planets by Right Ascension to the Midheaven and by Oblique Ascension to the Ascendant. The RA is the planet's position on the equator, the OA is the degree of RA rising when the planet is bodily on the horizon. It was customary before doing primary directions for a chart to calculate what was called a speculum, a table listing the astronomical coordinates of each planet and the angles. Typically, this would include longitude, latitude, declination, Right Ascension, Oblique Ascension, Meridian Distance, Ascensional Difference, pole and semi-arc, these all being worked out with trigonometry. With this information at hand, primary directions could then be employed in forecasting. This tedious requirement is why astrologers were referred to as mathematicians through much of history.

Note: The following description of primary directions is highly simplified and designed to only give a sense of how they are done. Seri-

ous readers should consult other more specialized sources to better understand the subject.

Directing a planet somewhere in its diurnal semi-arc (between the Ascendant and the Midheaven) to the Midheaven (MC) is relatively simple. The method is to subtract the RA of the MC from the RA of a planet which would, by rotation of the Earth, move to conjunct the MC. To find the RA of a planet, however, requires its absolute longitude, latitude, and declination, all of which are found in the typical ephemeris. The formula is derived from this relationship:

$$\frac{\cos \text{declination}}{\cos \text{longitude}} = \frac{\cos \text{latitude}}{\cos \text{RA}}$$

$$\cos \text{RA} \times \cos \text{declination} = \cos \text{latitude} \times \cos \text{longitude}$$

$$\cos \text{RA} = \frac{(\cos \text{lat} \times \cos \text{long})}{\cos \text{dec}}$$

$$\text{RA} = \text{arc cos} \frac{(\cos \text{lat} \times \cos \text{long})}{\cos \text{dec}}$$

There are adjustments necessary when using this formula depending on where the longitude is located relative to the cardinal points Aries, Cancer, Libra, and Capricorn. This involves changing from positive to negative numbers and adding or subtracting the longitudes of the cardinal points. When doing the calculation be sure to use the parentheses. Some calculators may differ in actual input sequence of commands.

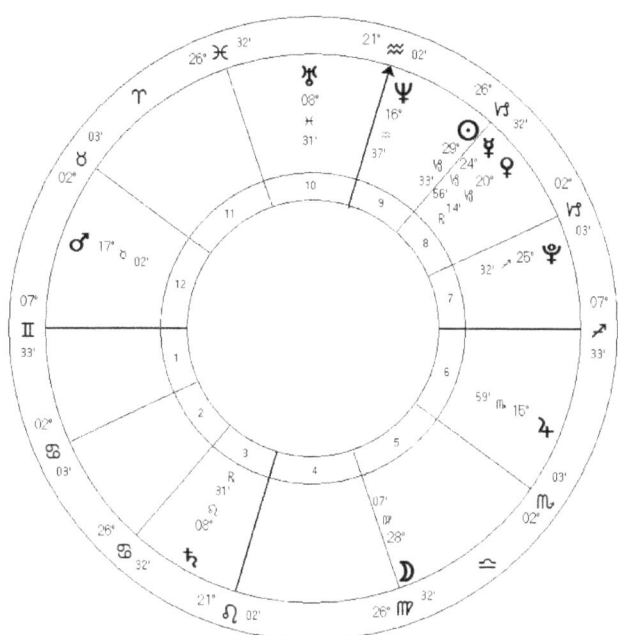

Example: Using the New Horizons Launch chart above, with longitude, latitude and declination data from an ephemeris, find the arc from Uranus to the Midheaven:

RA of MC = 323.424
Long Ur = 8Pi31 = 338d 31m = 338.517
Lat Ur = – 0d 44m = -0.733
Dec Ur = -9d 03m = -9.05

Using the above formula to convert Uranus longitude, latitude and declination positions to RA:

RA Ur = (cos -0.733 x cos 338.517) ÷ cos -9.05 = arc cos
= 19.579

This figure is obviously not right as it is. In this case subtract it from 360 = 340.42

RA Ur 340.42 – RAMC 323.424 = 16.999 (16h 59m)

Using a rate of a year per degree (see time values below), this means that at about 17 years from the launch (January 2023), Uranus will reach the Midheaven. Perhaps an abrupt or unique event may occur and change the mission.

Example: Using primary directions Saturn can be moved ahead in the zodiac to the IC and opposite the MC. This contact would not happen by rotation as Saturn would be moving away from the IC and toward the Ascendant, making it a converse direction.

First calculate the RA of Saturn given the following:

RA of IC = RAMC – 180 = 143.424
Sa longitude = 128d 32m = 128.53
Sa latitude = 0d 40m = 0.666
Sa declination = 18d 46m = 18.766

$$RA = arc\ cos\ \frac{(cos\ lat\ x\ cos\ long)}{cos\ dec}$$

(cos 0.666 x cos 128.53) ÷ cos 18.766 = arc cos = 131.136
= RA Sa

RA IC 143.424 – RA Sa 131.136 = 12.288 (12h 17m)

The IC conjunction with Saturn's position in RA occurs just over 12 years from the launch date. At a rate of 1 degree per year, this would be in early 2018. By solar arc, Saturn would conjunct the IC in May of 2008. Interestingly, New Horizon, which was in hibernation mode, crossed Saturn's orbit in on June 8, 2008.

Directing planets to the Ascendant or Descendant requires knowing a planet's RA when it is exactly on the horizon. This is complicated due to the fact that planets will rise and set at an oblique angle from the equator. Planets with extreme declinations may rise or set at times that are not so apparent when looking at a standard horoscope. To do these calculations the oblique ascension (OA) of the planet, which is the point on the equator that will rise at the same time the planet bodily crosses the horizon, is required. Since planets are not often exactly on the equator, there could be a big difference between these two points, the planet and the equatorial degree. Further, this situation is dependent on the geographical latitude, which varies the rising angle.

The oblique ascension OA of a point must be determined after determining its ascensional difference (AD) which is the difference between the RA of any body and its OA. This is found by subtracting the AD from the RA in the northern hemisphere, or the reverse for the southern.

OA = RA – AD

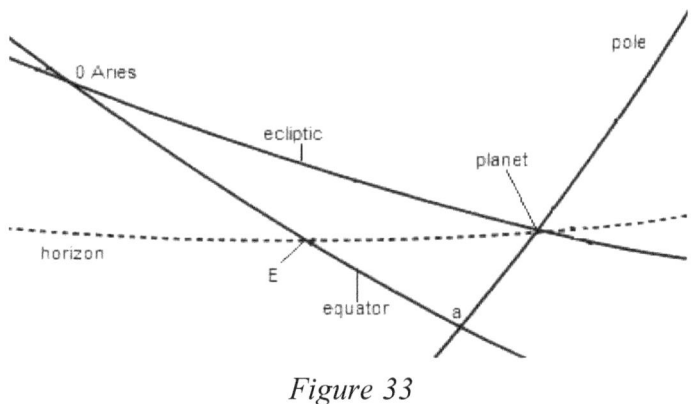

Figure 33

In Figure 33 a planet is located on the eastern horizon. A great circle from the pole of the equator is drawn through the planet to the horizon where it makes an angle equivalent to the geographical latitude, and is extended to the equator where it makes a right angle (a). A triangle E-planet-a is then formed. The point E on the equator that rises at the same time as the planet does is its OA. The planet's RA, located on the equator (at a), can be calculated from its longitude, latitude and declination. Given the geographical latitude, which is the same as the angle formed by E-planet-a, the side of the triangle E-a, the AD (Ascensional Difference), can be then be calculated.

Example: Finding the AD requires the declination and geographical latitude of the planet – not its celestial latitude. The example used

187

will be the primary direction from the Descendant to Pluto in the New Horizons Launch chart.

First compute the RA of the Descendant (7th house cusp) which is the RAMC – 90 = 323.424 – 90 = 233.424

Next calculate the RA of Pluto given:
Longitude = 25Sa32 = 265 32 or 265.533
Celestial Latitude = 7d 27m = 7.45
Declination = -15d 54m = -15.9

$$RA = arc \cos \frac{(\cos lat \times \cos long)}{\cos dec}$$

= (cos 7.45 x cos 265.533) ÷ cos (-15.9) = arc cos = 94.6
Subtract from 360 = 265.394 = RA of Pluto
Next calculate the AD of Pluto given geographical latitude = 28 N 24 or 28.4

AD = arc sin (tan declination x tan geographical lat)

(tan -15.9 x tan 28.4) = arc sin = -8.86

Then calculate OA which is RA – AD

265.394 + (-8.86) = 256.534

So as Earth rotates, the RA of the Descendant, which is 233.424, moves ahead in the zodiac. When it arrives at the oblique ascension of Pluto, which is 256.534, it will have traveled 23.11 degrees. Using a year per degree, Pluto will be on the west horizon in just over 23 years from January 2006, or in early 2029.

In contrast, the Descendant will advance by solar arc in the zodiac to the conjunction with Pluto in October, 2023. Here is a large discrepancy between primary directions and solar arc directions which treats all points as if on the ecliptic. The relative effectiveness of primaries vs solar arc remains untested (no serious scientific studies) with only anecdotal evidence reported.

There are two basic approaches to primaries, mundane position and zodiacal position. In zodiacal position the arcs are computed using the RA of the body as described above. In mundane position the distance between points is measured by their relative position within the houses. The distance of a semi-arc is equal to a square even though the distance may not equal 90 degrees.

Time values for primary directions include:

1. one degree for a year (Ptolemy)
2. Naibod arc or mean motion of Sun = 59' 8"
3. True motion of the Sun in RA, ranges from 54' to 66' (DeLuce)

Summary: Primary directions are based on the rotation of Earth where one degree of rotation corresponds to one year and one full rotation equals 360 years. In primary directions it is the actual bodily (on the horizon) rising or setting of a planet that counts for contacts between the Ascendant and a directed body. Directions in declination are also used. Primary directions is an old system, found in Ptolemy and developed over the centuries, that has been used to establish the primary events and also life periods of a nativity. It's logic follows from the complications of calculating the Ascendant and the houses.

Midpoints

Midpoints, used in Uranian astrology and Cosmobiology, are points that focus the principles or energies of two chart points. They are sensitive points in an event or natal chart, can be progressed or directed, and are also transiting points. To calculate a midpoint add the absolute longitudes of two chart points and divide by two. If the chart points are near an opposition, the calculation will result in a point on the axis between the two chart points, but not the one closest to the points. It may then be necessary to add or subtract 180.

Example: Find the midpoint of Mars and Pluto in the New Horizons launch chart.

1. Convert to absolute longitude:

Mars 17Ta02 = 47d 02m   or   47.033
Pluto 25Sa32 = 265 32   or   265.533

2. Add the two points:

47.033 + 265.533 = 312.566

3. Divide the sum by 2:

312.566 ÷ 2 = 156.283 = 156d 17m

4. Convert to zodiac: 156d 17m = 6Vi17

This result is the far midpoint between Mars and Pluto which are in a very wide opposition. The close midpoint would then be 6Pi17.

Composite Charts

A composite chart is a chart derived from two (or more) charts. The standard approach is to take like factors and calculate their midpoints. In other words, the midpoint of the two natal Suns becomes the Sun position in the composite chart. This calculation is most easily accomplished by converting all the planetary positions into absolute longitude.

Example: Moon in one chart (a) is at 26 Scorpio 37. The Moon in another (b) is at 13 Aries 22. Where is the composite Moon?

1. Convert to decimals, then to absolute, or true, longitude:
        a. 210 + 26.6167 =   236.6167
        b. 0 + 13.3667 =   13.3667
2. Add the two figures: =   249.9833
3. Divide by 2: =   124.9917 or 124d 59m

Although this figure corresponds to 4 degrees and 59 minutes of Leo, we need to consider if that point, or its opposite point in the zodiac is the midpoint we want to use. Since we know that these two Moon positions are not in opposition (if the second Moon was at 26 Taurus we'd have a close opposition), we can easily see that the closer midpoint would be at 4 degrees 59 minutes of Aquarius and the midpoint in Leo is the far midpoint. It has been the custom to use the closer midpoint for practical work, although midpoints between planets in exact opposition are often displayed in both positions. The close midpoint could also be found by adding 360 to the position of Moon (b) such that it equals 373.3667 which added to 236.6167 and divided by 2 equals 302.99 or 4 Aq 59. The main point to be learned here is that the computation of midpoints leads to the determination of an axis, and not a single position.

There are two common methods of creating houses into which the composite planets are placed. One method simply finds the midpoints of matching house cusps (which must be of the same house system!) and places these on the 12-house chart form. Another calculates the composite Midheaven, and then finds a derived Ascendant from a table of houses for the latitude in which the relationship is occurring. The other house cusps are likewise derived from this composite Midheaven.

Finally, composite charts built from more than two natal or event charts are possible. In such an instance, the absolute longitudes are added and then divided by the number of factors. For example, a composite chart derived from four natal charts will require that the four Sun positions are added up and then divided by 4 to obtain the composite Sun position.

Astro-Mapping

There are two major ways that a chart can be analyzed in terms of its location. One, the Radix Local Space Chart, involves the horizon coordinate system. The chart is presented as a 360 degree grid with the planetary positions given in azimuth shown as vectors radiating in specific directions from the birth location. For example, a planet at the Midheaven (in the northern hemisphere) would have an azimuth near to south and one setting would be roughly to the west. With precise figures for planetary azimuths, planet directions can be used locally or over long distances. The azimuth (and altitude) of each of the planets can be calculated using trigonometry, but this process will not be covered in this book.

More commonly a natal chart can be relocated to any other location. This change will be seen in the zodiacal degrees at the cusps of the houses but not in the planetary positions which will remain constant. Such charts are called relocated charts and are the basis of astrological cartographic maps that show with lines where planets were rising or culminating at the time of the event/birth. Relocated charts are easily calculated by doing the following:

1. Prepare to calculate the chart using the given time of the event/birth including the time zone and Daylight Saving time if it was in effect. Calculate the GMT as usual.

2. When calculating the LST, replace the birth location coordinates with those for the relocation. Do not change the time of the event/birth or time zone.

3. Calculate the chart angles and houses using this new LST. Calculate the planet positions using the GMT.

The result will be a chart with the planets in exactly the same zodiacal positions as for the original location, but in the context of a different Midheaven, Ascendant and intermediate houses. If the relocation was to the west of the original chart, the signs on the houses will move to positions earlier in the zodiac at a rate of very roughly a degree per each degree of terrestrial longitude. If relocated to the east, the houses will move ahead in the zodiac.

Planetary Period Systems

Planetary periods in time, designated by successive planetary rulerships according to a standardized system, were a core predictive technique in Hellenistic astrology. This technique, now known as zodiacal Releasing (aphesis), is an attempt to time the activation of the planets in the natal chart whereupon they become chronocrators or "time lords." The periods themselves, derived from real astronomical cycles of the planets, are blocks of time that are said to denote and describe the qualities of experience (presumably both subjective and objective) in a person's life. It appears that they were an application of astronomical tables useful for calculating planetary positions (before ephemerides) to natal dynamic analysis. In general, variations on a planet's synodic cycle were added to the date of birth in proscribed ways to designate periods when that planet would be dominant in life trends. For example, Venus and the sun (their synodic cycle) return to nearly the same positions every eight years. The planetary period for Venus in the zodiacal releasing technique is 8 years (the least period – see below), so at a point in life, determined by rules that allow for some variation based on the nature of individual horoscopes, an 8-year Venus-ruled period would be in effect and Venus would be the time lord. The actual effects/events during this period would be determined by Venus' dignity in the chart as well as a number of subperiods.

Planetary period systems are similar in principle to the dasas of Hindu astrology (Jyotish) which are an important part of that astrological system's predictive methodology. They are also similar in principle to the astrology of ancient Mesoamerica where blocks of time functioned as astrological signs. As stated above, planetary periods indicate times when a given planet expresses its power most directly, comes to the front, so to speak. The planet ruling a period becomes a vehicle for interpretation and shows links to specific areas of life. Subperiods with other planetary rulers complement or weaken the primary ruler and provide additional information. It is thought that stronger effects of planetary period rulership are experienced at the terminal phase of the period.

The profusion of complicated schemes involving planetary periods found in ancient writing are now being cataloged and experimented with. How well they work remains to be seen. Like much in astrology, it is very difficult to assign units and discriminate between real and imagined effects. It is entirely possible that planetary periods

may have been a complicated attempt to account for events not indicated by the visible planets and that, because the least years of the
planets are real synodic cycles, and these are applied in fractal-like
manner like progressions, genuine correlations between method and
reality do occur.

Planetary periods are established one planet at a time, which are
then called chronocrators or "Time-Lords." These time periods are at
least three in number, most of them relating to astronomical synch-
ronicities of the orbits of the planets and their relationship to the Sun
(synodic cycle). There are some issues that are being sorted out, for
example whether to use the 365 day civil year or the 360-day Egyptian year. For these reasons I will only set out the numerical value of
the traditional periods and leave the reader to explore the various
forms of the technique. The primary sources for information on the
Greek Planetary Periods are Ptolemy IV.10, Valens IV.1, Hermes,
and Bonatti. Delphic Oracle software produced by Curtis Manwar-
ing offers a great deal of information and, of course, calculations for
the techniques of Hellenistic astrology.

The *Least Years* of the planets

Saturn - 30 years: 29 synodic cycles in 30 years.
    (29 x 378.1 = 30.02 years)

Jupiter - 12 years: 11 synodic cycles in 12 years.
    (11 x 398.9 = 12.01 years)
Mars - 15 years: 7 synodic cycles in 15 years.
    (7 x 780 = 14.95 years)

Venus - 8 years: 5 synodic cycles equals 8 solar years.
    (5 x 584 = 8 years)

Sun - 19 years: Metonic cycle linking Sun and Moon.
    (19 x 365.24 = 6939.56 days, 235 x 29.53 = 6939.55 days)

Mercury - 20 years: 63 synodic cycles in 20 years.
    (115.9 x 63 = 19.99 years)

Moon - 25 years: 309 lunation cycles in 25 years.
   (29.53 x 309 = 24.98 years)

The *Greatest Years* of the planets

Sun's greatest year of 1461 = 4 x 365 + 1 year (4 x 365.25 = 1461). This is the Sothic year, the time needed for any calendar day to cycle through the entire seasonal year.

Venus' greatest year of 1151 may be related to the retrograding cycle of its five stationary points.

Jupiter's greatest year of 427 years = 36 sidereal cycles of 11.86 years.

Saturn's greatest year of 265 years = 9 sidereal cycles of 29.46 years.

Mars' greatest year of 284 years = 151 sidereal cycles of 1.88 years.

The *Great Years* of the planets are the sums of degrees allocated to each planet in Ptolemaic and Egyptian systems of bounds or terms. The great years may be approximate ratios of the 365.24-day solar year and planetary sidereal cycles. Venus' great year of 82 years = 133 sidereal cycles of 225 days and Mars' great year of 66 years = 35 sidereal cycles of 1.88 years. Interestingly, the Hindu dasas, which are very similar to the Western time periods, add up to 120 years, the same as the Sun's great year. There are also the *Mean Years* of the planets. The formula for these values is least years + great years divided by 2. This method doesn't compute for the Sun and Moon.

The planetary periods were subdivided in various ways after a starting point was determined by the individual horoscope. Valens began the sequence of periods with the Part of Fortune for matters of fortune, and matters of the body with the Part of Spirit. In this approach, the ruler of the sign that the Part is located in determines the first time-lord. Subsequent time-lords follow by rulership in zodiacal order. One method divides each of these primary periods into months equivalent to the planet's least years. Here the ruling time lord rules the first part of the entire period itself. After 17 years and 10 months, the time equivalent to all the time periods expressed in months, the cycle picks up at the opposite point in the zodiac (called "loosing of the bond") and continues in the same manner.

There are also variations on the Time-Lords of the minor periods. The *Decennia* uses the sum of the minor periods of the planets expressed in months. Each planet rules for 10 years and 9 months (129 months). This system begins with the Sun for a diurnal birth, the Moon for nocturnal birth. Another version begins with the first planet after the Ascendant. In either case, the next planet in zodiacal order rules the second period. Each of these periods is subdivided according to the order of the planets using the same time proportions of the least periods, but in months instead of years. This method is found in Valens 6 and Maternus 2:26, 6:33.

Another method is called the *Quarters*. In this scheme 129 years is divided into fourths or 4 cycles of 32y 3m. The first time-lord is determined by the planet following the prenatal new or full moon. Valens describes a time-lord system of 9 years for each planet that begins with the domicile ruler of the Moon, computed proportionally. All of the above methodologies are in the process of being recovered, worked out and tested and I refer the reader to more recent works on this subject.

Firdaria or Fardariyat

These planetary periods, having Arabic names, were used by Dorotheus and later by Abu Ma'shar. The *fardar* is a planetary period, one used to date historical events, an application of astrology that was permissible in ancient Islamic culture. The mighty fardar is 360 years, based on sums of zodiac signs and planets. The big fardar is 78 years shared by the 12 signs numbered 12 to 1, backwards in the zodiac. The middle fardar is 75 years, ruled by the 7 planets and nodes. Each planetary period is divided into 7ths (no nodes). The lord of the first rules the first period, the others follow in order of the exaltations. Ma'shar gives the order of these planetary periods according to exaltations:

196

Planet	exaltation	years ruled
Sun	19 Aries	10
Moon	3 Taurus	9
North Node	3 Gemini	3
Jupiter	15 Cancer	12
Mercury	15 Virgo	13
Saturn	21 Libra	11
South Node	3 Sagittarius	2
Mars	28 Capricorn	7
Venus	27 Pisces	8

The Firdaria according to Bonatti and Ibn Ezra is applied to nativities. They use the same planetary periods but in the Chaldean order. Diurnal births start with the Sun, nocturnal births start with the Moon. These planetary periods are easier to work with because their application is so consistent.

A note might be made about the very popular *Vimshotarri Dasa* system from Vedic astrology. It uses the same nine factors as the Firdaria and is also applied to nativities. The scheme works as follows: First there is a translation of the natal Moon's position in its lunar mansion (Nakshatra) into a portion of its planetary rulers period. The rest of the life is divided according to the usual order of the dasas. Subperiods are called bhuktis, and then further subperiods are called antardasas. Key to interpretation lies in placing the dasha ruler on the Ascendant and examining its relations with the other planets, particularly the bhukti subrulers.

Profections

Profections utilize the sequence of houses to determine the changing nature and qualities of time for an individual. One will notice that there is as little agreement among the ancients in regard to this technique as there was on the planetary periods. Maternus begins with, or profects, the Ascendant at the rate of $^1/_{12}$ of the zodiac per year. The subperiods are based on the division of the year into proportions that reflect the least periods of the planets. These are the Sun-53 days, Moon-71, Saturn-85, Jupiter-30, Mars-42, Venus-23, Mercury-57 = 361. The ruler of the current profection starts the year, it is followed by the next planet in zodiacal order, etc. See Maternus, Book 2:28.

Ptolemy profects one sign at a time but uses only the ruler of the profected sign. Valens (Valens 4) begins with a significator that rules the first year, and then moves ahead at a rate of one sign per year. If a planet occupies a sign, it rules the period but if there is no planet, then a transiting planet that happens to be in that sign rules the period. If there is no transiting planet, then the ruler of the sign rules the period. Manilius (Book 3) profects from the Ascendant, the succeeding months are ruled by the following signs. It appears that he uses 13 months per year. Dorotheus (Book 4) also profects from the Ascendant and the lords of the houses. Clearly much brush clearing (archaeoastrology) needs to be done with many of these ancient predictive techniques.

Chapter 11

Calculations, Exams and the Certification of Astrologers

Astrology is a subject that includes theory, research, its own history and, of course, practice. However, the majority of people who call themselves astrologers only identify with the later and are barely cognizant of the other dimensions of the subject. Because of this the public only knows astrology as horoscopes and readers. As a practice, astrology calls upon many skills and talents, and it can be argued that not all people have these in the right combination, making the interpretation of horoscopes something akin to musicianship. Some get it right away, others can labor for years and not get very far. But without strong professional standards, just about anyone can say they are an astrologer and go about the business of doing readings for people. In some cases, talent may succeed, but often enthusiastic and deluded self-promoters will hurt clients and damage the field's already battered public reputation. It is this problem that certification for astrologers attempts to address.

In the effort to qualify or certify astrologers a number of large astrological organizations have created standards and some of them include the requirement of chart calculation. In part, this was because these certification programs (USA organizations AFA and NCGR in particular) were put together by a generation of astrologers who had to know how to calculate a chart by hand as there was no alternative at the time. But it was also thought by the developers of certification exams that knowledge of chart calculations was valuable for two important reasons. The first is that anyone capable of calculating a horoscope would have at least some idea of what a horoscope is based on, i.e. the rotation of the Earth, coordinate systems, different kinds of time, planetary daily motions, etc., and this sort of knowledge would be expected from professionals in other disciplines. Without learning how to cast a chart, it is quite possible that a large number of people with professional certification would be sent into the world with a very weak knowledge of astronomy and thus be ignorant of basics – and also be easy targets for astrology's many critics. After all, it is only the astronomical realities of the horoscope that keep astrology as a practice from being not much more than a psychologically-informed divination system. The second reason is that, in the process of calculating a horoscope, much information is gleaned about the chart itself and this aids in interpretation. Examples include the daily motion of the Moon and planets, the duration of each rising sign, and the effects of declination and other measurements.

For about three quarters of the 20th century most astrologers calculated horoscopes using ephemerides and various interpolation tables. Logarithms, and sometimes slide rules, were used to manipulate figures. Then in the early 1970s came calculators, and by the late 1970s and early 1980s, computers. Suddenly, time-consuming horoscope calculations could be accomplished in split seconds. Complex and difficult to calculate techniques, and some that had been proposed but were rarely used, were now there to try out on the menus of the many astrology software packages that were being produced. Even certain kinds of interpretive summaries, like essential dignities and astrodynes, were possible in a single keystroke. With this came the question, why bother to cast charts by hand anymore? And following that, why should chart calculations be on professional astrology exams? Meanwhile, the generation that had created the exams was still dominant and as the years went by, many of them insisted on keeping this requirement. Then, during the late 1990s, the astrological organization ISAR adopted a professional certification exam that is focused primarily on interpretation and consulting and does not require the calculation of a chart, though there are some questions about the process and related astronomy. However, calculations remain on the AFA and NCGR-PAA exams. At the time of this writing (2017) there continues to be some buzz about doing something about this, but no consensus has been reached.

The deeper questions in all of this are not just about calculating charts, they are about what kind of knowledge is important to the professionalization of the field of astrology and how it should be tested. The standard routine of chart calculation is really fairly mindless. It's basically high school arithmetic and one can learn it and yet not understand much, if anything, about the astronomy and mathematics that lies behind the horoscope; coordinate systems, time, the motions of the solar system, trigonometry, etc. (It's this situation that this book is attempting to address.) From a broad perspective, astrological chart calculation does have a long tradition, however, and that may count for something. It is a major part of the history of astrology. There are, after all, other professions (eg. surveying, nursing) that, even in today's digital world, require traditional calculations and technical information for professional certifications or licenses. But if chart calculation is to be dropped from the list of professional requirements, what should replace it? What might a future exam look like?

We could begin solving this problem by laying out specific categories of subject material that would be addressed in questions on exams. The first of these should be the astronomy of the solar system. This topic is often taught at colleges and universities as part of an introductory astronomy course, and is sometimes a course of its own. Any professional astrologer should have a good scientific understanding of the solar system that would include its origin, evolution, description, and composition. Of course, the physical nature of the planets, including data such as size, composition and orbital periods should be considered foundational. An understanding of the geocentric versus heliocentric perspectives, and their place in the history of science, must be a focus topic and from there the range of daily motions of the planets, the phenomena of retrogradation, eclipses and the various types of cycles would be referenced. One possibility would be to require a first-year college course on astronomy from a reputable institution as part of a prerequisite to taking an astrology exam. An objection to this is that most astronomy courses in the academic spend little time on the information most relevant to someone studying astrology. Some astrology schools, however, do offer astronomy courses that place far more emphasis on matters essential to astrologers such as coordinate systems, the history of astronomy and the physical nature of solar system bodies. Perhaps courses like these should be required before taking exams.

The translation of planetary phenomena to ephemeris listings leads to the crucial topic in astronomy that pertains to the horoscope: co-ordinate systems. Exam takers should be required to understand the distinctions between the horizon, equatorial and ecliptic systems and should be able to answer questions about planetary positions in each and perhaps why certain measurements are done in one system rather than another, i.e. planet longitudes being charted against the ecliptic but declinations measured from the equator. While trigono-metric calculations shouldn't be required, some understanding how planets are located and translated between coordinate systems might be.

The ecliptic in particular should be emphasized, in particular the dis-tinction between the tropical and sidereal zodiacs. How is one zo-diac based on the Earth and its orbit around the Sun, and the other on its location against the background of stars? Every educated as-trologer should be able to explain to critics, who have a special taste for this apparent discrepancy, the rationale and differences. Related, and should be on exams, are the mechanics of precession, the nature of its two primary cycles (precession of the equinoxes and climatic precession – see page 12) and implications for the zodiac. In addi-tion, the obliquity and ellipticity cycles that are known to have con-nections to long-term climate change might be included under this category.

The change in rate of ascension of the signs involves knowledge of coordinate systems and the rotating Earth. This can be seen best in an animation or in a planetarium, but it is fundamental to the diurnal cycle that produces the houses. This phenomena has a long history of great value in interpretation. Unfortunately, these topics are barely treated in nearly all college and university introductory as-tronomy courses.

The topic of house systems will need to be on any professional exam. Knowledge of the major house systems, including their fun-damental logic, and what coordinate systems are employed to con-struct them, should be tested. Topics should include the division of the semi-arcs and the distortion of the horoscope at high latitudes, the varying angle between Midheaven and Ascendant over the course of a day, and the diurnal motion of planets through the houses. Testing of house systems should require the ability to read diagrams of the celestial sphere that depict various house systems and distinguish between them. Some knowledge of the history of house systems might be on this part of an exam.

Finally, the astronomical basis of the horoscope must be tested. This could be done in two stages. First, exam takers should be required to translate the horoscopic grid itself into the appropriate astronomical components, that is explain exactly what it is. Given a horoscope containing the sun, moon and only one or two planets, an examinee with an ephemeris should be able to roughly determine the time, date and the year it was calculated for. This knowledge would be extremely valuable in a situation where astrological software was malfunctioning. Additional questions could be asked about where each planet was in its cycle relative to the Sun (synodic cycle) or relative to other planets, both of which are relevant to interpretation. Details like the hourly motion of the angles and the risings and settings of planets during the period immediately following the time of the horoscope might also be questioned.

An exam requiring the above would certainly not be any easier than one that requires the calculation of a chart. It would, however, require precisely the kind of knowledge that would help in defining what astrology really is to the outside world and bring it in line with other subjects, particularly the sciences. Such insights generally do not come with knowing how to read from tables and calculate an astrology chart, which is the only requirement at the present time on the AFA and NCGR-PAA exams.

A possible compromise in all this would be to allow those taking astrological certification exams a choice between (1) a wide range of questions on the astronomy of the horoscope or (2) the calculation of a chart by hand, either being acceptable.

The separation of the astronomical and mathematical underpinnings of the horoscope, the primary tool of astrology, from interpretation and consulting does not bode well for the future of the field of astrology. The astronomy and mathematics in astrology, and its long history, is precisely what the subject needs to survive as a viable field of study and practice. In addition, astrology needs to embrace more enthusiastically the rigorous scientific study of its subject material and come to rely less on tradition and more on democratically-generated knowledge, by this I mean scientific studies. Without either of these, astrology has no backbone, fails as a real subject with a possible future in the academic world (where it once was), and becomes merely a kind of divination and pop psychology dominated by those with charisma and natural promotional and sales abilities.

Tables for Calculations

(All tables in this section calculated by the author using Apache Open Office *Calculate* and Astrolabe *Solar Fire* software except where otherwise noted.)

Daily Ephemeris

The ephemeris below is a 1-month sample of a typical planetary ephemeris. Across from each day is the sidereal time for midnight Greenwich Time and the positions of the Moon, Sun, Mercury, Venus and Mars at that time. The positions for Jupiter, Saturn, Uranus, Neptune and Pluto are found on the next page. Normally all the planets would be listed on one page, space considerations necessitated splitting the ephemeris.

Date	S.T.	Moon	Sun	Mercury	Venus	Mars
Jan 1 2006	06:42:01	22°Cp23'	10°Cp25'	25°Sg39'	00°Aq16'	R11°Ta04'
Jan 2 2006	06:45:58	07°Aq18'	11°Cp26'	27°Sg09'	29°Cp56'	11°Ta19'
Jan 3 2006	06:49:54	22°Aq10'	12°Cp27'	28°Sg39'	29°Cp34'	11°Ta34'
Jan 4 2006	06:53:51	06°Pi52'	13°Cp28'	00°Cp09'	29°Cp10'	11°Ta50'
Jan 5 2006	06:57:47	21°Pi17'	14°Cp29'	01°Cp40'	28°Cp43'	12°Ta07'
Jan 6 2006	07:01:44	05°Ar24'	15°Cp31'	03°Cp11'	28°Cp15'	12°Ta24'
Jan 7 2006	07:05:40	19°Ar12'	16°Cp32'	04°Cp43'	27°Cp45'	12°Ta41'
Jan 8 2006	07:09:37	02°Ta42'	17°Cp33'	06°Cp15'	27°Cp13'	12°Ta59'
Jan 9 2006	07:13:33	15°Ta56'	18°Cp34'	07°Cp48'	26°Cp39'	13°Ta18'
Jan 10 2006	07:17:30	28°Ta56'	19°Cp35'	09°Cp21'	26°Cp05'	13°Ta37'
Jan 11 2006	07:21:27	11°Ge44'	20°Cp36'	10°Cp54'	25°Cp29'	13°Ta56'
Jan 12 2006	07:25:23	24°Ge21'	21°Cp38'	12°Cp28'	24°Cp53'	14°Ta15'
Jan 13 2006	07:29:20	06°Cn48'	22°Cp39'	14°Cp03'	24°Cp17'	14°Ta36'
Jan 14 2006	07:33:16	19°Cn06'	23°Cp40'	15°Cp37'	23°Cp40'	14°Ta56'
Jan 15 2006	07:37:13	01°Le15'	24°Cp41'	17°Cp13'	23°Cp03'	15°Ta17'
Jan 16 2006	07:41:09	13°Le15'	25°Cp42'	18°Cp48'	22°Cp26'	15°Ta38'
Jan 17 2006	07:45:06	25°Le09'	26°Cp43'	20°Cp25	21°Cp50'	16°Ta00'
Jan 18 2006	07:49:02	06°Vi58'	27°Cp44'	22°Cp01'	21°Cp15'	16°Ta22'
Jan 19 2006	07:52:59	18°Vi45'	28°Cp45'	23°Cp39'	20°Cp41'	16°Ta44'
Jan 20 2006	07:56:56	00°Li35'	29°Cp46'	25°Cp16'	20°Cp08'	17°Ta07'
Jan 21 2006	08:00:52	12°Li30'	00°Aq47'	26°Cp55'	19°Cp36'	17°Ta30'
Jan 22 2006	08:04:49	24°Li37'	01°Aq48'	28°Cp34'	19°Cp06'	17°Ta53'
Jan 23 2006	08:08:45	07°Sc01'	02°Aq49'	00°Aq13'	18°Cp38'	18°Ta17'
Jan 24 2006	08:12:42	19°Sc47'	03°Aq50'	01°Aq53'	18°Cp12'	18°Ta41'
Jan 25 2006	08:16:38	02°Sg59'	04°Aq51'	03°Aq34'	17°Cp49'	19°Ta05'
Jan 26 2006	08:20:35	16°Sg41'	05°Aq52'	05°Aq16'	17°Cp27'	19°Ta29'
Jan 27 2006	08:24:31	00°Cp53'	06°Aq53'	06°Aq58'	17°Cp08'	19°Ta54'
Jan 28 2006	08:28:28	15°Cp32'	07°Aq54'	08°Aq40'	16°Cp51'	20°Ta19'
Jan 29 2006	08:32:25	00°Aq31'	08°Aq55'	10°Aq23'	16°Cp36'	20°Ta45'
Jan 30 2006	08:36:21	15°Aq43'	09°Aq56'	12°Aq07'	16°Cp24'	21°Ta10'

Date	Jupiter	Saturn	Uranus	Neptune	Pluto
Jan 1 2006	13°Sc18'	09°Le55'	R07°Pi43'	15°Aq58'	24°Sg53'
Jan 2 2006	13°Sc27'	09°Le51'	07°Pi45'	16°Aq00'	24°Sg55'
Jan 3 2006	13°Sc37'	09°Le47'	07°Pi47'	16°Aq02'	24°Sg57'
Jan 4 2006	13°Sc46'	09°Le43'	07°Pi50'	16°Aq04'	24°Sg59'
Jan 5 2006	13°Sc55'	09°Le39'	07°Pi52'	16°Aq06'	25°Sg02'
Jan 6 2006	14°Sc05'	09°Le34'	07°Pi54'	16°Aq08'	25°Sg04'
Jan 7 2006	14°Sc14'	09°Le30'	07°Pi57'	16°Aq10'	25°Sg06'
Jan 8 2006	14°Sc23'	09°Le26'	07°Pi59'	16°Aq12'	25°Sg08'
Jan 9 2006	14°Sc32'	09°Le21'	08°Pi02'	16°Aq14'	25°Sg10'
Jan 10 2006	14°Sc40'	09°Le17'	08°Pi04'	16°Aq16'	25°Sg12'
Jan 11 2006	14°Sc49'	09°Le12'	08°Pi07'	16°Aq18'	25°Sg14'
Jan 12 2006	14°Sc57'	09°Le08'	08°Pi09'	16°Aq20'	25°Sg16'
Jan 13 2006	15°Sc06'	09°Le03'	08°Pi12'	16°Aq23'	25°Sg18'
Jan 14 2006	15°Sc14'	08°Le59'	08°Pi15'	16°Aq25'	25°Sg20'
Jan 15 2006	15°Sc22'	08°Le54'	08°Pi17'	16°Aq27'	25°Sg22'
Jan 16 2006	15°Sc30'	08°Le49'	08°Pi20'	16°Aq29'	25°Sg24'
Jan 17 2006	15°Sc38'	08°Le45'	08°Pi23'	16°Aq31'	25°Sg26'
Jan 18 2006	15°Sc46'	08°Le40'	08°Pi26'	16°Aq33'	25°Sg28'
Jan 19 2006	15°Sc53'	08°Le35'	08°Pi28'	16°Aq36'	25°Sg30'
Jan 20 2006	16°Sc01'	08°Le30'	08°Pi31'	16°Aq38'	25°Sg32'
Jan 21 2006	16°Sc08'	08°Le25'	08°Pi34'	16°Aq40'	25°Sg34'
Jan 22 2006	16°Sc15'	08°Le21'	08°Pi37'	16°Aq42'	25°Sg36'
Jan 23 2006	16°Sc22'	08°Le16'	08°Pi40'	16°Aq44'	25°Sg38'
Jan 24 2006	16°Sc29'	08°Le11'	08°Pi43'	16°Aq47'	25°Sg40'
Jan 25 2006	16°Sc36'	08°Le06'	08°Pi46'	16°Aq49'	25°Sg42'
Jan 26 2006	16°Sc43'	08°Le01'	08°Pi49'	16°Aq51'	25°Sg44'
Jan 27 2006	16°Sc49'	07°Le56'	08°Pi52'	16°Aq53'	25°Sg45'
Jan 28 2006	16°Sc55'	07°Le51'	08°Pi55'	16°Aq56'	25°Sg47'
Jan 29 2006	17°Sc02'	07°Le46'	08°Pi58'	16°Aq58'	25°Sg49'
Jan 30 2006	17°Sc08'	07°Le41'	09°Pi01'	17°Aq00'	25°Sg51'

Date	S.T.	Moon	Sun	Mercury	Venus	Mars
Nov 25 1942	04:13:13	25°Ge53'	02°Sg05'	28°Sc39'	04°Sg10'	15°Sc39'
Nov 26 1942	04:17:10	07°Cn46'	03°Sg05'	00°Sg14'	05°Sg26'	16°Sc20'
Nov 27 1942	04:21:06	19°Cn36'	04°Sg06'	01°Sg48'	06°Sg41'	17°Sc01'
Nov 28 1942	04:25:03	01°Le23'	05°Sg07'	03°Sg23'	07°Sg57'	17°Sc43'
Nov 29 1942	04:28:59	13°Le14'	06°Sg07'	04°Sg58'	09°Sg12'	18°Sc24'

	Jupiter	Saturn	Uranus	Neptune	Pluto
Nov 25 1942	24°Cn58'R	09°Ge35'R	02°Ge35'R	01°Li36'	07°Le11' R
Nov 26 1942	24°Cn56'	09°Ge30'	02°Ge32'	01°Li38'	07°Le11'
Nov 27 1942	24°Cn53'	09°Ge25'	02°Ge30'	01°Li39'	07°Le10'
Nov 28 1942	24°Cn50'	09°Ge21'	02°Ge27'	01°Li40'	07°Le10'
Nov 29 1942	24°Cn47'	09°Ge16'	02°Ge25'	01°Li41'	07°Le09'

Ephemeris generated by Solar Fire astrological software published by Astrolabe, Inc.

Table of Midheavens and Ascendants

This table replicates part of what is found in a typical table of houses. Because it is designed for educational purposes, and also because of space restrictions and the practicality of avoiding tiny typefaces, it provides limited information within a relatively narrow range. It does contain the most important information, that is the Local Sidereal Time (LST), the Midheaven and Ascendants for seven latitudes. (*This table has been provided by Barry Orr.*)

LST	MC	25N	30N	35N	40N	45N	50N	55N
0h00'	0ar00	10ca31	12ca56	15ca34	18ca28	21ca42	25ca22	29ca37
0h04'	1ar05	11ca24	13ca49	16ca25	19ca17	22ca29	26ca07	0le18
0h08'	2ar11	12ca17	14ca41	17ca16	20ca07	23ca17	26ca52	0le60
0h12'	3ar16	13ca10	15ca33	18ca07	20ca56	24ca04	27ca37	1le41
0h16'	4ar22	14ca03	16ca24	18ca57	21ca45	24ca51	28ca21	2le22
0h20'	5ar27	14ca55	17ca16	19ca48	22ca34	25ca38	29ca05	3le03
0h24'	6ar32	15ca48	18ca08	20ca38	23ca22	26ca24	29ca50	3le44
0h28'	7ar37	16ca41	18ca59	21ca28	24ca11	27ca11	0le34	4le25
0h32'	8ar43	17ca33	19ca51	22ca19	24ca60	27ca58	1le18	5le06
0h36'	9ar48	18ca26	20ca42	23ca09	25ca48	28ca44	2le01	5le47
0h40'	10ar53	19ca18	21ca33	23ca59	26ca36	29ca30	2le45	6le28
0h44'	11ar58	20ca10	22ca25	24ca48	27ca24	0le16	3le29	7le08
0h48'	13ar03	21ca03	23ca16	25ca38	28ca12	1le02	4le13	7le49
0h52'	14ar08	21ca55	24ca07	26ca28	29ca01	1le48	4le56	8le29
0h56'	15ar12	22ca47	24ca58	27ca17	29ca48	2le34	5le40	9le10
1h00'	16ar17	23ca39	25ca49	28ca07	0le36	3le20	6le23	9le50
1h04'	17ar21	24ca31	26ca40	28ca56	1le24	4le06	7le06	10le30
1h08'	18ar26	25ca23	27ca30	29ca46	2le12	4le52	7le50	11le11
1h12'	19ar30	26ca15	28ca21	0le35	2le59	5le37	8le33	11le51
1h16'	20ar34	27ca07	29ca12	1le24	3le47	6le23	9le16	12le31
1h20'	21ar38	27ca59	0le03	2le14	4le35	7le08	9le59	13le11
1h24'	22ar42	28ca51	0le53	3le03	5le22	7le54	10le42	13le52
1h28'	23ar46	29ca43	1le44	3le52	6le10	8le39	11le25	14le32
1h32'	24ar50	0le35	2le35	4le41	6le57	9le25	12le08	15le12
1h36'	25ar53	1le27	3le25	5le30	7le44	10le10	12le51	15le52
1h40'	26ar57	2le19	4le16	6le20	8le32	10le55	13le34	16le32
1h44'	27ar60	3le11	5le07	7le09	9le19	11le41	14le17	17le12
1h48'	29ar03	4le03	5le57	7le58	10le06	12le26	14le60	17le52
1h52'	0ta06	4le55	6le48	8le47	10le54	13le11	15le42	18le32
1h56'	1ta08	5le47	7le38	9le36	11le41	13le56	16le25	19le12
2h00'	2ta11	6le39	8le29	10le25	12le28	14le41	17le08	19le52
2h04'	3ta13	7le31	9le20	11le14	13le15	15le26	17le51	20le32
2h08'	4ta16	8le23	10le10	12le03	14le02	16le12	18le33	21le12
2h12'	5ta18	9le15	11le01	12le52	14le50	16le57	19le16	21le51
2h16'	6ta19	10le07	11le51	13le41	15le37	17le42	19le59	22le31

LST	MC	25N	30N	35N	40N	45N	50N	55N
2h20'	7ta21	10le59	12le42	14le30	16le24	18le27	20le41	23le11
2h24'	8ta23	11le51	13le33	15le19	17le11	19le12	21le24	23le51
2h28'	9ta24	12le44	14le24	16le08	17le58	19le57	22le07	24le31
2h32'	10ta25	13le36	15le14	16le57	18le45	20le42	22le49	25le11
2h36'	11ta26	14le28	16le05	17le46	19le32	21le27	23le32	25le51
2h40'	12ta27	15le21	16le56	18le35	20le20	22le12	24le15	26le31
2h44'	13ta27	16le13	17le47	19le24	21le07	22le57	24le57	27le11
2h48'	14ta28	17le05	18le37	20le13	21le54	23le42	25le40	27le51
2h52'	15ta28	17le58	19le28	21le02	22le41	24le27	26le23	28le31
2h56'	16ta28	18le50	20le19	21le51	23le28	25le12	27le05	29le11
3h00'	17ta28	19le43	21le10	22le40	24le16	25le57	27le48	29le51
3h04'	18ta28	20le36	22le01	23le30	25le03	26le43	28le31	0vi31
3h08'	19ta27	21le28	22le52	24le19	25le50	27le28	29le14	1vi11
3h12'	20ta27	22le21	23le43	25le08	26le37	28le13	29le56	1vi50
3h16'	21ta26	23le14	24le34	25le57	27le25	28le58	0vi39	2vi30
3h20'	22ta25	24le07	25le25	26le47	28le12	29le43	1vi22	3vi10
3h24'	23ta23	24le60	26le16	27le36	28le59	0vi28	2vi04	3vi50
3h28'	24ta22	25le53	27le08	28le25	29le47	1vi13	2vi47	4vi31
3h32'	25ta21	26le46	27le59	29le15	0vi34	1vi58	3vi30	5vi11
3h36'	26ta19	27le39	28le50	0vi04	1vi21	2vi44	4vi13	5vi51
3h40'	27ta17	28le32	29le42	0vi53	2vi09	3vi29	4vi55	6vi31
3h44'	28ta15	29le25	0vi33	1vi43	2vi56	4vi14	5vi38	7vi11
3h48'	29ta13	0vi18	1vi24	2vi32	3vi44	4vi59	6vi21	7vi51
3h52'	0ge11	1vi11	2vi16	3vi22	4vi31	5vi45	7vi04	8vi31
3h56'	1ge08	2vi05	3vi07	4vi12	5vi19	6vi30	7vi47	9vi11
4h00'	2ge05	2vi58	3vi59	5vi01	6vi06	7vi15	8vi29	9vi51
4h04'	3ge03	3vi52	4vi50	5vi51	6vi54	8vi00	9vi12	10vi31
4h08'	3ge60	4vi45	5vi42	6vi40	7vi41	8vi46	9vi55	11vi11
4h12'	4ge57	5vi39	6vi34	7vi30	8vi29	9vi31	10vi38	11vi52
4h16'	5ge54	6vi32	7vi25	8vi20	9vi16	10vi16	11vi21	12vi32
4h20'	6ge50	7vi26	8vi17	9vi09	10vi04	11vi02	12vi04	13vi12
4h24'	7ge47	8vi20	9vi09	9vi59	10vi52	11vi47	12vi47	13vi52
4h28'	8ge43	9vi14	10vi01	10vi49	11vi39	12vi33	13vi30	14vi32
4h32'	9ge40	10vi07	10vi53	11vi39	12vi27	13vi18	14vi13	15vi13
4h36'	10ge36	11vi01	11vi44	12vi29	13vi15	14vi03	14vi56	15vi53
4h40'	11ge32	11vi55	12vi36	13vi19	14vi02	14vi49	15vi39	16vi33
4h44'	12ge28	12vi49	13vi28	14vi08	14vi50	15vi34	16vi22	17vi13
4h48'	13ge24	13vi43	14vi20	14vi58	15vi38	16vi20	17vi05	17vi54
4h52'	14ge20	14vi37	15vi12	15vi48	16vi26	17vi05	17vi48	18vi34
4h56'	15ge16	15vi31	16vi04	16vi38	17vi14	17vi51	18vi31	19vi14
5h00'	16ge11	16vi25	16vi57	17vi28	18vi01	18vi36	19vi14	19vi55
5h04'	17ge07	17vi20	17vi49	18vi18	18vi49	19vi22	19vi57	20vi35
5h08'	18ge02	18vi14	18vi41	19vi08	19vi37	20vi07	20vi40	21vi15
5h12'	18ge58	19vi08	19vi33	19vi58	20vi25	20vi53	21vi23	21vi56
5h16'	19ge53	20vi02	20vi25	20vi49	21vi13	21vi38	22vi06	22vi36
5h20'	20ge49	20vi56	21vi17	21vi39	22vi01	22vi24	22vi49	23vi16
5h24'	21ge44	21vi51	22vi10	22vi29	22vi49	23vi10	23vi32	23vi57
5h28'	22ge39	22vi45	23vi02	23vi19	23vi37	23vi55	24vi15	24vi37
5h32'	23ge34	23vi39	23vi54	24vi09	24vi24	24vi41	24vi58	25vi17

208

LST	MC	25N	30N	35N	40N	45N	50N	55N
5h36'	24ge30	24vi34	24vi46	24vi59	25vi12	25vi26	25vi41	25vi58
5h40'	25ge25	25vi28	25vi39	25vi49	26vi00	26vi12	26vi24	26vi38
5h44'	26ge20	26vi22	26vi31	26vi39	26vi48	26vi58	27vi08	27vi18
5h48'	27ge15	27vi17	27vi23	27vi30	27vi36	27vi43	27vi51	27vi59
5h52'	28ge10	28vi11	28vi15	28vi20	28vi24	28vi29	28vi34	28vi39
5h56'	29ge05	29vi06	29vi08	29vi10	29vi12	29vi14	29vi17	29vi20
6h00'	0ca00	0li00	0li00	0li00	0li00	0li00	0li00	0li00
6h04'	0ca55	0li54	0li52	0li50	0li48	0li46	0li43	0li40
6h08'	1ca50	1li49	1li45	1li40	1li36	1li31	1li26	1li21
6h12'	2ca45	2li43	2li37	2li30	2li24	2li17	2li09	2li01
6h16'	3ca40	3li38	3li29	3li21	3li12	3li02	2li52	2li42
6h20'	4ca35	4li32	4li21	4li11	3li60	3li48	3li36	3li22
6h24'	5ca30	5li26	5li14	5li01	4li48	4li34	4li19	4li02
6h28'	6ca26	6li21	6li06	5li51	5li36	5li19	5li02	4li43
6h32'	7ca21	7li15	6li58	6li41	6li23	6li05	5li45	5li23
6h36'	8ca16	8li09	7li50	7li31	7li11	6li50	6li28	6li03
6h40'	9ca11	9li04	8li43	8li21	7li59	7li36	7li11	6li44
6h44'	10ca07	9li58	9li35	9li11	8li47	8li22	7li54	7li24
6h48'	11ca02	10li52	10li27	10li02	9li35	9li07	8li37	8li04
6h52'	11ca58	11li46	11li19	10li52	10li23	9li53	9li20	8li45
6h56'	12ca53	12li40	12li11	11li42	11li11	10li38	10li03	9li25
7h00'	13ca49	13li35	13li03	12li32	11li59	11li24	10li46	10li05
7h04'	14ca44	14li29	13li56	13li22	12li46	12li09	11li29	10li46
7h08'	15ca40	15li23	14li48	14li12	13li34	12li55	12li12	11li26
7h12'	16ca36	16li17	15li40	15li02	14li22	13li40	12li55	12li06
7h16'	17ca32	17li11	16li32	15li52	15li10	14li26	13li38	12li47
7h20'	18ca28	18li05	17li24	16li41	15li58	15li11	14li21	13li27
7h24'	19ca24	18li59	18li16	17li31	16li45	15li57	15li04	14li07
7h28'	20ca20	19li53	19li07	18li21	17li33	16li42	15li47	14li47
7h32'	21ca17	20li46	19li59	19li11	18li21	17li27	16li30	15li28
7h36'	22ca13	21li40	20li51	20li01	19li08	18li13	17li13	16li08
7h40'	23ca10	22li34	21li43	20li51	19li56	18li58	17li56	16li48
7h44'	24ca06	23li28	22li35	21li40	20li44	19li44	18li39	17li28
7h48'	25ca03	24li21	23li26	22li30	21li31	20li29	19li22	18li08
7h52'	26ca00	25li15	24li18	23li20	22li19	21li14	20li05	18li49
7h56'	26ca57	26li08	25li10	24li09	23li06	21li60	20li48	19li29
8h00'	27ca55	27li02	26li01	24li59	23li54	22li45	21li31	20li09
8h04'	28ca52	27li55	26li53	25li48	24li41	23li30	22li13	20li49
8h08'	29ca49	28li49	27li44	26li38	25li29	24li15	22li56	21li29
8h12'	0le47	29li42	28li36	27li28	26li16	25li01	23li39	22li09
8h16'	1le45	0sc35	29li27	28li17	27li04	25li46	24li22	22li49
8h20'	2le43	1sc28	0sc18	29li07	27li51	26li31	25li05	23li29
8h24'	3le41	2sc21	1sc10	29li56	28li39	27li16	25li47	24li09
8h28'	4le39	3sc14	2sc01	0sc45	29li26	28li02	26li30	24li49
8h32'	5le38	4sc07	2sc52	1sc35	0sc13	28li47	27li13	25li29
8h36'	6le37	5sc00	3sc44	2sc24	1sc01	29li32	27li56	26li10
8h40'	7le35	5sc53	4sc35	3sc13	1sc48	0sc17	28li38	26li50
8h44'	8le34	6sc46	5sc26	4sc03	2sc35	1sc02	29li21	27li30
8h48'	9le33	7sc39	6sc17	4sc52	3sc23	1sc47	0sc04	28li10

LST	MC	25N	30N	35N	40N	45N	50N	55N
8h52'	10le33	8sc32	7sc08	5sc41	4sc10	2sc32	0sc46	28li49
8h56'	11le32	9sc24	7sc59	6sc30	4sc57	3sc17	1sc29	29li29
9h00'	12le32	10sc17	8sc50	7sc20	5sc44	4sc03	2sc12	0sc09
9h04'	13le32	11sc10	9sc41	8sc09	6sc32	4sc48	2sc55	0sc49
9h08'	14le32	12sc02	10sc32	8sc58	7sc19	5sc33	3sc37	1sc29
9h12'	15le32	12sc55	11sc23	9sc47	8sc06	6sc18	4sc20	2sc09
9h16'	16le33	13sc47	12sc13	10sc36	8sc53	7sc03	5sc03	2sc49
9h20'	17le33	14sc39	13sc04	11sc25	9sc40	7sc48	5sc45	3sc29
9h24'	18le34	15sc32	13sc55	12sc14	10sc28	8sc33	6sc28	4sc09
9h28'	19le35	16sc24	14sc46	13sc03	11sc15	9sc18	7sc11	4sc49
9h32'	20le36	17sc16	15sc36	13sc52	12sc02	10sc03	7sc53	5sc29
9h36'	21le37	18sc09	16sc27	14sc41	12sc49	10sc48	8sc36	6sc09
9h40'	22le39	19sc01	17sc18	15sc30	13sc36	11sc33	9sc19	6sc49
9h44'	23le41	19sc53	18sc09	16sc19	14sc23	12sc18	10sc01	7sc29
9h48'	24le42	20sc45	18sc59	17sc08	15sc10	13sc03	10sc44	8sc09
9h52'	25le44	21sc37	19sc50	17sc57	15sc58	13sc48	11sc27	8sc48
9h56'	26le47	22sc29	20sc40	18sc46	16sc45	14sc34	12sc09	9sc28
10h00'	27le49	23sc21	21sc31	19sc35	17sc32	15sc19	12sc52	10sc08
10h04'	28le52	24sc13	22sc22	20sc24	18sc19	16sc04	13sc35	10sc48
10h08'	29le54	25sc05	23sc12	21sc13	19sc06	16sc49	14sc18	11sc28
10h12'	0vi57	25sc57	24sc03	22sc02	19sc54	17sc34	15sc00	12sc08
10h16'	2vi00	26sc49	24sc53	22sc51	20sc41	18sc19	15sc43	12sc48
10h20'	3vi03	27sc41	25sc44	23sc40	21sc28	19sc05	16sc26	13sc28
10h24'	4vi07	28sc33	26sc35	24sc30	22sc16	19sc50	17sc09	14sc08
10h28'	5vi10	29sc25	27sc25	25sc19	23sc03	20sc35	17sc52	14sc48
10h32'	6vi14	0sa17	28sc16	26sc08	23sc50	21sc21	18sc35	15sc28
10h36'	7vi18	1sa09	29sc07	26sc57	24sc38	22sc06	19sc18	16sc08
10h40'	8vi22	2sa01	29sc57	27sc46	25sc25	22sc52	20sc01	16sc49
10h44'	9vi26	2sa53	0sa48	28sc36	26sc13	23sc37	20sc44	17sc29
10h48'	10vi30	3sa45	1sa39	29sc25	27sc01	24sc23	21sc27	18sc09
10h52'	11vi34	4sa37	2sa30	0sa14	27sc48	25sc08	22sc10	18sc49
10h56'	12vi39	5sa29	3sa20	1sa04	28sc36	25sc54	22sc54	19sc30
11h00'	13vi43	6sa21	4sa11	1sa53	29sc24	26sc40	23sc37	20sc10
11h04'	14vi48	7sa13	5sa02	2sa43	0sa12	27sc26	24sc20	20sc50
11h08'	15vi52	8sa05	5sa53	3sa32	0sa59	28sc12	25sc04	21sc31
11h12'	16vi57	8sa57	6sa44	4sa22	1sa48	28sc58	25sc47	22sc11
11h16'	18vi02	9sa50	7sa35	5sa12	2sa36	29sc44	26sc31	22sc52
11h20'	19vi07	10sa42	8sa27	6sa01	3sa24	0sa30	27sc15	23sc32
11h24'	20vi12	11sa34	9sa18	6sa51	4sa12	1sa16	27sc59	24sc13
11h28'	21vi17	12sa27	10sa09	7sa41	5sa00	2sa02	28sc42	24sc54
11h32'	22vi23	13sa19	11sa01	8sa32	5sa49	2sa49	29sc26	25sc35
11h36'	23vi28	14sa12	11sa52	9sa22	6sa38	3sa36	0sa10	26sc16
11h40'	24vi33	15sa05	12sa44	10sa12	7sa26	4sa22	0sa55	26sc57
11h44'	25vi38	15sa57	13sa36	11sa03	8sa15	5sa09	1sa39	27sc38
11h48'	26vi44	16sa50	14sa27	11sa53	9sa04	5sa56	2sa23	28sc19
11h52'	27vi49	17sa43	15sa19	12sa44	9sa53	6sa43	3sa08	29sc00
11h56'	28vi55	18sa36	16sa11	13sa35	10sa43	7sa31	3sa53	29sc42
12h00'	0li00	19sa29	17sa04	14sa26	11sa32	8sa18	4sa38	0sa23
12h04'	1li05	20sa23	17sa56	15sa17	12sa22	9sa06	5sa23	1sa05

210

LST	MC	25N	30N	35N	40N	45N	50N	55N
12h08'	2li11	21sa16	18sa48	16sa08	13sa11	9sa53	6sa08	1sa47
12h12'	3li16	22sa09	19sa41	16sa60	14sa01	10sa41	6sa53	2sa29
12h16'	4li22	23sa03	20sa34	17sa51	14sa52	11sa29	7sa39	3sa11
12h20'	5li27	23sa57	21sa27	18sa43	15sa42	12sa18	8sa24	3sa53
12h24'	6li32	24sa51	22sa20	19sa35	16sa32	13sa06	9sa10	4sa35
12h28'	7li37	25sa45	23sa13	20sa27	17sa23	13sa55	9sa56	5sa18
12h32'	8li43	26sa39	24sa07	21sa20	18sa14	14sa44	10sa43	6sa01
12h36'	9li48	27sa34	25sa01	22sa13	19sa05	15sa33	11sa29	6sa44
12h40'	10li53	28sa28	25sa54	23sa05	19sa57	16sa23	12sa16	7sa27
12h44'	11li58	29sa23	26sa49	23sa59	20sa48	17sa12	13sa03	8sa10
12h48'	13li03	0cp18	27sa43	24sa52	21sa40	18sa02	13sa50	8sa54
12h52'	14li08	1cp13	28sa38	25sa45	22sa33	18sa53	14sa38	9sa37
12h56'	15li12	2cp09	29sa32	26sa39	23sa25	19sa43	15sa25	10sa21
13h00'	16li17	3cp04	0cp27	27sa33	24sa18	20sa34	16sa13	11sa05
13h04'	17li21	4cp00	1cp23	28sa28	25sa11	21sa25	17sa02	11sa50
13h08'	18li26	4cp56	2cp18	29sa23	26sa04	22sa16	17sa50	12sa35
13h12'	19li30	5cp53	3cp14	0cp18	26sa58	23sa08	18sa39	13sa20
13h16'	20li34	6cp49	4cp10	1cp13	27sa52	24sa00	19sa29	14sa05
13h20'	21li38	7cp46	5cp07	2cp08	28sa46	24sa53	20sa18	14sa51
13h24'	22li42	8cp43	6cp03	3cp04	29sa41	25sa46	21sa09	15sa36
13h28'	23li46	9cp41	7cp00	4cp01	0cp36	26sa39	21sa59	16sa23
13h32'	24li50	10cp38	7cp58	4cp57	1cp32	27sa33	22sa50	17sa09
13h36'	25li53	11cp36	8cp55	5cp54	2cp28	28sa27	23sa41	17sa56
13h40'	26li57	12cp34	9cp53	6cp52	3cp24	29sa21	24sa33	18sa44
13h44'	27li60	13cp33	10cp52	7cp49	4cp21	0cp16	25sa25	19sa32
13h48'	29li03	14cp32	11cp50	8cp48	5cp18	1cp12	26sa17	20sa20
13h52'	0sc06	15cp31	12cp49	9cp46	6cp15	2cp07	27sa11	21sa08
13h56'	1sc08	16cp30	13cp49	10cp45	7cp13	3cp04	28sa04	21sa58
14h00'	2sc11	17cp30	14cp48	11cp45	8cp12	4cp01	28sa58	22sa47
14h04'	3sc13	18cp30	15cp49	12cp45	9cp11	4cp58	29sa53	23sa37
14h08'	4sc16	19cp31	16cp49	13cp45	10cp11	5cp56	0cp48	24sa28
14h12'	5sc18	20cp32	17cp50	14cp46	11cp11	6cp55	1cp44	25sa19
14h16'	6sc19	21cp33	18cp52	15cp47	12cp11	7cp54	2cp41	26sa11
14h20'	7sc21	22cp35	19cp54	16cp49	13cp13	8cp54	3cp38	27sa03
14h24'	8sc23	23cp37	20cp56	17cp51	14cp14	9cp54	4cp36	27sa56
14h28'	9sc24	24cp39	21cp59	18cp54	15cp17	10cp56	5cp34	28sa50
14h32'	10sc25	25cp42	23cp02	19cp58	16cp20	11cp57	6cp33	29sa45
14h36'	11sc26	26cp45	24cp06	21cp01	17cp24	12cp60	7cp33	0cp40
14h40'	12sc27	27cp49	25cp10	22cp06	18cp28	14cp03	8cp34	1cp36
14h44'	13sc27	28cp53	26cp15	23cp11	19cp33	15cp07	9cp36	2cp33
14h48'	14sc28	29cp57	27cp20	24cp17	20cp39	16cp12	10cp38	3cp30
14h52'	15sc28	1aq02	28cp26	25cp23	21cp45	17cp18	11cp42	4cp29
14h56'	16sc28	2aq08	29cp32	26cp30	22cp52	18cp24	12cp46	5cp29
15h00'	17sc28	3aq13	0aq39	27cp37	23cp60	19cp32	13cp52	6cp29
15h04'	18sc28	4aq20	1aq46	28cp46	25cp08	20cp40	14cp58	7cp31
15h08'	19sc27	5aq26	2aq54	29cp55	26cp18	21cp49	16cp05	8cp33
15h12'	20sc27	6aq34	4aq02	1aq04	27cp28	22cp59	17cp14	9cp37
15h16'	21sc26	7aq41	5aq11	2aq14	28cp39	24cp10	18cp23	10cp42
15h20'	22sc25	8aq49	6aq21	3aq25	29cp51	25cp22	19cp34	11cp49

211

LST	MC	25N	30N	35N	40N	45N	50N	55N
15h24'	23sc23	9aq58	7aq31	4aq37	1aq04	26cp35	20cp46	12cp57
15h28'	24sc22	11aq07	8aq42	5aq49	2aq17	27cp50	21cp60	14cp06
15h32'	25sc21	12aq16	9aq53	7aq02	3aq32	29cp05	23cp14	15cp16
15h36'	26sc19	13aq26	11aq05	8aq16	4aq47	0aq21	24cp30	16cp29
15h40'	27sc17	14aq37	12aq17	9aq30	6aq03	1aq39	25cp48	17cp43
15h44'	28sc15	15aq48	13aq31	10aq45	7aq21	2aq58	27cp07	18cp58
15h48'	29sc13	16aq59	14aq44	12aq01	8aq39	4aq18	28cp27	20cp16
15h52'	0sa11	18aq11	15aq58	13aq18	9aq58	5aq39	29cp49	21cp35
15h56'	1sa08	19aq24	17aq13	14aq35	11aq18	7aq01	1aq13	22cp57
16h00'	2sa05	20aq37	18aq29	15aq54	12aq39	8aq25	2aq38	24cp20
16h04'	3sa03	21aq50	19aq45	17aq13	14aq01	9aq50	4aq05	25cp46
16h08'	3sa60	23aq04	21aq01	18aq32	15aq24	11aq16	5aq34	27cp14
16h12'	4sa57	24aq18	22aq19	19aq53	16aq48	12aq44	7aq05	28cp45
16h16'	5sa54	25aq33	23aq37	21aq14	18aq13	14aq13	8aq38	0aq18
16h20'	6sa50	26aq48	24aq55	22aq36	19aq39	15aq44	10aq12	1aq54
16h24'	7sa47	28aq04	26aq14	23aq59	21aq06	17aq16	11aq49	3aq33
16h28'	8sa43	29aq20	27aq34	25aq22	22aq34	18aq49	13aq27	5aq15
16h32'	9sa40	0pi36	28aq54	26aq47	24aq03	20aq23	15aq08	6aq60
16h36'	10sa36	1pi53	0pi14	28aq12	25aq33	21aq59	16aq51	8aq48
16h40'	11sa32	3pi11	1pi35	29aq37	27aq04	23aq37	18aq35	10aq40
16h44'	12sa28	4pi29	2pi57	1pi04	28aq36	25aq16	20aq22	12aq34
16h48'	13sa24	5pi47	4pi19	2pi31	0pi09	26aq56	22aq11	14aq33
16h52'	14sa20	7pi05	5pi42	3pi58	1pi43	28aq37	24aq03	16aq35
16h56'	15sa16	8pi24	7pi05	5pi27	3pi18	0pi20	25aq56	18aq41
17h00'	16sa11	9pi43	8pi29	6pi55	4pi53	2pi04	27aq51	20aq51
17h04'	17sa07	11pi03	9pi53	8pi25	6pi30	3pi50	29aq49	23aq04
17h08'	18sa02	12pi23	11pi17	9pi55	8pi07	5pi36	1pi48	25aq21
17h12'	18sa58	13pi43	12pi42	11pi26	9pi45	7pi24	3pi50	27aq43
17h16'	19sa53	15pi03	14pi07	12pi57	11pi23	9pi13	5pi53	0pi08
17h20'	20sa49	16pi24	15pi33	14pi28	13pi03	11pi03	7pi58	2pi37
17h24'	21sa44	17pi45	16pi59	16pi00	14pi43	12pi53	10pi05	5pi09
17h28'	22sa39	19pi06	18pi25	17pi32	16pi23	14pi45	12pi14	7pi45
17h32'	23sa34	20pi27	19pi51	19pi05	18pi04	16pi38	14pi24	10pi24
17h36'	24sa30	21pi49	21pi18	20pi38	19pi45	18pi31	16pi35	13pi06
17h40'	25sa25	23pi11	22pi44	22pi11	21pi27	20pi25	18pi47	15pi51
17h44'	26sa20	24pi32	24pi11	23pi45	23pi09	22pi19	21pi01	18pi38
17h48'	27sa15	25pi54	25pi38	25pi18	24pi52	24pi14	23pi15	21pi27
17h52'	28sa10	27pi16	27pi06	26pi52	26pi34	26pi09	25pi29	24pi17
17h56'	29sa05	28pi38	28pi33	28pi26	28pi17	28pi05	27pi45	27pi08
18h00'	0cp00	0ar00	0ar00	0ar00	0ar00	0ar00	0ar00	0ar00
18h04'	0cp55	1ar22	1ar27	1ar34	1ar43	1ar55	2ar15	2ar52
18h08'	1cp50	2ar44	2ar54	3ar08	3ar26	3ar51	4ar31	5ar43
18h12'	2cp45	4ar06	4ar22	4ar42	5ar08	5ar46	6ar45	8ar33
18h16'	3cp40	5ar28	5ar49	6ar15	6ar51	7ar41	8ar59	11ar22
18h20'	4cp35	6ar49	7ar16	7ar49	8ar33	9ar35	11ar13	14ar09
18h24'	5cp30	8ar11	8ar42	9ar22	10ar15	11ar29	13ar25	16ar54
18h28'	6cp26	9ar33	10ar09	10ar55	11ar56	13ar22	15ar36	19ar36
18h32'	7cp21	10ar54	11ar35	12ar28	13ar37	15ar15	17ar46	22ar15
18h36'	8cp16	12ar15	13ar01	13ar60	15ar17	17ar07	19ar55	24ar51

212

LST	MC	25N	30N	35N	40N	45N	50N	55N
18h40'	9cp11	13ar36	14ar27	15ar32	16ar57	18ar57	22ar02	27ar23
18h44'	10cp07	14ar57	15ar53	17ar03	18ar37	20ar47	24ar07	29ar52
18h48'	11cp02	16ar17	17ar18	18ar34	20ar15	22ar36	26ar10	2ta17
18h52'	11cp58	17ar37	18ar43	20ar05	21ar53	24ar24	28ar12	4ta39
18h56'	12cp53	18ar57	20ar07	21ar35	23ar30	26ar10	0ta11	6ta56
19h00'	13cp49	20ar17	21ar31	23ar05	25ar07	27ar56	2ta09	9ta09
19h04'	14cp44	21ar36	22ar55	24ar33	26ar42	29ar40	4ta04	11ta19
19h08'	15cp40	22ar55	24ar18	26ar02	28ar17	1ta23	5ta57	13ta25
19h12'	16cp36	24ar13	25ar41	27ar29	29ar51	3ta04	7ta49	15ta27
19h16'	17cp32	25ar31	27ar03	28ar56	1ta24	4ta44	9ta38	17ta26
19h20'	18cp28	26ar49	28ar25	0ta23	2ta56	6ta23	11ta25	19ta20
19h24'	19cp24	28ar07	29ar46	1ta48	4ta27	8ta01	13ta09	21ta12
19h28'	20cp20	29ar24	1ta06	3ta13	5ta57	9ta37	14ta52	23ta00
19h32'	21cp17	0ta40	2ta26	4ta38	7ta26	11ta11	16ta33	24ta45
19h36'	22cp13	1ta56	3ta46	6ta01	8ta54	12ta44	18ta11	26ta27
19h40'	23cp10	3ta12	5ta05	7ta24	10ta21	14ta16	19ta48	28ta06
19h44'	24cp06	4ta27	6ta23	8ta46	11ta47	15ta47	21ta22	29ta42
19h48'	25cp03	5ta42	7ta41	10ta07	13ta12	17ta16	22ta55	1ge15
19h52'	26cp00	6ta56	8ta58	11ta28	14ta36	18ta44	24ta26	2ge46
19h56'	26cp57	8ta10	10ta15	12ta47	15ta59	20ta10	25ta55	4ge14
20h00'	27cp55	9ta23	11ta31	14ta06	17ta21	21ta35	27ta22	5ge40
20h04'	28cp52	10ta36	12ta47	15ta25	18ta42	22ta59	28ta47	7ge03
20h08'	29cp49	11ta49	14ta02	16ta42	20ta02	24ta21	0ge11	8ge25
20h12'	0aq47	13ta01	15ta16	17ta59	21ta21	25ta42	1ge33	9ge44
20h16'	1aq45	14ta12	16ta29	19ta15	22ta39	27ta02	2ge53	11ge02
20h20'	2aq43	15ta23	17ta43	20ta30	23ta57	28ta21	4ge12	12ge17
20h24'	3aq41	16ta34	18ta55	21ta44	25ta13	29ta39	5ge30	13ge31
20h28'	4aq39	17ta44	20ta07	22ta58	26ta28	0ge55	6ge46	14ge44
20h32'	5aq38	18ta53	21ta18	24ta11	27ta43	2ge10	8ge00	15ge54
20h36'	6aq37	20ta02	22ta29	25ta23	28ta56	3ge25	9ge14	17ge03
20h40'	7aq35	21ta11	23ta39	26ta35	0ge09	4ge38	10ge26	18ge11
20h44'	8aq34	22ta19	24ta49	27ta46	1ge21	5ge50	11ge37	19ge18
20h48'	9aq33	23ta26	25ta58	28ta56	2ge32	7ge01	12ge46	20ge23
20h52'	10aq33	24ta34	27ta06	0ge05	3ge42	8ge11	13ge55	21ge27
20h56'	11aq32	25ta40	28ta14	1ge14	4ge52	9ge20	15ge02	22ge29
21h00'	12aq32	26ta47	29ta21	2ge23	6ge00	10ge28	16ge08	23ge31
21h04'	13aq32	27ta52	0ge28	3ge30	7ge08	11ge36	17ge14	24ge31
21h08'	14aq32	28ta58	1ge34	4ge37	8ge15	12ge42	18ge18	25ge31
21h12'	15aq32	0ge03	2ge40	5ge43	9ge21	13ge48	19ge22	26ge30
21h16'	16aq33	1ge07	3ge45	6ge49	10ge27	14ge53	20ge24	27ge27
21h20'	17aq33	2ge11	4ge50	7ge54	11ge32	15ge57	21ge26	28ge24
21h24'	18aq34	3ge15	5ge54	8ge59	12ge36	17ge00	22ge27	29ge20
21h28'	19aq35	4ge18	6ge58	10ge02	13ge40	18ge03	23ge27	0ca15
21h32'	20aq36	5ge21	8ge01	11ge06	14ge43	19ge04	24ge26	1ca10
21h36'	21aq37	6ge23	9ge04	12ge09	15ge46	20ge06	25ge24	2ca04
21h40'	22aq39	7ge25	10ge06	13ge11	16ge47	21ge06	26ge22	2ca57
21h44'	23aq41	8ge27	11ge08	14ge13	17ge49	22ge06	27ge19	3ca49
21h48'	24aq42	9ge28	12ge10	15ge14	18ge49	23ge05	28ge16	4ca41
21h52'	25aq44	10ge29	13ge11	16ge15	19ge49	24ge04	29ge12	5ca32

213

LST	MC	25N	30N	35N	40N	45N	50N	55N
21h56'	26aq47	11ge30	14ge11	17ge15	20ge49	25ge02	0ca07	6ca23
22h00'	27aq49	12ge30	15ge12	18ge15	21ge48	25ge59	1ca02	7ca13
22h04'	28aq52	13ge30	16ge11	19ge15	22ge47	26ge56	1ca56	8ca02
22h08'	29aq54	14ge29	17ge11	20ge14	23ge45	27ge53	2ca49	8ca52
22h12'	0pi57	15ge28	18ge10	21ge12	24ge42	28ge48	3ca43	9ca40
22h16'	2pi00	16ge27	19ge08	22ge11	25ge39	29ge44	4ca35	10ca28
22h20'	3pi03	17ge26	20ge07	23ge08	26ge36	0ca39	5ca27	11ca16
22h24'	4pi07	18ge24	21ge05	24ge06	27ge32	1ca33	6ca19	12ca04
22h28'	5pi10	19ge22	22ge02	25ge03	28ge28	2ca27	7ca10	12ca51
22h32'	6pi14	20ge19	22ge60	25ge59	29ge24	3ca21	8ca01	13ca37
22h36'	7pi18	21ge17	23ge57	26ge56	0ca19	4ca14	8ca51	14ca24
22h40'	8pi22	22ge14	24ge53	27ge52	1ca14	5ca07	9ca42	15ca09
22h44'	9pi26	23ge11	25ge50	28ge47	2ca08	5ca60	10ca31	15ca55
22h48'	10pi30	24ge07	26ge46	29ge42	3ca02	6ca52	11ca21	16ca40
22h52'	11pi34	25ge04	27ge42	0ca37	3ca56	7ca44	12ca10	17ca25
22h56'	12pi39	25ge60	28ge37	1ca32	4ca49	8ca35	12ca58	18ca10
23h00'	13pi43	26ge56	29ge33	2ca27	5ca42	9ca26	13ca47	18ca55
23h04'	14pi48	27ge51	0ca28	3ca21	6ca35	10ca17	14ca35	19ca39
23h08'	15pi52	28ge47	1ca22	4ca15	7ca27	11ca07	15ca22	20ca23
23h12'	16pi57	29ge42	2ca17	5ca08	8ca20	11ca58	16ca10	21ca06
23h16'	18pi02	0ca37	3ca11	6ca01	9ca12	12ca48	16ca57	21ca50
23h20'	19pi07	1ca32	4ca06	6ca55	10ca03	13ca37	17ca44	22ca33
23h24'	20pi12	2ca26	4ca59	7ca47	10ca55	14ca27	18ca31	23ca16
23h28'	21pi17	3ca21	5ca53	8ca40	11ca46	15ca16	19ca17	23ca59
23h32'	22pi23	4ca15	6ca47	9ca33	12ca37	16ca05	20ca04	24ca42
23h36'	23pi28	5ca09	7ca40	10ca25	13ca28	16ca54	20ca50	25ca25
23h40'	24pi33	6ca03	8ca33	11ca17	14ca18	17ca42	21ca36	26ca07
23h44'	25pi38	6ca57	9ca26	12ca09	15ca08	18ca31	22ca21	26ca49
23h48'	26pi44	7ca51	10ca19	13ca00	15ca59	19ca19	23ca07	27ca31
23h52'	27pi49	8ca44	11ca12	13ca52	16ca49	20ca07	23ca52	28ca13
23h56'	28pi55	9ca37	12ca04	14ca43	17ca38	20ca54	24ca37	28ca55

Solar-Sidereal Correction Table

Hours	minutes / seconds						
	0	**10**	**20**	**30**	**40**	**50**	**60**
0	0	0:02	0:03	0:05	0:07	0:08	0:10
1	0:10	0:11	0:13	0:15	0:16	0:18	0:20
2	0:20	0:21	0:23	0:25	0:26	0:28	0:29
3	0:30	0:31	0:33	0:34	0:36	0:38	0:39
4	0:39	0:41	0:43	0:44	0:46	0:47	0:49
5	0:49	0:51	0:52	0:54	0:56	0:57	0:59
6	0:59	1:01	1:02	1:04	1:06	1:07	1:09
7	1:09	1:10	1:12	1:14	1:15	1:17	1:19
8	1:19	1:20	1:22	1:24	1:25	1:27	1:28
9	1:29	1:30	1:32	1:33	1:35	1:37	1:38
10	1:38	1:40	1:42	1:43	1:45	1:46	1:48
11	1:48	1:50	1:51	1:53	1:55	1:56	1:58
12	1:58	2:00	2:01	2:03	2:05	2:06	2:08
13	2:08	2:09	2:11	2:13	2:14	2:16	2:18
14	2:18	2:19	2:21	2:23	2:24	2:26	2:27
15	2:28	2:29	2:31	2:32	2:34	2:36	2:37
16	2:37	2:39	2:41	2:42	2:44	2:45	2:47
17	2:47	2:49	2:50	2:52	2:54	2:55	2:57
18	2:57	2:59	3:00	3:02	3:04	3:05	3:07
19	3:07	3:08	3:10	3:12	3:13	3:15	3:17
20	3:17	3:18	3:20	3:22	3:23	3:25	3:26
21	3:27	3:28	3:30	3:31	3:33	3:35	3:36
22	3:36	3:38	3:40	3:41	3:43	3:44	3:46
23	3:46	3:48	3:49	3:51	3:53	3:54	3:56

Midheaven Interpolation Tables

	0m 10s	0m 20s	0m 30s	0m 40s	0m 50s	1m 00s	1m 10s	1m 20s
30m	1.3	2.5	3.8	5.0	6.3	7.5	8.8	10.0
35m	1.5	2.9	4.4	5.8	7.3	8.8	10.2	11.7
40m	1.7	3.3	5.0	6.7	8.3	10.0	11.7	13.3
45m	1.9	3.8	5.6	7.5	9.4	11.3	13.1	15.0
50m	2.1	4.2	6.3	8.3	10.4	12.5	14.6	16.7
55m	2.3	4.6	6.9	9.2	11.5	13.8	16.0	18.3
60m	2.5	5.0	7.5	10.0	12.5	15.0	17.5	20.0
65m	2.7	5.4	8.1	10.8	13.5	16.3	19.0	21.7
70m	2.9	5.8	8.8	11.7	14.6	17.5	20.4	23.3
75m	3.1	6.3	9.4	12.5	15.6	18.8	21.9	25.0
80m	3.3	6.7	10.0	13.3	16.7	20.0	23.3	26.7
85m	3.5	7.1	10.6	14.2	17.7	21.3	24.8	28.3
90m	3.8	7.5	11.3	15.0	18.8	22.5	26.3	30.0
95m	4.0	7.9	11.9	15.8	19.8	23.8	27.7	31.7
100m	4.2	8.3	12.5	16.7	20.8	25.0	29.2	33.3
105m	4.4	8.8	13.1	17.5	21.9	26.3	30.6	35.0
110m	4.6	9.2	13.8	18.3	22.9	27.5	32.1	36.7
115m	4.8	9.6	14.4	19.2	24.0	28.8	33.5	38.3
120m	5.0	10.0	15.0	20.0	25.0	30.0	35.0	40.0

	1m 30s	1m 40s	1m 50s	2m 00s	2m 10s	2m 20s	2m 30s	2m 40s
30m	11.3	12.5	13.8	15.0	16.3	17.5	18.8	20.0
35m	13.1	14.6	16.0	17.5	19.0	20.4	21.9	23.3
40m	15.0	16.7	18.3	20.0	21.7	23.3	25.0	26.7
45m	16.9	18.8	20.6	22.5	24.4	26.3	28.1	30.0
50m	18.8	20.8	22.9	25.0	27.1	29.2	31.3	33.3
55m	20.6	22.9	25.2	27.5	29.8	32.1	34.4	36.7
60m	22.5	25.0	27.5	30.0	32.5	35.0	37.5	40.0
65m	24.4	27.1	29.8	32.5	35.2	37.9	40.6	43.3
70m	26.3	29.2	32.1	35.0	37.9	40.8	43.8	46.7
75m	28.1	31.3	34.4	37.5	40.6	43.8	46.9	50.0
80m	30.0	33.3	36.7	40.0	43.3	46.7	50.0	53.3
85m	31.9	35.4	39.0	42.5	46.0	49.6	53.1	56.7
90m	33.8	37.5	41.3	45.0	48.8	52.5	56.3	60.0
95m	35.6	39.6	43.5	47.5	51.5	55.4	59.4	63.3
100m	37.5	41.7	45.8	50.0	54.2	58.3	62.5	66.7
105m	39.4	43.8	48.1	52.5	56.9	61.3	65.6	70.0
110m	41.3	45.8	50.4	55.0	59.6	64.2	68.8	73.3
115m	43.1	47.9	52.7	57.5	62.3	67.1	71.9	76.7
120m	45.0	50.0	55.0	60.0	65.0	70.0	75.0	80.0

	2m 50s	3m 00s	3m 10s	3m 20s	3m 30s	3m 40s	3m 50s	4m 00s
30m	21.3	22.5	23.8	25.0	26.3	27.5	28.8	30.0
35m	24.8	26.3	27.7	29.2	30.6	32.1	33.5	35.0
40m	28.3	30.0	31.7	33.3	35.0	36.7	38.3	40.0
45m	31.9	33.8	35.6	37.5	39.4	41.3	43.1	45.0
50m	35.4	37.5	39.6	41.7	43.8	45.8	47.9	50.0
55m	39.0	41.3	43.5	45.8	48.1	50.4	52.7	55.0
60m	42.5	45.0	47.5	50.0	52.5	55.0	57.5	60.0
65m	46.0	48.8	51.5	54.2	56.9	59.6	62.3	65.0
70m	49.6	52.5	55.4	58.3	61.3	64.2	67.1	70.0
75m	53.1	56.3	59.4	62.5	65.6	68.8	71.9	75.0
80m	56.7	60.0	63.3	66.7	70.0	73.3	76.7	80.0
85m	60.2	63.8	67.3	70.8	74.4	77.9	81.5	85.0
90m	63.8	67.5	71.3	75.0	78.8	82.5	86.3	90.0
95m	67.3	71.3	75.2	79.2	83.1	87.1	91.0	95.0
100m	70.8	75.0	79.2	83.3	87.5	91.7	95.8	100.0
105m	74.4	78.8	83.1	87.5	91.9	96.3	100.6	105.0
110m	77.9	82.5	87.1	91.7	96.3	100.8	105.4	110.0
115m	81.5	86.3	91.0	95.8	100.6	105.4	110.2	115.0
120m	85.0	90.0	95.0	100.0	105.0	110.0	115.0	120.0

Ascendant Interpolation Tables

	0° 0'	0° 20'	0° 30'	0° 40'	0°50'	1°00'	1°10'	1°20'
5'	0.2	0.3	0.5	0.7	0.8	1.0	1.2	1.3
10'	0.3	0.7	1.0	1.3	1.7	2.0	2.3	2.7
15'	0.5	1.0	1.5	2.0	2.5	3.0	3.5	4.0
20'	0.7	1.3	2.0	2.7	3.3	4.0	4.7	5.3
25'	0.8	1.7	2.5	3.3	4.2	5.0	5.8	6.7
30'	1.0	2.0	3.0	4.0	5.0	6.0	7.0	8.0
35'	1.2	2.3	3.5	4.7	5.8	7.0	8.2	9.3
40'	1.3	2.6	4.0	5.3	6.6	8.0	9.3	10.6
45'	1.5	3.0	4.5	6.0	7.5	9.0	10.5	12.0
50'	1.7	3.3	5.0	6.7	8.3	10.0	11.7	13.3
55'	1.8	3.6	5.5	7.3	9.1	11.0	12.8	14.6
1°	2.0	4.0	6.0	8.0	10.0	12.0	14.0	16.0
1° 5'	2.1	4.3	6.5	8.6	10.8	13.0	15.1	17.3
1° 10'	2.3	4.6	7.0	9.3	11.6	14.0	16.3	18.6
1° 15'	2.5	5.0	7.5	10.0	12.5	15.0	17.5	20.0
1° 20'	2.6	5.3	8.0	10.6	13.3	16.0	18.6	21.3
1° 25'	2.8	5.6	8.5	11.3	14.1	17.0	19.8	22.6
1° 30'	3.0	5.9	9.0	12.0	14.9	18.0	21.0	23.9
1° 35'	3.1	6.3	9.5	12.6	15.8	19.0	22.1	25.3
1° 40'	3.3	6.6	10.0	13.3	16.6	20.0	23.3	26.6
1° 45'	3.5	6.9	10.5	14.0	17.4	21.0	24.5	27.9
1° 50'	3.6	7.3	11.0	14.6	18.3	22.0	25.6	29.3
1° 55'	3.8	7.6	11.5	15.3	19.1	23.0	26.8	30.6

	0° 0'	0° 20'	0° 30'	0° 40'	0° 50'	1° 00'	1° 10'	1° 20'
2°	4.0	7.9	12.0	16.0	19.9	24.0	28.0	31.9
2° 5'	4.1	8.3	12.5	16.6	20.8	25.0	29.1	33.3
2° 10'	4.3	8.6	13.0	17.3	21.6	26.0	30.3	34.6
2° 15'	4.5	8.9	13.5	18.0	22.4	27.0	31.5	35.9
2° 20'	4.6	9.2	14.0	18.6	23.2	28.0	32.6	37.2
2° 25'	4.8	9.6	14.5	19.3	24.1	29.0	33.8	38.6
2° 30'	5.0	9.9	15.0	20.0	24.9	30.0	35.0	39.9
2° 35'	5.1	10.2	15.5	20.6	25.7	31.0	36.1	41.2
2° 40'	5.3	10.6	16.0	21.3	26.6	32.0	37.3	42.6
2° 45'	5.4	10.9	16.5	21.9	27.4	33.0	38.4	43.9
2° 50'	5.6	11.2	17.0	22.6	28.2	34.0	39.6	45.2
2° 55'	5.8	11.6	17.5	23.3	29.1	35.0	40.8	46.6
3°	5.9	11.9	18.0	23.9	29.9	36.0	41.9	47.9
3° 5'	6.1	12.2	18.5	24.6	30.7	37.0	43.1	49.2
3° 10'	6.3	12.5	19.0	25.3	31.5	38.0	44.3	50.5
3° 15'	6.4	12.9	19.5	25.9	32.4	39.0	45.4	51.9
3° 20'	6.6	13.2	20.0	26.6	33.2	40.0	46.6	53.2
3° 25'	6.8	13.5	20.5	27.3	34.0	41.0	47.8	54.5
3° 30'	6.9	13.9	21.0	27.9	34.9	42.0	48.9	55.9
3° 35'	7.1	14.2	21.5	28.6	35.7	43.0	50.1	57.2
3° 40'	7.3	14.5	22.0	29.3	36.5	44.0	51.3	58.5
3° 45'	7.4	14.9	22.5	29.9	37.4	45.0	52.4	59.9
3° 50'	7.6	15.2	23.0	30.6	38.2	46.0	53.6	61.2
3° 55'	7.8	15.5	23.5	31.3	39.0	47.0	54.8	62.5
4°	7.9	15.8	24.0	31.9	39.8	48.0	55.9	63.8

	1° 30'	1° 40'	1° 50'	2° 00'	2° 10'	2° 20'	2° 30'	2° 40'
5'	1.5	1.7	1.8	2.0	2.2	2.3	2.5	2.7
10'	3.0	3.3	3.7	4.0	4.3	4.7	5.0	5.3
15'	4.5	5.0	5.5	6.0	6.5	7.0	7.5	8.0
20'	6.0	6.7	7.3	8.0	8.7	9.3	10.0	10.7
25'	7.5	8.3	9.2	10.0	10.8	11.7	12.5	13.3
30'	9.0	10.0	11.0	12.0	13.0	14.0	15.0	16.0
35'	10.5	11.7	12.8	14.0	15.2	16.3	17.5	18.7
40'	12.0	13.3	14.6	16.0	17.3	18.6	20.0	21.3
45'	13.5	15.0	16.5	18.0	19.5	21.0	22.5	24.0
50'	15.0	16.7	18.3	20.0	21.7	23.3	25.0	26.7
55'	16.5	18.3	20.1	22.0	23.8	25.6	27.5	29.3
1°	18.0	20.0	22.0	24.0	26.0	28.0	30.0	32.0
1° 5'	19.5	21.6	23.8	26.0	28.1	30.3	32.5	34.6
1° 10'	21.0	23.3	25.6	28.0	30.3	32.6	35.0	37.3
1° 15'	22.5	25.0	27.5	30.0	32.5	35.0	37.5	40.0
1° 20'	24.0	26.6	29.3	32.0	34.6	37.3	40.0	42.6
1° 25'	25.5	28.3	31.1	34.0	36.8	39.6	42.5	45.3
1° 30'	27.0	30.0	32.9	36.0	39.0	41.9	45.0	48.0
1° 35'	28.5	31.6	34.8	38.0	41.1	44.3	47.5	50.6
1° 40'	30.0	33.3	36.6	40.0	43.3	46.6	50.0	53.3
1° 45'	31.5	35.0	38.4	42.0	45.5	48.9	52.5	56.0

	1° 30'	1° 40'	1° 50'	2° 00'	2° 10'	2° 20'	2° 30'	2° 40'
1° 50'	33.0	36.6	40.3	44.0	47.6	51.3	55.0	58.6
1° 55'	34.5	38.3	42.1	46.0	49.8	53.6	57.5	61.3
2°	36.0	40.0	43.9	48.0	52.0	55.9	60.0	64.0
2° 5'	37.5	41.6	45.8	50.0	54.1	58.3	62.5	66.6
2° 10'	39.0	43.3	47.6	52.0	56.3	60.6	65.0	69.3
2° 15'	40.5	45.0	49.4	54.0	58.5	62.9	67.5	72.0
2° 20'	42.0	46.6	51.2	56.0	60.6	65.2	70.0	74.6
2° 25'	43.5	48.3	53.1	58.0	62.8	67.6	72.5	77.3
2° 30'	45.0	50.0	54.9	60.0	65.0	69.9	75.0	80.0
2° 35'	46.5	51.6	56.7	62.0	67.1	72.2	77.5	82.6
2° 40'	48.0	53.3	58.6	64.0	69.3	74.6	80.0	85.3
2° 45'	49.5	54.9	60.4	66.0	71.4	76.9	82.5	87.9
2° 50'	51.0	56.6	62.2	68.0	73.6	79.2	85.0	90.6
2° 55'	52.5	58.3	64.1	70.0	75.8	81.6	87.5	93.3
3°	54.0	59.9	65.9	72.0	77.9	83.9	90.0	95.9
3° 5'	55.5	61.6	67.7	74.0	80.1	86.2	92.5	98.6
3° 10'	57.0	63.3	69.5	76.0	82.3	88.5	95.0	101.3
3° 15'	58.5	64.9	71.4	78.0	84.4	90.9	97.5	103.9
3° 20'	60.0	66.6	73.2	80.0	86.6	93.2	100.0	106.6
3° 25'	61.5	68.3	75.0	82.0	88.8	95.5	102.5	109.3
3° 30'	63.0	69.9	76.9	84.0	90.9	97.9	105.0	111.9
3° 35'	64.5	71.6	78.7	86.0	93.1	100.2	107.5	114.6
3° 40'	66.0	73.3	80.5	88.0	95.3	102.5	110.0	117.3
3° 45'	67.5	74.9	82.4	90.0	97.4	104.9	112.5	119.9
3° 50'	69.0	76.6	84.2	92.0	99.6	107.2	115.0	122.6
3° 55'	70.5	78.3	86.0	94.0	101.8	109.5	117.5	125.3
4°	72.0	79.9	87.8	96.0	103.9	111.8	120.0	127.9

	2° 50'	3° 00'	3° 10'	3° 20'	3° 30'	3° 40'	3° 50'	4° 00'
5'	2.8	3.0	3.2	3.3	3.5	3.7	3.8	4.0
10'	5.7	6.0	6.3	6.7	7.0	7.3	7.7	8.0
15'	8.5	9.0	9.5	10.0	10.5	11.0	11.5	12.0
20'	11.3	12.0	12.7	13.3	14.0	14.7	15.3	16.0
25'	14.2	15.0	15.8	16.7	17.5	18.3	19.2	20.0
30'	17.0	18.0	19.0	20.0	21.0	22.0	23.0	24.0
35'	19.8	21.0	22.2	23.3	24.5	25.7	26.8	28.0
40'	22.6	24.0	25.3	26.6	28.0	29.3	30.6	32.0
45'	25.5	27.0	28.5	30.0	31.5	33.0	34.5	36.0
50'	28.3	30.0	31.7	33.3	35.0	36.7	38.3	40.0
55'	31.1	33.0	34.8	36.6	38.5	40.3	42.1	44.0
1°	34.0	36.0	38.0	40.0	42.0	44.0	46.0	48.0
1° 5'	36.8	39.0	41.1	43.3	45.5	47.6	49.8	52.0
1° 10'	39.6	42.0	44.3	46.6	49.0	51.3	53.6	56.0
1° 15'	42.5	45.0	47.5	50.0	52.5	55.0	57.5	60.0
1° 20'	45.3	48.0	50.6	53.3	56.0	58.6	61.3	64.0
1° 25'	48.1	51.0	53.8	56.6	59.5	62.3	65.1	68.0
1° 30'	50.9	54.0	57.0	59.9	63.0	66.0	68.9	72.0
1° 35'	53.8	57.0	60.1	63.3	66.5	69.6	72.8	76.0

	2° 50'	3° 00'	3° 10'	3° 20'	3° 30'	3° 40'	3° 50'	4° 00'
1° 40'	56.6	60.0	63.3	66.6	70.0	73.3	76.6	80.0
1° 45'	59.4	63.0	66.5	69.9	73.5	77.0	80.4	84.0
1° 50'	62.3	66.0	69.6	73.3	77.0	80.6	84.3	88.0
1° 55'	65.1	69.0	72.8	76.6	80.5	84.3	88.1	92.0
2°	67.9	72.0	76.0	79.9	84.0	88.0	91.9	96.0
2° 5'	70.8	75.0	79.1	83.3	87.5	91.6	95.8	100.0
2° 10'	73.6	78.0	82.3	86.6	91.0	95.3	99.6	104.0
2° 15'	76.4	81.0	85.5	89.9	94.5	99.0	103.4	108.0
2° 20'	79.2	84.0	88.6	93.2	98.0	102.6	107.2	112.0
2° 25'	82.1	87.0	91.8	96.6	101.5	106.3	111.1	116.0
2° 30'	84.9	90.0	95.0	99.9	105.0	110.0	114.9	120.0
2° 35'	87.7	93.0	98.1	103.2	108.5	113.6	118.7	124.0
2° 40'	90.6	96.0	101.3	106.6	112.0	117.3	122.6	128.0
2° 45'	93.4	99.0	104.4	109.9	115.5	120.9	126.4	132.0
2° 50'	96.2	102.0	107.6	113.2	119.0	124.6	130.2	136.0
2° 55'	99.1	105.0	110.8	116.6	122.5	128.3	134.1	140.0
3°	101.9	108.0	113.9	119.9	126.0	131.9	137.9	144.0
3° 5'	104.7	111.0	117.1	123.2	129.5	135.6	141.7	148.0
3° 10'	107.5	114.0	120.3	126.5	133.0	139.3	145.5	152.0
3° 15'	110.4	117.0	123.4	129.9	136.5	142.9	149.4	156.0
3° 20'	113.2	120.0	126.6	133.2	140.0	146.6	153.2	160.0
3° 25'	116.0	123.0	129.8	136.5	143.5	150.3	157.0	164.0
3° 30'	118.9	126.0	132.9	139.9	147.0	153.9	160.9	168.0
3° 35'	121.7	129.0	136.1	143.2	150.5	157.6	164.7	172.0
3° 40'	124.5	132.0	139.3	146.5	154.0	161.3	168.5	176.0
3° 45'	127.4	135.0	142.4	149.9	157.5	164.9	172.4	180.0
3° 50'	130.2	138.0	145.6	153.2	161.0	168.6	176.2	184.0
3° 55'	133.0	141.0	148.8	156.5	164.5	172.3	180.0	188.0
4°	135.8	144.0	151.9	159.8	168.0	175.9	183.8	192.0

	4° 10'	4° 20'	4° 30'	4° 40'	4° 50'	5° 00'
5'	4.2	4.3	4.5	4.7	4.8	5.0
10'	8.3	8.7	9.0	9.3	9.7	10.0
15'	12.5	13.0	13.5	14.0	14.5	15.0
20'	16.7	17.3	18.0	18.7	19.3	20.0
25'	20.8	21.7	22.5	23.3	24.2	25.0
30'	25.0	26.0	27.0	28.0	29.0	30.0
35'	29.2	30.3	31.5	32.7	33.8	35.0
40'	33.3	34.6	36.0	37.3	38.6	40.0
45'	37.5	39.0	40.5	42.0	43.5	45.0
50'	41.7	43.3	45.0	46.7	48.3	50.0
55'	45.8	47.6	49.5	51.3	53.1	55.0
1°	50.0	52.0	54.0	56.0	58.0	60.0
1° 5'	54.1	56.3	58.5	60.6	62.8	65.0
1° 10'	58.3	60.6	63.0	65.3	67.6	70.0
1° 15'	62.5	65.0	67.5	70.0	72.5	75.0
1° 20'	66.6	69.3	72.0	74.6	77.3	80.0
1° 25'	70.8	73.6	76.5	79.3	82.1	85.0
	4° 10'	4° 20'	4° 30'	4° 40'	4° 50'	5° 00'

1° 30'	75.0	77.9	81.0	84.0	86.9	90.0
1° 35'	79.1	82.3	85.5	88.6	91.8	95.0
1° 40'	83.3	86.6	90.0	93.3	96.6	100.0
1° 45'	87.5	90.9	94.5	98.0	101.4	105.0
1° 50'	91.6	95.3	99.0	102.6	106.3	110.0
1° 55'	95.8	99.6	103.5	107.3	111.1	115.0
2°	100.0	103.9	108.0	112.0	115.9	120.0
2° 5'	104.1	108.3	112.5	116.6	120.8	125.0
2° 10'	108.3	112.6	117.0	121.3	125.6	130.0
2° 15'	112.5	116.9	121.5	126.0	130.4	135.0
2° 20'	116.6	121.2	126.0	130.6	135.2	140.0
2° 25'	120.8	125.6	130.5	135.3	140.1	145.0
2° 30'	125.0	129.9	135.0	140.0	144.9	150.0
2° 35'	129.1	134.2	139.5	144.6	149.7	155.0
2° 40'	133.3	138.6	144.0	149.3	154.6	160.0
2° 45'	137.4	142.9	148.5	153.9	159.4	165.0
2° 50'	141.6	147.2	153.0	158.6	164.2	170.0
2° 55'	145.8	151.6	157.5	163.3	169.1	175.0
3°	149.9	155.9	162.0	167.9	173.9	180.0
3° 5'	154.1	160.2	166.5	172.6	178.7	185.0
3° 10'	158.3	164.5	171.0	177.3	183.5	190.0
3° 15'	162.4	168.9	175.5	181.9	188.4	195.0
3° 20'	166.6	173.2	180.0	186.6	193.2	200.0
3° 25'	170.8	177.5	184.5	191.3	198.0	205.0
3° 30'	174.9	181.9	189.0	195.9	202.9	210.0
3° 35'	179.1	186.2	193.5	200.6	207.7	215.0
3° 40'	183.3	190.5	198.0	205.3	212.5	220.0
3° 45'	187.4	194.9	202.5	209.9	217.4	225.0
3° 50'	191.6	199.2	207.0	214.6	222.2	230.0
3° 55'	195.8	203.5	211.5	219.3	227.0	235.0
4°	199.9	207.8	216.0	223.9	231.8	240.0

Tables of Daily Planetary Motion

Daily Motion of the Planets

	Mean	Maximum
Sun	0°59'08"	1°03'00"
Moon	13°10'35"	16°30'00"
Mercury	1°23'00"	2°25'00"
Venus	1°12'00"	1°22'00"
Mars	0°31'27"	0°52'00"
Ceres	0°12'40"	0°30'00"
Jupiter	0°04'59"	0°15'40"
Saturn	0°02'01"	0°08'48"
Chiron	0°02'00"	0°10'00"
Uranus	0°00'42"	0°04'00"
Neptune	0°00'24"	0°02'25"
Pluto	0°00'15"	0°02'30"

GMT — Planetary Daily Motion in minutes of a degree

GMT	5	10	15	20	25	30	35	40
0	0.0	0.0	0.0	0.0	0.0	0.0	0.0	0.0
1	0.2	0.4	0.6	0.8	1.0	1.3	1.5	1.7
2	0.4	0.8	1.3	1.7	2.1	2.5	2.9	3.3
3	0.6	1.3	1.9	2.5	3.1	3.8	4.4	5.0
4	0.8	1.7	2.5	3.3	4.2	5.0	5.8	6.7
5	1.0	2.1	3.1	4.2	5.2	6.3	7.3	8.3
6	1.2	2.5	3.8	5.0	6.3	7.5	8.7	10.0
7	1.5	2.9	4.4	5.8	7.3	8.8	10.2	11.7
8	1.7	3.3	5.0	6.7	8.3	10.0	11.7	13.3
9	1.9	3.8	5.6	7.5	9.4	11.3	13.1	15.0
10	2.1	4.2	6.3	8.3	10.4	12.5	14.6	16.7
11	2.3	4.6	6.9	9.2	11.5	13.8	16.0	18.3
12	2.5	5.0	7.5	10.0	12.5	15.0	17.5	20.0
13	2.7	5.4	8.1	10.8	13.5	16.3	19.0	21.7
14	2.9	5.8	8.8	11.7	14.6	17.5	20.4	23.3
15	3.1	6.3	9.4	12.5	15.6	18.8	21.9	25.0
16	3.3	6.7	10.0	13.3	16.7	20.0	23.3	26.7
17	3.5	7.1	10.6	14.2	17.7	21.3	24.8	28.3
18	3.7	7.5	11.3	15.0	18.8	22.5	26.2	30.0
19	4.0	7.9	11.9	15.8	19.8	23.8	27.7	31.7
20	4.2	8.3	12.5	16.7	20.8	25.0	29.2	33.3
21	4.4	8.8	13.1	17.5	21.9	26.3	30.6	35.0
22	4.6	9.2	13.8	18.3	22.9	27.5	32.1	36.7
23	4.8	9.6	14.4	19.2	24.0	28.8	33.5	38.3
24	5.0	10.0	15.0	20.0	25.0	30.0	35.0	40.0

	45	50	55	60	65	70	75	80
0	0.0	0.0	0.0	0.0	0.0	0.0	0.0	0.0
1	1.9	2.1	2.3	2.5	2.7	2.9	3.1	3.3
2	3.8	4.2	4.6	5.0	5.4	5.8	6.3	6.7
3	5.6	6.2	6.9	7.5	8.1	8.8	9.4	10.0
4	7.5	8.3	9.2	10.0	10.8	11.7	12.5	13.3
5	9.4	10.4	11.5	12.5	13.5	14.6	15.6	16.7
6	11.3	12.5	13.8	15.0	16.2	17.5	18.8	20.0
7	13.1	14.6	16.0	17.5	19.0	20.4	21.9	23.3
8	15.0	16.7	18.3	20.0	21.7	23.3	25.0	26.7
9	16.9	18.7	20.6	22.5	24.4	26.3	28.1	30.0
10	18.8	20.8	22.9	25.0	27.1	29.2	31.3	33.3
11	20.6	22.9	25.2	27.5	29.8	32.1	34.4	36.7
12	22.5	25.0	27.5	30.0	32.5	35.0	37.5	40.0
13	24.4	27.1	29.8	32.5	35.2	37.9	40.6	43.3
14	26.3	29.2	32.1	35.0	37.9	40.8	43.8	46.7
15	28.1	31.2	34.4	37.5	40.6	43.8	46.9	50.0
16	30.0	33.3	36.7	40.0	43.3	46.7	50.0	53.3
17	31.9	35.4	39.0	42.5	46.0	49.6	53.1	56.7
18	33.8	37.5	41.3	45.0	48.7	52.5	56.3	60.0
19	35.6	39.6	43.5	47.5	51.5	55.4	59.4	63.3
20	37.5	41.7	45.8	50.0	54.2	58.3	62.5	66.7
21	39.4	43.7	48.1	52.5	56.9	61.3	65.6	70.0
22	41.3	45.8	50.4	55.0	59.6	64.2	68.8	73.3
23	43.1	47.9	52.7	57.5	62.3	67.1	71.9	76.7
24	45.0	50.0	55.0	60.0	65.0	70.0	75.0	80.0

	85	90	95	100	105	110	115	120
0	0.0	0.0	0.0	0.0	0.0	0.0	0.0	0.0
1	3.5	3.8	4.0	4.2	4.4	4.6	4.8	5.0
2	7.1	7.5	7.9	8.3	8.8	9.2	9.6	10.0
3.	10.6	11.3	11.9	12.5	13.1	13.7	14.4	15.0
4	14.2	15.0	15.8	16.7	17.5	18.3	19.2	20.0
5	17.7	18.8	19.8	20.8	21.9	22.9	24.0	25.0
6	21.3	22.5	23.7	25.0	26.3	27.5	28.8	30.0
7	24.8	26.3	27.7	29.2	30.6	32.1	33.5	35.0
8	28.3	30.0	31.7	33.3	35.0	36.7	38.3	40.0
9	31.9	33.8	35.6	37.5	39.4	41.2	43.1	45.0
10	35.4	37.5	39.6	41.7	43.8	45.8	47.9	50.0
11	39.0	41.3	43.5	45.8	48.1	50.4	52.7	55.0
12	42.5	45.0	47.5	50.0	52.5	55.0	57.5	60.0
13	46.0	48.8	51.5	54.2	56.9	59.6	62.3	65.0
14	49.6	52.5	55.4	58.3	61.3	64.2	67.1	70.0
15	53.1	56.3	59.4	62.5	65.6	68.7	71.9	75.0
16	56.7	60.0	63.3	66.7	70.0	73.3	76.7	80.0
17	60.2	63.8	67.3	70.8	74.4	77.9	81.5	85.0
18	63.8	67.5	71.2	75.0	78.8	82.5	86.3	90.0
19	67.3	71.3	75.2	79.2	83.1	87.1	91.0	95.0
20	70.8	75.0	79.2	83.3	87.5	91.7	95.8	100.0
21	74.4	78.8	83.1	87.5	91.9	96.2	100.6	105.0
22	77.9	82.5	87.1	91.7	96.3	100.8	105.4	110.0
23	81.5	86.3	91.0	95.8	100.6	105.4	110.2	115.0
24	85.0	90.0	95.0	100.0	105.0	110.0	115.0	120.0

	125	130	135	140	145	150	155	160
0.	0.0	0.0	0.0	0.0	0.0	0.0	0.0	0.0
1.	5.2	5.4	5.6	5.8	6.0	6.3	6.5	6.7
2.	10.4	10.8	11.3	11.7	12.1	12.5	12.9	13.3
3	15.6	16.3	16.9	17.5	18.1	18.8	19.4	20.0
4	20.8	21.7	22.5	23.3	24.2	25.0	25.8	26.7
5	26.0	27.1	28.1	29.2	30.2	31.3	32.3	33.3
6	31.2	32.5	33.8	35.0	36.3	37.5	38.7	40.0
7	36.5	37.9	39.4	40.8	42.3	43.8	45.2	46.7
8	41.7	43.3	45.0	46.7	48.3	50.0	51.7	53.3
9	46.9	48.8	50.6	52.5	54.4	56.3	58.1	60.0
10	52.1	54.2	56.3	58.3	60.4	62.5	64.6	66.7
11	57.3	59.6	61.9	64.2	66.5	68.8	71.0	73.3
12	62.5	65.0	67.5	70.0	72.5	75.0	77.5	80.0
13	67.7	70.4	73.1	75.8	78.5	81.3	84.0	86.7
14	72.9	75.8	78.8	81.7	84.6	87.5	90.4	93.3
15	78.1	81.3	84.4	87.5	90.6	93.8	96.9	100.0
16	83.3	86.7	90.0	93.3	96.7	100.0	103.3	106.7
17	88.5	92.1	95.6	99.2	102.7	106.3	109.8	113.3
18	93.7	97.5	101.3	105.0	108.8	112.5	116.2	120.0
19	99.0	102.9	106.9	110.8	114.8	118.8	122.7	126.7
20	104.2	108.3	112.5	116.7	120.8	125.0	129.2	133.3
21	109.4	113.8	118.1	122.5	126.9	131.3	135.6	140.0
22	114.6	119.2	123.8	128.3	132.9	137.5	142.1	146.7
23	119.8	124.6	129.4	134.2	139.0	143.8	148.5	153.3
24	125.0	130.0	135.0	140.0	145.0	150.0	155.0	160.0

	165	170	175	180	185	190	195	200
0	0.0	0.0	0.0	0.0	0.0	0.0	0.0	0.0
1	6.9	7.1	7.3	7.5	7.7	7.9	8.1	8.3
2	13.8	14.2	14.6	15.0	15.4	15.8	16.3	16.7
3	20.6	21.2	21.9	22.5	23.1	23.7	24.4	25.0
4	27.5	28.3	29.2	30.0	30.8	31.6	32.5	33.3
5	34.4	35.4	36.5	37.5	38.5	39.6	40.6	41.7
6.	41.3	42.5	43.8	45.0	46.2	47.5	48.8	50.0
7	48.1	49.6	51.0	52.5	54.0	55.4	56.9	58.3
8.	55.0	56.7	58.3	60.0	61.7	63.3	65.0	66.7
9	61.9	63.7	65.6	67.5	69.4	71.2	73.1	75.0
10	68.8	70.8	72.9	75.0	77.1	79.1	81.3	83.3
11	75.6	77.9	80.2	82.5	84.8	87.0	89.4	91.7
12	82.5	85.0	87.5	90.0	92.5	94.9	97.5	100.0
13	89.4	92.1	94.8	97.5	100.2	102.9	105.6	108.3
14	96.3	99.2	102.1	105.0	107.9	110.8	113.8	116.7
15	103.1	106.2	109.4	112.5	115.6	118.7	121.9	125.0
16	110.0	113.3	116.7	120.0	123.3	126.6	130.0	133.3
17	116.9	120.4	124.0	127.5	131.0	134.5	138.1	141.7
18	123.8	127.5	131.3	135.0	138.7	142.4	146.3	150.0
19	130.6	134.6	138.5	142.5	146.5	150.3	154.4	158.3
20	137.5	141.7	145.8	150.0	154.2	158.2	162.5	166.7
21	144.4	148.7	153.1	157.5	161.9	166.2	170.6	175.0
22	151.3	155.8	160.4	165.0	169.6	174.1	178.8	183.3
23	158.1	162.9	167.7	172.5	177.3	182.0	186.9	191.7
24	165.0	170.0	175.0	180.0	185.0	190.0	195.0	200.0

	205	210	215	220	225
0.0	0.0	0.0	0.0	0.0	0.0
1.0	8.5	8.8	9.0	9.2	9.4
2.0	17.1	17.5	17.9	18.3	18.8
3.0	25.6	26.3	26.9	27.5	28.1
4.0	34.2	35.0	35.8	36.7	37.5
5.0	42.7	43.8	44.8	45.8	46.9
6.0	51.3	52.5	53.7	55.0	56.3
7.0	59.8	61.3	62.7	64.2	65.6
8.0	68.3	70.0	71.7	73.3	75.0
9.0	76.9	78.8	80.6	82.5	84.4
10.0	85.4	87.5	89.6	91.7	93.8
11.0	94.0	96.3	98.5	100.8	103.1
12.0	102.5	105.0	107.5	110.0	112.5
13.0	111.0	113.8	116.5	119.2	121.9
14.0	119.6	122.5	125.4	128.3	131.3
15.0	128.1	131.3	134.4	137.5	140.6
16.0	136.7	140.0	143.3	146.7	150.0
17.0	145.2	148.8	152.3	155.8	159.4
18.0	153.8	157.5	161.2	165.0	168.8
19.0	162.3	166.3	170.2	174.2	178.1
20.0	170.8	175.0	179.2	183.3	187.5
21.0	179.4	183.8	188.1	192.5	196.9
22.0	187.9	192.5	197.1	201.7	206.3
23.0	196.5	201.3	206.0	210.8	215.6
24.0	205.0	210.0	215.0	220.0	225.0

Lunar daily motion in degrees and minutes

GMT	11d45m	12d00m	12d15m	12d30m	12d45m	13d00m	13d15m
0							
1	00:29	00:30	00:30	00:31	00:31	00:32	00:33
2	00:58	01:00	01:01	01:02	01:03	01:05	01:06
3	01:28	01:30	01:31	01:33	01:35	01:37	01:39
4	01:57	02:00	02:02	02:05	02:07	02:10	02:12
5	02:26	02:30	02:33	02:36	02:39	02:42	02:45
6	02:56	03:00	03:03	03:07	03:11	03:15	03:18
7	03:25	03:30	03:34	03:38	03:43	03:47	03:51
8	03:55	04:00	04:05	04:10	04:15	04:20	04:25
9	04:24	04:30	04:35	04:41	04:46	04:52	04:58
10	04:53	05:00	05:06	05:12	05:18	05:25	05:31
11	05:23	05:30	05:36	05:43	05:50	05:57	06:04
12	05:52	06:00	06:07	06:15	06:22	06:30	06:37
13	06:21	06:30	06:38	06:46	06:54	07:02	07:10
14	06:51	07:00	07:08	07:17	07:26	07:35	07:43
15	07:20	07:30	07:39	07:48	07:58	08:07	08:16
16	07:50	08:00	08:10	08:20	08:30	08:40	08:50
17	08:19	08:30	08:40	08:51	09:01	09:12	09:23
18	08:48	09:00	09:11	09:22	09:33	09:45	09:56
19	09:18	09:30	09:41	09:53	10:05	10:17	10:29
20	09:47	10:00	10:12	10:25	10:37	10:50	11:02
21	10:16	10:30	10:43	10:56	11:09	11:22	11:35
22	10:46	11:00	11:13	11:27	11:41	11:54	12:08
23	11:15	11:30	11:44	11:58	12:13	12:27	12:41
24	11:45	12:00	12:15	12:30	12:45	12:59	13:15

GMT	13d30m	13d45m	14d00m	14d15m	14d30m	14d45m	15d00m
0							
1	00:33	00:34	00:35	00:35	00:36	00:36	00:37
2	01:07	01:08	01:10	01:11	01:12	01:13	01:15
3	01:41	01:43	01:45	01:46	01:48	01:50	01:52
4	02:15	02:17	02:20	02:22	02:25	02:27	02:30
5	02:48	02:51	02:55	02:58	03:01	03:04	03:07
6	03:22	03:26	03:30	03:33	03:37	03:41	03:45
7	03:56	04:00	04:05	04:09	04:13	04:18	04:22
8	04:30	04:34	04:40	04:45	04:50	04:55	05:00
9	05:03	05:09	05:15	05:20	05:26	05:31	05:37
10	05:37	05:43	05:50	05:56	06:02	06:08	06:15
11	06:11	06:18	06:25	06:31	06:38	06:45	06:52
12	06:45	06:52	07:00	07:07	07:15	07:22	07:30
13	07:18	07:26	07:35	07:43	07:51	07:59	08:07
14	07:52	08:01	08:10	08:18	08:27	08:36	08:45
15	08:26	08:35	08:45	08:54	09:03	09:13	09:22
16	09:00	09:09	09:20	09:30	09:40	09:50	10:00
17	09:33	09:44	09:55	10:05	10:16	10:26	10:37

GMT	13d30m	13d45m	14d00m	14d15m	14d30m	14d45m	15d00m
18	10:07	10:18	10:30	10:41	10:52	11:03	11:15
19	10:41	10:53	11:05	11:16	11:28	11:40	11:52
20	11:15	11:27	11:40	11:52	12:05	12:17	12:30
21	11:48	12:01	12:15	12:28	12:41	12:54	13:07
22	12:22	12:36	12:50	13:03	13:17	13:31	13:45
23	12:56	13:10	13:25	13:39	13:53	14:08	14:22
24	13:30	13:44	14:00	14:15	14:30	14:45	15:00

GMT	15d15m	15d30m	15d45m	16h00m	16d15m	16d30m
0						
1	00:38	00:38	00:39	00:40	00:40	00:41
2	01:16	01:17	01:18	01:20	01:21	01:22
3	01:54	01:56	01:58	02:00	02:01	02:03
4	02:32	02:35	02:37	02:40	02:42	02:45
5	03:10	03:13	03:16	03:20	03:23	03:26
6	03:48	03:52	03:56	04:00	04:03	04:07
7	04:26	04:31	04:35	04:40	04:44	04:48
8	05:05	05:10	05:15	05:20	05:25	05:30
9	05:43	05:48	05:54	06:00	06:05	06:11
10	06:21	06:27	06:33	06:40	06:46	06:52
11	06:59	07:06	07:13	07:20	07:26	07:33
12	07:37	07:45	07:52	08:00	08:07	08:15
13	08:15	08:23	08:31	08:40	08:48	08:56
14	08:53	09:02	09:11	09:20	09:28	09:37
15	09:31	09:41	09:50	10:00	10:09	10:18
16	10:10	10:20	10:30	10:40	10:50	11:00
17	10:48	10:58	11:09	11:20	11:30	11:41
18	11:26	11:37	11:48	12:00	12:11	12:22
19	12:04	12:16	12:28	12:40	12:51	13:03
20	12:42	12:55	13:07	13:20	13:32	13:45
21	13:20	13:33	13:46	14:00	14:13	14:26
22	13:58	14:12	14:26	14:40	14:53	15:07
23	14:36	14:51	15:05	15:20	15:34	15:48
24	15:15	15:30	15:45	16:00	16:15	16:30

Table of Diurnal Proportional Logarithms

	0	1	2	3	4	5	6	7
	3.1584	1.3802	1.0792	.9031	.7782	.6812	.6021	.5351
1	3.1584	1.3730	1.0756	.9007	.7763	.6798	.6009	.5341
2	2.8573	1.3660	1.0720	.8983	.7745	.6784	.5997	.5331
3	2.6812	1.3590	1.0685	.8959	.7728	.6769	.5985	.5320
4	2.5563	1.3522	1.0649	.8935	.7710	.6755	.5973	.5310
5	2.4594	1.3454	1.0615	.8912	.7692	.6741	.5961	.5300
6	2.3802	1.3388	1.0580	.8888	.7674	.6726	.5949	.5290
7	2.3133	1.3323	1.0546	.8865	.7657	.6712	.5937	.5279
8	2.2553	1.3259	1.0512	.8842	.7639	.6698	.5925	.5269
9	2.2041	1.3195	1.0478	.8819	.7622	.6684	.5913	.5259
10	2.1584	1.3133	1.0444	.8796	.7604	.6670	.5902	.5249
11	2.1170	1.3071	1.0411	.8773	.7587	.6656	.5890	.5239
12	2.0792	1.3010	1.0378	.8751	.7570	.6642	.5878	.5229
13	2.0444	1.2950	1.0345	.8728	.7552	.6628	.5867	.5219
14	2.0122	1.2891	1.0313	.8706	.7535	.6614	.5855	.5209
15	1.9823	1.2833	1.0280	.8683	.7518	.6601	.5843	.5199
16	1.9542	1.2775	1.0248	.8661	.7501	.6587	.5832	.5189
17	1.9279	1.2719	1.0216	.8639	.7484	.6573	.5820	.5179
18	1.9031	1.2663	1.0185	.8617	.7467	.6559	.5809	.5169
19	1.8796	1.2607	1.0153	.8595	.7451	.6546	.5797	.5159
20	1.8573	1.2553	1.0122	.8573	.7434	.6532	.5786	.5149
21	1.8361	1.2499	1.0091	.8552	.7417	.6519	.5774	.5139
22	1.8159	1.2445	1.0061	.8530	.7401	.6505	.5763	.5129
23	1.7966	1.2393	1.0030	.8509	.7384	.6492	.5752	.5120
24	1.7782	1.2341	1.0000	.8487	.7368	.6478	.5740	.5110
25	1.7604	1.2289	.9970	.8466	.7351	.6465	.5729	.5100
26	1.7434	1.2239	.9940	.8445	.7335	.6451	.5718	.5090
27	1.7270	1.2188	.9910	.8424	.7319	.6438	.5707	.5081
28	1.7112	1.2139	.9881	.8403	.7302	.6425	.5695	.5071
29	1.6960	1.2090	.9852	.8382	.7286	.6412	.5684	.5061
30	1.6812	1.2041	.9823	.8361	.7270	.6398	.5673	.5051
31	1.6670	1.1993	.9794	.8341	.7254	.6385	.5662	.5042
32	1.6532	1.1946	.9765	.8320	.7238	.6372	.5651	.5032
33	1.6398	1.1899	.9737	.8300	.7222	.6359	.5640	.5023
34	1.6269	1.1852	.9708	.8279	.7206	.6346	.5629	.5013
35	1.6143	1.1806	.9680	.8259	.7190	.6333	.5618	.5004
36	1.6021	1.1761	.9652	.8239	.7175	.6320	.5607	.4994
37	1.5902	1.1716	.9625	.8219	.7159	.6307	.5596	.4984
38	1.5786	1.1671	.9597	.8199	.7143	.6294	.5585	.4975
39	1.5673	1.1627	.9570	.8179	.7128	.6282	.5574	.4965
40	1.5563	1.1584	.9542	.8159	.7112	.6269	.5563	.4956
41	1.5456	1.1540	.9515	.8140	.7097	.6256	.5552	.4947
42	1.5351	1.1498	.9488	.8120	.7081	.6243	.5541	.4937
43	1.5249	1.1455	.9462	.8101	.7066	.6231	.5531	.4928
44	1.5149	1.1413	.9435	.8081	.7050	.6218	.5520	.4918
45	1.5051	1.1372	.9409	.8062	.7035	.6205	.5509	.4909
46	1.4956	1.1331	.9383	.8043	.7020	.6193	.5498	.4900

	0	1	2	3	4	5	6	7
47	1.4863	1.1290	.9356	.8023	.7005	.6180	.5488	.4890
48	1.4771	1.1249	.9331	.8004	.6990	.6168	.5477	.4881
49	1.4682	1.1209	.9305	.7985	.6975	.6155	.5466	.4872
50	1.4594	1.1170	.9279	.7966	.6960	.6143	.5456	.4863
51	1.4508	1.1130	.9254	.7948	.6945	.6131	.5445	.4853
52	1.4424	1.1091	.9228	.7929	.6930	.6118	.5435	.4844
53	1.4341	1.1053	.9203	.7910	.6915	.6106	.5424	.4835
54	1.4260	1.1015	.9178	.7891	.6900	.6094	.5414	.4826
55	1.4180	1.0977	.9153	.7873	.6885	.6081	.5403	.4817
56	1.4102	1.0939	.9128	.7855	.6871	.6069	.5393	.4808
57	1.4025	1.0902	.9104	.7836	.6856	.6057	.5382	.4798
58	1.3949	1.0865	.9079	.7818	.6841	.6045	.5372	.4789
59	1.3875	1.0828	.9055	.7800	.6827	.6033	.5361	.4780
60	1.3802	1.0792	.9031	.7782	.6812	.6021	.5351	.4771

	8	9	10	11	12	13	14	15
	.4771	.4260	.3802	.3388	.3010	.2663	.2341	.2041
1	.4762	.4252	.3795	.3382	.3004	.2657	.2336	.2036
2	.4753	.4244	.3788	.3375	.2998	.2652	.2331	.2032
3	.4744	.4236	.3780	.3368	.2992	.2646	.2325	.2027
4	.4735	.4228	.3773	.3362	.2986	.2640	.2320	.2022
5	.4726	.4220	.3766	.3355	.2980	.2635	.2315	.2017
6	.4717	.4212	.3759	.3349	.2974	.2629	.2310	.2012
7	.4708	.4204	.3752	.3342	.2968	.2624	.2305	.2008
8	.4699	.4196	.3745	.3336	.2962	.2618	.2300	.2003
9	.4691	.4188	.3737	.3329	.2956	.2613	.2295	.1998
10	.4682	.4180	.3730	.3323	.2950	.2607	.2289	.1993
11	.4673	.4172	.3723	.3316	.2944	.2602	.2284	.1988
12	.4664	.4164	.3716	.3310	.2939	.2596	.2279	.1984
13	.4655	.4156	.3709	.3303	.2933	.2591	.2274	.1979
14	.4646	.4149	.3702	.3297	.2927	.2585	.2269	.1974
15	.4638	.4141	.3695	.3291	.2921	.2580	.2264	.1969
16	.4629	.4133	.3688	.3284	.2915	.2574	.2259	.1965
17	.4620	.4125	.3681	.3278	.2909	.2569	.2254	.1960
18	.4611	.4117	.3674	.3271	.2903	.2564	.2249	.1955
19	.4603	.4110	.3667	.3265	.2897	.2558	.2244	.1950
20	.4594	.4102	.3660	.3259	.2891	.2553	.2239	.1946
21	.4585	.4094	.3653	.3252	.2885	.2547	.2234	.1941
22	.4577	.4086	.3646	.3246	.2880	.2542	.2229	.1936
23	.4568	.4079	.3639	.3239	.2874	.2536	.2224	.1932
24	.4559	.4071	.3632	.3233	.2868	.2531	.2218	.1927
25	.4551	.4063	.3625	.3227	.2862	.2526	.2213	.1922
26	.4542	.4055	.3618	.3220	.2856	.2520	.2208	.1918
27	.4534	.4048	.3611	.3214	.2850	.2515	.2203	.1913
28	.4525	.4040	.3604	.3208	.2845	.2510	.2198	.1908
29	.4516	.4033	.3597	.3201	.2839	.2504	.2193	.1903
30	.4508	.4025	.3590	.3195	.2833	.2499	.2188	.1899
31	.4499	.4017	.3583	.3189	.2827	.2493	.2183	.1894
32	.4491	.4010	.3576	.3183	.2821	.2488	.2178	.1889
33	.4482	.4002	.3570	.3176	.2816	.2483	.2173	.1885

	8	9	10	11	12	13	14	15
34	.4474	.3995	.3563	.3170	.2810	.2477	.2169	.1880
35	.4466	.3987	.3556	.3164	.2804	.2472	.2164	.1876
36	.4457	.3979	.3549	.3158	.2798	.2467	.2159	.1871
37	.4449	.3972	.3542	.3151	.2793	.2461	.2154	.1866
38	.4440	.3964	.3535	.3145	.2787	.2456	.2149	.1862
39	.4432	.3957	.3529	.3139	.2781	.2451	.2144	.1857
40	.4424	.3949	.3522	.3133	.2775	.2445	.2139	.1852
41	.4415	.3942	.3515	.3126	.2770	.2440	.2134	.1848
42	.4407	.3934	.3508	.3120	.2764	.2435	.2129	.1843
43	.4399	.3927	.3502	.3114	.2758	.2430	.2124	.1839
44	.4390	.3919	.3495	.3108	.2753	.2424	.2119	.1834
45	.4382	.3912	.3488	.3102	.2747	.2419	.2114	.1829
46	.4374	.3905	.3481	.3096	.2741	.2414	.2109	.1825
47	.4366	.3897	.3475	.3089	.2736	.2409	.2104	.1820
48	.4357	.3890	.3468	.3083	.2730	.2403	.2099	.1816
49	.4349	.3882	.3461	.3077	.2724	.2398	.2095	.1811
50	.4341	.3875	.3454	.3071	.2719	.2393	.2090	.1806
51	.4333	.3868	.3448	.3065	.2713	.2388	.2085	.1802
52	.4325	.3860	.3441	.3059	.2707	.2382	.2080	.1797
53	.4316	.3853	.3434	.3053	.2702	.2377	.2075	.1793
54	.4308	.3846	.3428	.3047	.2696	.2372	.2070	.1788
55	.4300	.3838	.3421	.3041	.2691	.2367	.2065	.1784
56	.4292	.3831	.3415	.3034	.2685	.2362	.2061	.1779
57	.4284	.3824	.3408	.3028	.2679	.2356	.2056	.1775
58	.4276	.3817	.3401	.3022	.2674	.2351	.2051	.1770
59	.4268	.3809	.3395	.3016	.2668	.2346	.2046	.1765
60	.4260	.3802	.3388	.3010	.2663	.2341	.2041	.1761

	16	17	18	19	20	21	22	23
	.1761	.1498	.1249	.1015	.0792	.0580	.0378	.0185
1	.1756	.1493	.1245	.1011	.0788	.0576	.0375	.0182
2	.1752	.1489	.1241	.1007	.0785	.0573	.0371	.0179
3	.1747	.1485	.1237	.1003	.0781	.0570	.0368	.0175
4	.1743	.1481	.1233	.0999	.0777	.0566	.0365	.0172
5	.1738	.1476	.1229	.0996	.0774	.0563	.0361	.0169
6	.1734	.1472	.1225	.0992	.0770	.0559	.0358	.0166
7	.1729	.1468	.1221	.0988	.0767	.0556	.0355	.0163
8	.1725	.1464	.1217	.0984	.0763	.0552	.0352	.0160
9	.1720	.1459	.1213	.0980	.0759	.0549	.0348	.0157
10	.1716	.1455	.1209	.0977	.0756	.0546	.0345	.0153
11	.1711	.1451	.1205	.0973	.0752	.0542	.0342	.0150
12	.1707	.1447	.1201	.0969	.0749	.0539	.0339	.0147
13	.1702	.1443	.1197	.0965	.0745	.0535	.0335	.0144
14	.1698	.1438	.1193	.0962	.0741	.0532	.0332	.0141
15	.1694	.1434	.1189	.0958	.0738	.0529	.0329	.0138
16	.1689	.1430	.1186	.0954	.0734	.0525	.0326	.0135
17	.1685	.1426	.1182	.0950	.0731	.0522	.0322	.0132
18	.1680	.1422	.1178	.0947	.0727	.0518	.0319	.0129
19	.1676	.1417	.1174	.0943	.0724	.0515	.0316	.0125
20	.1671	.1413	.1170	.0939	.0720	.0512	.0313	.0122

	16	17	18	19	20	21	22	23
21	.1667	.1409	.1166	.0935	.0716	.0508	.0309	.0119
22	.1663	.1405	.1162	.0932	.0713	.0505	.0306	.0116
23	.1658	.1401	.1158	.0928	.0709	.0501	.0303	.0113
24	.1654	.1397	.1154	.0924	.0706	.0498	.0300	.0110
25	.1649	.1392	.1150	.0920	.0702	.0495	.0296	.0107
26	.1645	.1388	.1146	.0917	.0699	.0491	.0293	.0104
27	.1640	.1384	.1142	.0913	.0695	.0488	.0290	.0101
28	.1636	.1380	.1138	.0909	.0692	.0484	.0287	.0098
29	.1632	.1376	.1134	.0905	.0688	.0481	.0284	.0095
30	.1627	.1372	.1130	.0902	.0685	.0478	.0280	.0091
31	.1623	.1368	.1126	.0898	.0681	.0474	.0277	.0088
32	.1619	.1363	.1123	.0894	.0678	.0471	.0274	.0085
33	.1614	.1359	.1119	.0891	.0674	.0468	.0271	.0082
34	.1610	.1355	.1115	.0887	.0670	.0464	.0267	.0079
35	.1605	.1351	.1111	.0883	.0667	.0461	.0264	.0076
36	.1601	.1347	.1107	.0880	.0663	.0458	.0261	.0073
37	.1597	.1343	.1103	.0876	.0660	.0454	.0258	.0070
38	.1592	.1339	.1099	.0872	.0656	.0451	.0255	.0067
39	.1588	.1335	.1095	.0868	.0653	.0448	.0251	.0064
40	.1584	.1331	.1091	.0865	.0649	.0444	.0248	.0061
41	.1579	.1326	.1088	.0861	.0646	.0441	.0245	.0058
42	.1575	.1322	.1084	.0857	.0642	.0438	.0242	.0055
43	.1571	.1318	.1080	.0854	.0639	.0434	.0239	.0052
44	.1566	.1314	.1076	.0850	.0635	.0431	.0235	.0049
45	.1562	.1310	.1072	.0846	.0632	.0428	.0232	.0045
46	.1558	.1306	.1068	.0843	.0628	.0424	.0229	.0042
47	.1553	.1302	.1064	.0839	.0625	.0421	.0226	.0039
48	.1549	.1298	.1061	.0835	.0621	.0418	.0223	.0036
49	.1545	.1294	.1057	.0832	.0618	.0414	.0220	.0033
50	.1540	.1290	.1053	.0828	.0615	.0411	.0216	.0030
51	.1536	.1286	.1049	.0825	.0611	.0408	.0213	.0027
52	.1532	.1282	.1045	.0821	.0608	.0404	.0210	.0024
53	.1528	.1278	.1041	.0817	.0604	.0401	.0207	.0021
54	.1523	.1274	.1037	.0814	.0601	.0398	.0204	.0018
55	.1519	.1270	.1034	.0810	.0597	.0394	.0201	.0015
56	.1515	.1266	.1030	.0806	.0594	.0391	.0197	.0012
57	.1510	.1261	.1026	.0803	.0590	.0388	.0194	.0009
58	.1506	.1257	.1022	.0799	.0587	.0384	.0191	.0006
59	.1502	.1253	.1018	.0795	.0583	.0381	.0188	.0003
60	.1498	.1249	.1015	.0792	.0580	.0378	.0185	.0000

Table of Delta T Correction

From the *Astronomical Almanac* published annually by the Nautical Almanac Offices of the US Naval Observatory (Washington)

1900.0	-2.72	1941.0	24.83	1982.0	52.17
1901.0	-1.54	1942.0	25.30	1983.0	52.96
1902.0	-0.02	1943.0	25.70	1984.0	53.79
1903.0	1.24	1944.0	26.24	1985.0	54.34
1904.0	2.64	1945.0	26.77	1986.0	54.87
1905.0	3.86	1946.0	27.28	1987.0	55.32
1906.0	5.37	1947.0	27.78	1988.0	55.82
1907.0	6.14	1948.0	28.25	1989.0	56.30
1908.0	7.75	1949.0	28.71	1990.0	56.86
1909.0	9.13	1950.0	29.15	1991.0	57.57
1910.0	10.46	1951.0	29.57	1992.0	58.31
1911.0	11.53	1952.0	29.97	1993.0	59.12
1912.0	13.36	1953.0	30.36	1994.0	59.98
1913.0	14.65	1954.0	30.72	1995.0	60.78
1914.0	16.01	1955.0	31.07	1996.0	61.63
1915.0	17.20	1956.0	31.35	1997.0	62.29
1916.0	18.24	1957.0	31.68	1998.0	62.97
1917.0	19.06	1958.0	32.18	1999.0	63.47
1918.0	20.25	1959.0	32.68	2000.0	63.83
1919.0	20.95	1960.0	33.15	2001.0	64.09
1920.0	21.16	1961.0	33.59	2002.0	64.30
1921.0	22.25	1962.0	34.00	2003.0	64.47
1922.0	22.41	1963.0	34.47	2004.0	64.57
1923.0	23.03	1964.0	35.03	2005.0	64.69
1924.0	23.49	1965.0	35.73	2006.0	64.85
1925.0	23.62	1966.0	36.54	2007.0	65.15
1926.0	23.86	1967.0	37.43	2008.0	65.46
1927.0	24.49	1968.0	38.29	2009.0	65.78
1928.0	24.34	1969.0	39.20	2010.0	66.07
1929.0	24.08	1970.0	40.18	2011.0	66.35
1930.0	24.02	1971.0	41.17	2012.0	66.50
1931.0	24.00	1972.0	42.23	2013.0	67.20
1932.0	23.87	1973.0	43.37	2014.0	67.70
1933.0	23.95	1974.0	44.49	2015.0	68.00
1934.0	23.86	1975.0	45.48	2016.0	68.50
1935.0	23.93	1976.0	46.46	2017.0	69.00
1936.0	23.73	1977.0	47.52	2018.0	69.50
1937.0	23.92	1978.0	48.53	2019.0	70.00
1938.0	23.96	1979.0	49.59	2020.0	70.50
1939.0	24.02	1980.0	50.54		
1940.0	24.33	1981.0	51.38		

References and Additional Sources on Chart Calculations

Bradley, A.D. *Mathematics of Air and Marine Navigation*. American Book Company. 1942. Contains useful information on spherical astronomy and trigonometry as well as 5-place logarithm tables.

Bradley, Donald A. *Solar and Lunar Returns*. St. Paul: Llewellyn Publications. 1968. Bradley, who uses sidereal astrology, explains how to do returns and how to convert from the tropical to the sidereal zodiac.

Foreman, Patricia. *Computers and Astrology*. Burlington, VT: Good Earth Publications. 1992. Don't be misled by the title, this is an excellent book on house systems, astrological conventions, time zones and coordinates of cities, etc. It also has a large astrological dictionary.

Dalton, Joseph G. *The Spherical Basis of Astrology*. McCoy Publishing. 1893. This table of houses is probably the most widely-distributed volume in its class. The tables are for the Placidus system, though the explanation of the system is not correct. But the print is large and easy to read so the book is generally useful.

DeLuce, Robert. *Complete Method of Prediction*. New York: ASI Publishers. 1935, 1978. Although this is an older book, it contains much information on astrological calculations: primary directions, progressions. DeLuce also discusses the philosophy and mechanics of the celestial sphere.

Hand, Robert. *Essays on Astrology*. Gloucester, MA: Para Research, 1982. Contains several technical articles including one on calculating house cusps in extreme latitudes.

Houlding, Deborah. *The Houses: Temples of the Sky*. Mansfield, U.K. Ascella Publications. 1998. A good discussion of the history and nature of house systems in astrology. A portion of this book appeared in the August/September 2002 issue of The Mountain Astrologer.

Hooper, Alfred. *Makers of Mathematics*. Random House. 1948. Excellent popular history of mathematics from ancient times to Newton and a bit beyond.

Jayne, Charles A. *Progressions and Directions*. Astrological Bureau. 1973. Small but detailed information on the technical side of the topic. Contains tables of Right Ascensions.

Jones, J. Allen Jr. *Easy Tables*. Hollywood, CA: Golden Seal Research. 1960. This small book was a classic in the 1960's and 1970's. It offers simple instructions for casting charts and a number of handy tables to make the work easier.

Leo, Alan. *Casting the Horoscope*. London: L.N. Fowler & Co. 1912. This is one of the last great all-encompassing text on astrological calculations. While some of the methods are a bit cumbersome, Leo does offer good descriptions of how the various house systems work and also gives the logic behind many predictive techniques. The book contains trigonometrical formulae and many tables including a 10-day ephemeris from 1861-1913.

Leo, Alan. *The Progressed Horoscope*. London: L.N. Fowler & Co. 1913. An excellent early 20th century work on secondary progressions and also primary directions. Contains delineations of progressed and directed aspects and relevant trigonometrical formulae.

Lorenz, Dona Marie. *Tools of Astrology: Houses*. Topanga, CA: Eomega Grove Press. 1973. This out-of-print book is unusual in that it treats house systems in some technical detail and offers tables for various systems.

Makransky, Bob. *Primary Directions: A Primer of Calculation*. Occidental, CA: Dear Brutus Press. 1988. This is a book for mainly for technically-minded astrologers who are conversant in trigonometry, and for computer programmers who wish to understand astronomical mathematics relevant to astrology. It does cover far more than primary directions and offers an informed commentary on houses systems and other astrological conventions.

Martin, Benjamin. *The Young Trigonometer's Compleat Guide Being the Mystery and Rationale of Spherical Trigonometry Made Clear and Easy*. London. 1736. Benjamin Martin was a prolific writer and amateur scientist. The book is filled with classic calculation methods useful to astronomers, navigators and astrologers.

Mayo, Jeff. *How to Cast a Natal Chart*. London: L.N. Fowler & Co. 1967. Jeff Mayo wrote a series of small and very practical books on astrology titled "The Astrologer's Handbook Series." These include *The Astrologer's Astronomical Handbook* and *How to Read the Ephemeris*.

Michelsen, Neil F., *The Michelsen Book of Tables*. San Diego: ACS. 1997. This is an excellent compilation of tables for chart casting and also includes instructions on casting horoscopes. Placidus and Koch tables are included as well as instructions for chart calculations by Rob Hand and Joshua Brackett.

Munkasey, Michael P. *An Astrological House Formulary*. https://www.scribd.com/doc/6495552/An-Astrological-House-Formulary. Twenty-two house systems are outlined and the trigonometrical formulae for most of them is presented in this outline-essay. There is also an excellent set of astronomical terms related to the celestial sphere and house calculations that are defined.

NCGR. *Essentials of Intermediate Astrology*. National Council for Geocosmic Research. 1995. This collection of essays offers information on astronomy for astrologers and instructions on calculating progressed charts and solar arc directions.

Nielsen, Kaj L., and John H. Vanlonkhuyzen. *An Outline of Plane and Spherical Trigonometry*. Barnes and Noble. 1946. A basic text that outlines the major topics in trigonometry in great detail. Contains logarithmic and trigonometric tables.

Noonan, George C. *Spherical Astronomy for Astrologers*. American Federation of Astrologers. 1974. A small book that is technical with some interesting insights about spherical trigonometry, if you can navigate the indirect and incomplete arrangement of material that is his presentation. Contains tables of natural trigonometric functions.

North, J.D. *Horoscopes and History*. London: the Warburg Institute. 1986. North is academic, dense and full of math, basically communicating to a few dozen experts in the field, and he's smug toward astrology. He is successful in keeping some important definitions of things astrological out of the reach, and participation, of all but the most mathematically knowledgeable astrologers; but he does offer us a history of house systems.

Scofield, Bruce. Making Time out of Space: An Introduction to Planetary Periods. *The Mountain Astrologer*, Feb/Mar 1998. (Posted on Alabe.com) Contains a summary of the Hellenistic and Arabic planetary period schemes.

Sepharial. *Directional Astrology*. Philadelphia: David McKay, 1921.
Considers primary directions in detail and contains tables for doing so.

Van Brummelen, Glen. *The Mathematics of the Heavens and the Earth*. Princeton: Princeton University Press. 2009. Covers the history of trigonometry in mathematical detail and manages to skewer astrology whenever possible in spite of the fact that the history of trigonometry was partly, if not mostly, driven by the needs of the astrologer and that many of the contributions to the methodology were actually made by astrologers.

Wikipedia. (https://en.wikipedia.org/wiki/ Celestial_coordinate_system#Converting_coordinates.) Wikipedia's entry on coordinate systems and conversions between them. Contains the standard notation for coordinates and trigonometrical formulae.

About the Author

Bruce Scofield began a lifelong study of astrology in 1967 and since the mid 1970s has been an astrological consultant specializing in psychological analysis, relationships and electional astrology. He is the author of, or contributor to, many books and a large number of articles on astrology and other topics. He has served on the education committee of the National Center for Geocosmic Research (NCGR), as president of the Professional Astrologers Alliance (PAA), and he teaches for Kepler College. He holds an M.A. in history and a Ph.D. in geosciences. His website is www.onereed.com

Also from One Reed Publications
www.onereed.com

The Circuitry of the Self: Astrology and the Developmental Model, by Bruce Scofield. 2001. $12.95.

Signs of Time: An Introduction to Mesoamerican Astrology. by Bruce Scofield: 1993 - $11.95.

Foreseeing the Future: Evangeline Adams and Astrology in America, by Karen Christino. 2002. $14.95.

See also:

Day-Signs: Native American Astrology from Ancient Mexico. By Bruce Scofield. 2017. The Wessex Astrologer.

How to Practice Mayan Astrology. Bruce Scofield and Barry Orr. 2006. Bear & Company.

What Astrology is and How to Use it, by Bruce Scofield. 2021. The Wessex Astrologer.